The Laptop Handbook: Setups and Techniques of the Modern Performer

Jason Emsley

Course Technology PTR

A part of Cengage Learning

COURSE TECHNOLOGY
CENGAGE Learning

Australia • Brazil • Japan • Korea • Mexico • Singapore • Spain • United Kingdom • United States

COURSE TECHNOLOGY
CENGAGE Learning™

The Laptop DJ Handbook: Setups and Techniques of the Modern Performer
Jason Emsley

Publisher and General Manager, Course Technology PTR: Stacy L. Hiquet

Associate Director of Marketing: Sarah Panella

Manager of Editorial Services: Heather Talbot

Marketing Manager: Mark Hughes

Acquisitions Editor: Orren Merton

Project Editor/Copy Editor: Cathleen D. Small

Technical Reviewer: G.W. Childs IV

Interior Layout Tech: MPS Limited, a Macmillan Company

Cover Designer: Luke Fletcher

Indexer: Sharon Shock

Proofreader: Chuck Hutchinson

For product information and technology assistance, contact us at
Cengage Learning Customer & Sales Support, 1-800-354-9706

For permission to use material from this text or product, submit all requests online at **www.cengage.com/permissions**
Further permissions questions can be emailed to
permissionrequest@cengage.com

All trademarks are the property of their respective owners.

All images © Cengage Learning unless otherwise noted.

Library of Congress Control Number: 2010922099

ISBN-13: 978-1-4354-5664-8

ISBN-10: 1-4354-5664-5

Course Technology, a part of Cengage Learning
20 Channel Center Street
Boston, MA 02210
USA

Cengage Learning is a leading provider of customized learning solutions with office locations around the globe, including Singapore, the United Kingdom, Australia, Mexico, Brazil, and Japan. Locate your local office at: **international.cengage.com/region**

Cengage Learning products are represented in Canada by Nelson Education, Ltd.

For your lifelong learning solutions, visit **courseptr.com**

Visit our corporate website at **cengage.com**

Printed in the United States of America
1 2 3 4 5 6 7 12 11 10

Dedicated to my loving, patient wife and family.

Acknowledgments

I would like to acknowledge a handful of individuals and groups of people who, in different ways, all influenced me to start (and finish) this project.

- My friends and colleagues at Native Instruments

- The Los Angeles–based collective of techno freaks, Droid Behavior

- Tobias Becker of Platzhirsch Schallplatten

- My phenomenally patient and supportive editors, Orren Merton, Cathleen Small, and G.W. Childs

- The multitudes of writers, producers, DJs, and music fans who contribute to music culture's all-engrossing, ever-changing discourse

About the Author

Jason Emsley is a California-bred, London-based DJ/producer whose pursuit of electronic music found him a home several years ago on the seminal Cologne, Germany–based techno label, Platzhirsch Schallplatten, and upon the influential Kompakt booking roster. After three years of working from the Los Angeles–based Native Instruments office, he and his wife packed up and sailed off to explore further opportunities in Europe. Currently, Jason continues to work in a freelance capacity for Native Instruments as their UK-based DJ product specialist.

During the course of writing this book, Jason designed and opened his recording studio in East London. The Format Project is a room full of audio hardware and software where he continues to host product trainings, assist and collaborate with like-minded artists, design sound, and produce his own blend of electronic music.

Contents

Chapter 8
Traktor Pro: The Controller Manager   153

Chapter 9
Serato Scratch Live   187

Chapter 10
Intro to Ableton Live   231

Chapter 11
Ableton Live: The Clip Concept   271

Chapter 12
DJing with Ableton Live   297

Chapter 13
Parting Thoughts for Next Time

Introduction

The Laptop DJ Handbook: Setups and Techniques of the Modern Performer is the first book in a two-part series intended to encourage DJs to embrace the various tools emerging from contemporary digital DJ culture. In this first text, much of the introductory material caters to readers ranging from those with virtually no experience to those with a fair degree of awareness concerning the digital DJ realm; however, the approach is specifically devised for varied understandings of both computers and DJ technology. This text should be used as a companion to the user manuals included with the products discussed throughout the following chapters.

What You Will Find in This Book

Among other things, you will discover:

- An introduction to DJ history, evolution, culture, and concepts.

- The digital DJ life: Why laptops and hard drives are the new record crates.

- Descriptions, workflow, and examples of advanced performance techniques and stage setups catering to contemporary digital DJ sets.

- The essential features of industry-leading DJ performance software, such as Traktor Scratch Pro, Serato Scratch Live, and Ableton Live.

- How to augment your DJ sets with hardware controllers ranging from the APC40, Launchpad, Faderfox, and Kontrol X1 devices to external instruments, such as hardware drum machines or the Native Instruments Maschine groovebox.

Companion Website Downloads

Supplemental project file setups for the Ableton Live chapters can be downloaded from www.formatproject.com/djhandbook1.zip.

1 Redefining the DJ

Ask your friends, teachers, work colleagues, acquaintances, parents, musicians, the young, the old, or DJs themselves to define what it means to be a DJ. What is the answer?

Does DJing possess an unequivocal definition? Maybe. More importantly, does DJing *need* defining? Probably not.

What is the common thread? In its broadest sense, DJing is performing audio (music) to an audience of some form.

Part of what makes the art of DJing so difficult to pigeonhole is how often its methodologies shift. Historically, DJing has been a form of musical playback unilaterally instructed by the prerecorded output of musicians. Today, that old relationship is transformed. Unquestionably, the artist-as-DJ and DJ-as-artist paradigms have gained steam over the last century, so much so that at present, musicians are equally as likely to take the stage as DJs, as DJs are to chase their muse into the studio. At the heart of these transformations, and therefore this book, sits music technology.

From phonograph, to tape, to CD, to hard drives, one ingredient never changes: the audience.

Where Do We Start?

No matter what style of music we play or the way in which we play it, something all DJs share is the mixture of uncertainty and excitement experienced while becoming part of a global music culture. Whether it began at a party; on TV; through videogames; at a record shop, art gallery, nightclub, underground, or trade show; or in a bedroom, the fundamental message is pretty similar: We all have to start somewhere.

Fifteen years ago, this process was relatively simple. You probably owned some music—if not, you bought some. You spent more time at the record shop. You went to a retailer and bought some headphones, two turntables, a mixer, and maybe some speakers. You practiced anywhere you could. You performed anywhere you could. The peace and quiet of your family and neighbors was nowhere on the list.

1

Today, assuming Internet retailers didn't put your local music store out of business, the experience is totally different. Walking up to a sales associate and explaining that you want be a DJ is like walking into a butcher and asking for a piece of meat. What cut would you like, sir?

Options

Depending on your experience as a DJ, the prepurchase decision will probably be sandwiched between extremely exciting and exceptionally overwhelming. On one side, the financial expense can be enough to turn most people away. On the other, DJs today are presented with a wealth of tools with which to perform and experiment in ways that were unimaginable 15 years ago...at much less cost.

Famed multimedia artist John Oswald said, "Musical instruments produce sounds. Composers produce music. Musical instruments reproduce music. Tape recorders, radios, disc players, etc., reproduce sound." In effect, the unique sound of a scratch DJ's performance transforms turntables—traditionally used to "reproduce sound"—into an instrument used to reproduce music. The celebrated efforts of scratch pioneers such as Grandmaster Flash helped shape the sounds of turntablism into what would eventually become composition in its own right, with the DJ-as-composer producing new forms of music.

Turntables, laptops, Digital Vinyl Systems (DVS), effects units, drum machines, synthesizers, modular software, even iPhones and iPads—these are just some of the hardware tools—instruments—available to contemporary DJs.

So how do DJs benefit from having so many options? With options come opportunities.

DJs have the rare advantage of being at the epicenter of an industry in which sampling in any form possible is encouraged. Think about the relatively recent history of hip-hop, house, and techno. Despite the copyright legalities of how and where the samples are ripped, fundamentally, they exist at the heart of DJ culture and will continue to do so with or without the permission of the recording industry's legal system. Needless to say, a mind-blowing world of sonic potential surrounds us. As musician and music theorist Chris Cutler wrote, "In the new situation, it is only what is not recorded that belongs to its participants while what is recorded is placed inevitably in the public domain."

Note: These days, a sample is generally understood as a digitally captured sound file. Often, samples are taken—captured—from prerecorded music and used in the composition and/or performance of a new form of music; in other words, individual drum sounds, loops, vocals, and so on. (Think James Brown whoops and shouts.)

Sorry, but here comes some philosophical stuff. Close your eyes for a moment and just listen. Our vision dominates our senses, so give your hearing a few seconds to acclimate. Depending on your environment, there will be different forms of information engulfing you from three dimensions. If you are in a quiet room in your house, pay attention to the clock, sounds from other rooms, your neighbor's muffled television. If it's *very* quiet, listen to your breath. Go outside for a second and listen to your neighborhood. If you are at work, listen to productivity. If you're at school, listen to your classmates. If you're in a coffee shop, listen to the caffeinated stranger prattle on about his problems. When you're out in the city, listen to the cars, buses, the subway, commuters, and general human traffic. If you're fortunate enough to be out in some semblance of nature, listen when your feet meet the sand, waves crashing, wind in the trees, children playing, dogs barking....

Hopefully, you can see where this is going. Anything audible is up for grabs, ready for, as Chris Cutler put it, "the public domain" of the music world. Think of how many tracks you've heard with city or nature sounds, politicians, random radio feed, or samples snatched from music history's archives.

Combine the surrounding world with the last hundred years of recorded music history and you, as a DJ, have an unfathomable pool of content from which to draw. Amplify it; edit; loop; remix; layer synthesizers, drum machines, effects, vinyl records...or just play one track and mix it with another. The point? There is no prescribed format to what or how you play as a performing DJ.

Goals of This Project

Although there are several reasons, both personal and professional, why I have chosen to write this series of books, one of my primary motivations for writing *The Laptop DJ Handbook* is to engender a somewhat abstract thought process into a digital DJ culture that often speaks with a concrete tongue. Sometimes it's helpful to take a step back and look at DJ culture as a whole, rather than immediately buying into marketing histrionics that are as often as misleading as they are insular. Look at *all* of the tools and consider how to creatively mesh them; don't just focus on the bullet points of one.

Due to the scope of this project, *The Laptop DJ Handbook* is split into two parts. This book, *Part 1*, caters as much to curious or aspiring DJs as it does to DJs with slightly more experience behind them—a resource to help grease the "wheels of steel." However, the mix of system optimization with history, technical data with techniques, and abstract concepts with absolutes will hopefully find a place within the reading of any DJ or fan of digital DJ culture and technology.

Part 2 simply pushes digital DJing up the next logical step. Written with somewhat more practiced DJs/producers in mind, the structure of *Part 1* is developed and expanded through the use of advanced techniques, performance methods, and stage setups. More on this later...

An unavoidable byproduct of exciting new technology is the all-too-often dry language of user documentation. Nevertheless, communication between members of any culture can be difficult unless participants take the time to learn the lingo. Product manuals do contain essential information, a fact that shouldn't be taken lightly. This handbook is not designed to replace them. Rather, through a combination of explanation and example, it is my goal to offer insight, tips, and techniques that bridge the various product manuals. It would be interesting to comprehensively unravel each product within these two books; unfortunately, the scope of the overall project presents certain limitations requiring me to focus my considerations. Each product has been chosen for the power it presents to contemporary DJs on the stage, in the studio, and in between. I encourage you to peruse each book as you see fit; pick through chapters of interest, within which you may discover something new, or read from beginning to end.

No matter what level or style of DJ you are, I hope that while reading these books you find the inspiration to push yourself outside of your comfort zone. Remember, most of the DJ culture's best ideas arose out of accidents and experimentation.

Online Content

As mentioned a moment ago, reading through user documentation can be painfully tedious; we all share the impulse to tear open our presents and play. To help make the reading more interesting, the online portion of these manuals will help provide visual feedback for certain conceptual processes.

Point your browser to www.formatproject.com/djhandbook1.zip. There you can search for the title of this book, my name, or the book's ISBN, and you will be taken to the page for this book. And there, you will find various download folders containing the project files as covered throughout this text. (Significantly more content—including screen-capture videos—will be provided within *Part 2*.)

2 The Evolution of DJing

After nearly a century of evolution, DJ culture has matured into an immensely diverse arena of autonomous breeds and performance methodologies. Despite years of change and adaptation, the primary defining characteristic of DJing has remained consistent: the unifying behavior of performing some type of audio to some form of audience.

Today, a sizable percentage of that audience can be found partying inside one of the world's multitude of nightclubs. The DJ's milieu, nightclubs are purpose-built environments where we bathe our ears in a special type of amplified sound—they're not just dimly lit to make us look better (though it helps). One positive byproduct of a club's poor visibility is our heightened sense of, among other things, *music*.

Although it would be interesting to delve headlong into a thoroughly exhaustive project on DJ culture, for me to accomplish my goals with these books, the primary focus remains on the characteristics that outline a modern DJ performance. There was no way around the fact that conscious omissions had to be made; DJ culture is simply too vast to fit an unabridged approach within this chapter. However, this decision does not free me from the desire to provide you with a condensed synopsis of DJ culture's pivotal events and personas.

As the cliché goes, it's a lot easier to see where you're going once you understand where you've been.

History

Although the term *DJ* was conceived much later, during the early 1900s those we now refer to as DJs were generally bound either to the field of radio broadcasting or to the tenets of musical experimentation. Within the last century, the expansion of the DJ profession has grown in depth and scope to encompass myriad types of radio DJs, nightclub DJs, tuntablists, high-art experimentalists, mobile-event DJs, and, of course, the industry foundation of bedroom DJs. The venues within which these music aficionados perform range from beautifully appointed studios owned by multinational radio conglomerates to massive nightclubs capable of housing thousands of partiers; from one-off, illegal warehousers to intimate loft parties; from wedding celebrations to corporate-sponsored events and tradeshows; from bedrooms to worldwide performance

5

competitions; and from festivals to the hidden chambers of high art's sonic experimentation.

Presently, the popular understanding of what it means be a DJ is well reflected within videogame developer Activision's release of *DJ Hero*, a game that places DJs center stage inside the upper echelons of rock-star notoriety.

The method of music transmission has also evolved to use a massive range of platforms; radio DJs nowadays broadcast through any combination of AM, FM, shortwave, digital, and Internet radio. Nightclub DJs and others have evolved from long-held traditions of two turntables and a two-channel DJ mixer into elaborate stage configurations consisting of multiple laptops, drum machines, effect units, and more.

From Science and Experimentation

One must wonder what Thomas Edison or Emile Berliner would do if presented with the cultural significance of their early inventions. Edison's development of the phonograph cylinder in 1877 marked history with an unprecedented reality: The entirety of the audible world could be permanently stored onto a medium specifically designed for on-demand playback.

Figure 2.1 Thomas Alva Edison with his early phonograph cylinder.

Berliner took the concept one step further. Edison's cylinder presented obvious marketable disadvantages, so in 1887 Berliner squashed it, literally. The result was a flattened gramophone disc capable of indefinite reproduction from a single master copy—somewhat similar to the 12-inch vinyl EP still common with DJs today. Remarkably, it would be decades before the medium saw any (by today's standards) widespread commercial success. Yet, vinyl's prosperity would never have been realized without the help of another category of DJ, every modern DJ's namesake—the radio jock.

Figure 2.2 Emile Berliner and his early phonograph disc.

The first decade of the 20th century has numerous accounts of engineers fiddling with various radio technologies. The year 1906 saw Canadian Reginald A. Fessenden transmit the first receivable radio waves. One year later, American Lee de Forest fabricated the *triode*, a crucial piece of technology that served as the catalyst to commercial radio's explosion—hence why he is often trumpeted as the "father of radio."

Interestingly, avant-garde composers were some of the first to embrace the gramophone. German composer Stefan Wolpe purportedly took to the decks at a *Dada* event in the 1920s and employed eight (yes, eight) gramophone turntables to simultaneously play records at variable speeds. In 1922/23, Hungarian composer László Moholy-Nagy wrote two texts within which he ponders the gramophone's use as a musical instrument, beating scratch pioneers Grand Wizard Theodore and Grandmaster Flash to the punch by more than 50 years. The year 1939 saw American composer John Cage arrange *Imaginary Landscape No. 1*, a composition requiring the use of two variable-speed turntables to perform using frequency-based tone recordings. Cage would go on to compose *Cartridge Music* in 1960, whereupon inanimate objects were "played" by musicians using old phonograph cartridges.

Despite the fact that art and science embraced the turntable early on, decades passed before DJ culture conceptualized the turntable as a standalone musical instrument. Once it did, it began by accident.

To Popular Culture

Still nameless, it wasn't until the early 1940s that individual radio DJs gained widespread exposure—a position solidified once the advertising world saw radio's potential within post–World War II markets. It took innovative radio personalities such as Martin Block to cement the foundation upon which DJs have built their home within the music industry. As the '40s drew to a close, record labels recognized the playlists of Block and his cohorts as a band's primary breaking force. Around this time, abundant dubious sources claim to have coined the term *disc jockey*; nonetheless, it is certain that the term arose because of Block and his superstar contemporaries.

Increasingly, DJs shaped the manner in which popular culture consumed and understood music. Terms such as *rock 'n roll* and *rhythm'n blues* were popularized by DJs in the '50s to classify the music they played.

Fundamentally, a DJ is a salesman. Radio DJs sell a sponsor; club DJs sell a sound; scratch DJs sell the concept of turntable-as-instrument; avant-garde DJs sell high art, and so on. Historically, the relationships between a DJ's success (financially, anyhow) and his listenership have been mutually inclusive; there is a reason why it's called DJ *culture*.

In the early days of radio, DJs were a democratizing source of fresh music that often transcended contemporaneous social and racial barriers. Home stereos provided desegregated access to musical diversity within a time of debilitating social isolation. With radio, the masses now had instant access to multiple channels of shifting musical content, yet few people with whom to share it. Given that society remains gregarious to the end, specialized DJ-focused nightclubs began to sprout up across the U.S. and Europe. This became especially evident as radio jocks migrated into the nightclub environment, and events catering to specific styles of music and dancing grew global roots.

For centuries, groups of musicians have performed for crowds. All of a sudden, bands found themselves replaced by a dynamic sound source able to supply hours of stylistically different music. For music fans, DJs proved to be receptive to the communal mood of a dance floor. For promoters and venues, DJs provided a simple, cost-effective solution to an evening's musical programming.

Creative DJs embraced this opportunity and experimented with interesting new methods of playing records. The most resourceful of the lot utilized equipment to its fullest, often completely bypassing the intended design. One turntable turned into two or more; dancers responded favorably to percussive tracks by way of sweat; seamless mixing hypnotized the dance floor; dragging vinyl across a stylus conveyed voice and expression: aggression, sadness, comedy, and percussion; EQ manipulation generated controlled tension; but most importantly, as much as the world's music influenced DJs, DJs now equally influenced the world's music. Decades later, this theme continues to influence the culture of the disc jockey.

To Genre

One way or another, DJs have consistently managed to irritate the music industry. As hobby grew into profession, professionalism brought power. Before too long, DJs no longer begged record labels for promos—at some point labels wised up to the shifting climate and saw that consumer purchasing decisions often followed radio and club DJ playlists. Predictably, shady business practices eventually permeated radio. *Payola* in particular—effectively, incentives (generally financial) from a record label to a DJ for regular airplay of a particular track (or tracks) to increase the perception of popularity. Thankfully, as club culture grew from infancy into disco, DJs were given the conditions and the organs to shape a body of musical culture that persists as I write this sentence.

Reggae

Few musical genres can claim to have directly impacted modern DJ culture as much as the Jamaican reggae artists of the '50s, '60s, and early '70s. Innovative techniques were developed that sparked the deconstruction of barriers segregating stage and studio; producers rose in prominence, and their experiments with alternate mixdowns—dubs—of original tracks became commonplace, thus predicting remix culture. Studio effects were brought onstage while both DJs and MCs entered the studio, and the notion of a DJ and his *sound system* suffused Jamaican culture as the DJ-as-artist paradigm was born.

Note: The DJ versus the MC: Simply stated, DJs perform/play/scratch/mix the percussive beat structures over which the MC vocalizes his creative lyricism.

One of reggae's important contributions to the audio world was that it heavily influenced the sound of studio production. At its heart, this began with Jamaican DJs and their sound systems. Competitive crews and their mobile setups battled for supremacy by setting up massive, custom-built kits, commonly known as *sounds,* in open-air dance venues. Respect and recognition reigned supreme, as crews took pride in the sonic character of their gear and, of course, the unique records they brought to bear.

Pioneers such as Coxsone Dodd, King Tubby, and legendary Lee "Scratch" Perry were heavily influential in the development of reggae's trailblazing studio accomplishments. As multitrack recorders initially entered the market, Dodd and contemporaries sampled the rhythms of existing tracks and created new percussion-only takes, or *versions.* Segregated rhythms were now primed for the entry of the DJ's or MC's vocal freestyling, called *toasting.* Humorously, Dodd is known to be among the first DJs to rub off and/or alter artist and track names from his vinyl in order to retain musical secrecy.

Taking a step further, King Tubby developed dub techniques early in the 1970s, unintentionally predicting the future of remixing. Beyond the version, a dub is a full reworking of original material. Fundamentally, the dub (doubling) process imagined and developed music for a particular setting: the outdoor dance party. The first results were *dubplate* acetates—exclusively individual, one-off test pressings that deteriorate after a handful of plays. Much as dance music is produced for massive club systems, dub was crafted for individual Jamaican sound systems. The process itself generally detached the rhythms from a track, reworked frequency content through boosted lows and highs, and applied layer upon layer of magnified reverbs and protracted delays (echoes).

Dance music ranging from dub techno to dubstep can thank reggae for its pivotal focus on shaping pounding low-end, sculpting glistening highs, and envisaging distant spacious effect treatments. Likewise, hip-hop MCs and DJs, more than any other, but also jungle, drum 'n bass, UK garage, and so on all share collective nods in Jamaica's direction for establishing many fundamentals of their craft and culture.

Hip-Hop

Historically, DJs and hip-hop culture go hand in hand. They are the drummer, the bassist, the guitarist, and the backing vocalist—basically, DJs serve as hip-hop's backbone. Thus, it should come as no surprise that a Jamaican founded the genre. As the story goes, Jamaican immigrant Clive Campbell, or DJ Kool Herc, was so influenced by his homeland's DJ culture that he imported the idea of the sound system to West Brooklyn, New York.

When Herc's sets shifted from reggae to funk, people started to dance. Once he perceived the effectiveness of drum breaks on the dance floor, he mixed back and forth between the breaks of duplicate records to extend percussive sections. As a result, his dance floor lost it. The combination of Herc's Jamaica-inspired MCs and utilization of beat-based backing tracks proved irresistible. Thus, in 1974, hip-hop was born.

Shortly thereafter, Joseph Saddler, or Grandmaster Flash, took influence from Herc's style and raised the bar. By all accounts, Flash was motivated early on by another contemporary, Pete DJ Jones. Unlike Herc, Jones' mixes were seamlessly segued together so as not to distract the groove on the dance floor with sloppy mixing. Extracted from disco, Flash began to evaluate the hip-hop mix under the same principles. Using his *clock theory* concept, Flash affixed stickers to his vinyl to mark the location of particular breaks. Applying this to his *quick mix theory*, he shot back and forth between records to extend selected breaks and layer beats to creative effect. Further, he also fathered *punch phrasing* to thrust in snippets of, for example, vocals from another record. Ever the innovator, at one point Flash even began to experiment with drum machines alongside his DJ sets.

In 1977, as Flash developed and mastered his techniques, a young DJ Grand Wizard Theodore discovered scratching...accidentally. Ostensibly, Theodore was playing music in his house, and as mothers do, his told him to turn it down. Having held the platter still while she chided him, he immediately identified the creative significance

Figure 2.3 Grandmaster Flash.

of moving vinyl back and forth across a stylus. The importance of Theodore's discovery extends to the core of DJ culture by lending musical credibility to the craft. Scratching turned the turntable into an instrument—the contemporary guitar.

In 1983, pop music got its first proper taste of DJ culture via Grandmixer D.ST. Effectively serving as the percussive force behind Herbie Hancock's track "Rockit," turntables were permanently embedded inside the ears of the MTV generation. Once "Rockit" reached the music video circuit, it went on to win a Grammy and five MTV Music Video Awards, and thus the notion of DJ-as-artist was presented to pop culture.

As luminaries go, perhaps the greatest role model in early hip-hop's DJ culture was Afrika Bambaataa. As founder of the Zulu Nation, Bambaataa believed in an organization that unified hip-hop. Beyond the oft-applied ethnocentrism amongst DJ communities, through Zulu Nation, Bambaataa put himself forward in a social, communal context to blend the unifying effects of dance and music culture—pulling kids away from gangs and guiding them into music. Musically, no stone was left unturned; Bambaataa was a fervent collector of danceable records. His diverse taste is obvious when you consider that Bambaataa created a track widely considered as one of the most influential precursors to modern dance music, "Planet Rock."

Ironically, the triumvirate of Herc, Flash, and Bambaataa represents a vital aspect not only of early hip-hop, but more loosely of all-encompassing, genre-free DJ culture. Herc embodied perception, crowd awareness, and an appreciation of sound; Flash epitomized technical proficiency, work ethic, and attention to detail; while Bambaataa personified an understanding of DJ culture's youth movement and the powerful substance behind musical analysis and exploration.

Figure 2.4 Hip-hop visionary, Afrika Bambaataa.

Turntablism

The turntable has always appealed to the avant-garde musical realm for its obvious instrumental potential. From early experimental compositions arose avant-garde turntablists such as Christian Marclay. Marclay's experiments with turntables and DJing began in parallel with hip-hop around the mid '70s. With methods inspired from punk rock as well as the Dada and Fluxus art schools, he attempted to find a middle ground between pop music, DJ culture, and high art. Never spending more than a dollar on thrift store–purchased music, Marclay intentionally maimed and wounded records in order to coax new music out of damaged vinyl. On other occasions, he would cut portions (think pie slices) out of a few different EPs and then mix, match, and glue them back together as a new EP.

One project in particular, 1985's *Record Without a Cover*, exemplifies Marclay's artist-as-DJ experiments in that he managed to express the life of a primary DJ tool, vinyl. The release was precisely as it sounds: a limited, uncovered record that was intentionally unprotected. All damage wrought through transport, storage, and use was individual to each copy—its "life." In addition to a person's intangible musical experiences, *Record Without a Cover* also made each person's listening *physically* unique. Although it was not exactly a record for the typical dance floor, Marclay challenged cultural understandings of how to physically interact with vinyl.

Although not directly influenced by hip-hop's formative years, Marclay expressed a strong understanding of it. In an interview with *Music* magazine, Marclay explained, "HipHop didn't grow out of that kind of white, nerdy high art culture. It came out of the streets. It was a simple, direct way to make music. And also a cheap way. Rather than expensive musical instruments, it was just some cheap records and a couple of turntables. There's an economic reason for this happening. And in some strange way these two movements—the Experimental music and the HipHop culture—have kind of grown separately and there are very little interactions between the two, until now."

Modern hip-hop is less about the DJ and more about the lyricist. As the MC hyped the crowd, he gradually became bolder. As he became more brazen, he became more innovative. Lyrics birthed messages fans could identify with, and MCs gained the attention of the crowd. As commercial interest grew and hip-hop went mainstream, the DJ's position was diminished, and he was relegated to obscurity. The DJ, who once single-handedly transplanted the "band" front stage, was once again stuck back in the corner. Auspiciously, turntablism remained fundamental to hip-hop's four pillars: DJ, MC, break dancing, and graffiti. As Marclay said, there was very little interaction between hip-hop culture and experimental music, *until now. ...*

Figure 2.5 DJ Spooky performing at the Tate Modern Museum, London.

Around 1990, unrelenting study inspired DJ Steve Dee to originate *beat juggling*: the distinctive postmodern cut-and-paste process whereupon a DJ dexterously manipulates a mixer's crossfader to single out intricate beats across two or more decks. Since then, dozens of terms have emerged to describe various performance complexities—for example, those mastered by the pivotal U.S. DJ crews of the '90s: the San Francisco

Bay Area's Invisibl Skratch Piklz as well New York's X-Ecutioners and California's Beat Junkies. In the mid-'90s Qbert, of the now dissolved Skratch Piklz, introduced the *crab*: snapping four fingers against the crossfader's on/off state while the thumb springs, or returns the crossfader to the on/off state (depending on crossfader configuration).

From opposite coasts, American DJs Shadow and Spooky have managed to continually shape their own versions of turntablism and DJ culture; in short, the former through the studio-centric re-appropriation of the rare and long-lost sounds of the world, and the latter through highly conceptualized multimedia DJ performances.

Many modern-day DJs, such as the World DMC Champs Germany's Rafik, and the U.S.'s Shiftee, Craze, and Klever, have incorporated the power of software-based DVS systems into their performances. In particular, merging Traktor Scratch Pro with the Maschine and X1 controllers, Rafik has fashioned an impressive model of retrospective turntablism combined with progressive controllerism. There is simply no way for my words to do justice to Rafik's performance. Watch it at www.youtube.com/nativeinstruments.

Without question, turntablists exist as one of the DJ culture's most critical defining factions. The DJ-as-artist paradigm is well exemplified through a turntablist's knack at turning existing music into entirely new cut-and-paste compositions. Making new music out of old music is a postmodern theme that has flourished within DJ culture for decades. However, turntablists continue to push this thematic boundary in the realm of live performance. Paraphrasing Qbert's thoughts from the Doug Pray film, *Scratch*, individual scratch techniques are like words in a language. As DJ culture expands its techniques, it expands its language. As it develops its language, DJs are able to broaden their expression. As DJs further the potential to express themselves, they evolve the DJ-as-artist paradigm.

Disco

For most people, disco summons images of garish nightclubs, gaudy attire, tight pants, excessive partying, Studio 54, *Saturday Night Fever*, and the Village People. To be sure, late disco's decadence was ever-present on the tail end of the '70s and early '80s; however, few people are aware of the musical movement represented by its underground beginnings. Blended ideologies of freedom, release, sexual autonomy, and the collective mind were given life inside New York's multiracial gay communities at a time of monumental social transformation. Societal perceptions of sex and sexuality loosened, minority civil rights finally began to make some headway, the Vietnam War fostered kinship between peace-loving Americans, and the growing narcissism of '70s rock music pushed hordes of people toward new forms of music.

DJ pioneers such as Francis Grasso and David Mancuso helped fabricate the literal and figurative spaces within which many continue to party today. What's more, each role model independently fostered fundamental techniques and ideologies that persist through many of their DJ progeny.

Grasso visualized a DJ set as more than a sequence of prerecorded music; he believed in the individual journey of each evening. The showmanship of Grasso's performances erased the common view of DJs as venue accessories and in its place established the night-club industry's rock-star lynchpin. The pursuit of this goal began at the New York club The Sanctuary and bequeathed several rudimentary techniques that persist to this day. Among them are the *slip-cue*—finding and maintaining a record's cue position while the turntable platter continues to spin beneath the slipmat—and *beatmatching*—using a turntable's pitch control to maintain matched tempos between two or more decks. Further, Grasso is also said to have mixed duplicate records to extend sections of a song for the dance floor, nearly simultaneous to Kool Herc's experiments with pre-hip-hop funk records.

Where Grasso's early Sanctuary experience yielded the key technical and performance manifestations of modern DJs, the days of Mancuso's Loft club represent the realization of abstractions on the ultimate dancing environment. The Loft is widely considered to be the simultaneous birth of modern nightclubs and disco music—a rejection of New York's growing nightclub exclusivity and pretension. Rather, the Loft's principles were based around a love of music, a love of dancing, a love of people, and a love of sound. Mancuso transmuted these ideas into a custom-designed space created to achieve his aspirations: the perfect environment through which to enjoy the combined power of music and atmosphere.

In addition to the direction disco steered nightclub futures and DJ techniques, it also had enormous impact on the wider music industry. The first commercial club mixer was developed: David Rosner and Louis Bozak's 1971 Bozak mixer. (It's no coincidence that David Rosner designed the sound systems of both the Sanctuary and the Loft.) Eventually, record labels recognized the power of a club DJ's playlist—music heard while out at night often translated to sales via club-goers. Thus, labels supplemented in-demand DJs with upfront releases.

Disco gave birth to the 12-inch single in direct response to both consumer and DJ demand—behavior only since repeated with the development of compressed digital formats, such as the MP3. The remix was commodified; whereas reggae remixed dubs for individuals, producers such as Tom Moulton and disco DJs such as Shep Pettibone, Walter Gibbons, François Kevorkian, and Larry Levan remixed extended intro and outro "club" versions for DJs and the public.

Unlike the insular principles of sole use propelled through reggae's vinyl label deface-ment, the disco mentality of founders such as Mancuso cultivated a society of DJs who believed in the sharing and archiving of musical knowledge. Today, this mentality could be loosely compared with peer-to-peer networks (at some level), a la carte

Internet radio, music blogging, online music journalism, and an attitude of "This is who made it, this is what it sounds like, and this is why I love it."

Disco died a hard death in the very late '70s and early '80s. A backlash against the ostentatious pomp that Studio 54 and its ilk exemplified was one of a dozen reasons behind disco's demise; however, disco's last gasp began, as is typical, once the major labels saw profitability in the genre and shoved it down the world's throat. The adverse reaction was for dance music to return underground. Among other examples, disco's next evolution began when Larry Levan set New York's Paradise Garage in motion; Frankie Knuckles moved to Chicago and primed the Warehouse for the birth of house music; and Detroit futurists Juan Atkins, Derrick May, and Kevin Saunderson awoke techno.

Figure 2.6 The former Paradise Garage.

House

There was a time when house was more than just a style of music. Chicago house-heads in the '80s were *house* in the same way that today people who embody hip-hop culture are *hip-hop*. The term *house* emerged not from any stylistic underpinnings linked to it today, but rather from roughly 1977 onward within Frankie Knuckles' resident club, the Warehouse. Effectively, one well-known story behind the creation of house music explains that Chicago club-goers would shop specifically for music they heard at Knuckles' Warehouse.

Emerging out of a predominately gay, black, and Hispanic music community, the house mentality was not taken seriously throughout Chicago for several years, basically due to unfortunate, regressive prejudice. As the popularity of the Warehouse grew, the early '80s saw some of the city's more open-minded straight DJs venture to the Warehouse and take the experience outside of Chicago's west side. In 1983 Knuckles moved on and opened his own club, the Power Plant. In response, the Warehouse owners started the Music Box venue and established another of house music's early DJ innovators, Ron Hardy. While the two were reportedly friends, independent styles aided in further diversifying the development of house music's umbrella of subgenres. Knuckles personified house's disco soul, whereas Hardy epitomized its emergent experimentalism.

In alignment with pushing the DJ performance forward, Knuckles, Hardy, and those who followed after began toying with new performance ideas. Knuckles bought a Roland TR-909 from one of techno's originators, Derrick May, as a percussive tool for use within the Warehouse—a performance technique employed by early house legends Farley "Jackmaster" Funk, with his Roland TR-808, and additionally by Jesse Saunders. Around the same time, Hardy and Knuckles implemented local producers' reel-to-reel recordings into their sets, which further engendered the DIY aesthetic into Chicago's homegrown scene. This manner of thinking set an example that hastily spread across Chicago with the release of Jesse Saunders' track "On and On." Generally considered one of the first true house tracks, the simple rhythm structure and straightforward melodic content spurred the subsequent explosion of bedroom producers.

The expansion of home studios combined with the welcoming nature of the house's early professors and allowed the music to mature on its own accord for years. Removed from the contaminating touch of the major music industry, Knuckles and Hardy created a metaphorical Petri dish, within which Chicago's house DJ producers proliferated. This framework not only nurtured house legends such as Chez Damier, Marshall Jefferson, Larry Heard, Lil Louis, and Derrick Carter, but it also provided the foundation upon which DJ Pierre and Marshall Jefferson partly established the sound of the acid house movement with Phuture's timeless "Acid Tracks" release—squelching Roland's TB-303 sound into the sonic archives alongside their TR-808 and TR-909 drum machines.

Significantly, global ripple effects arose out of the early Chicago house years, particularly within the UK and across Europe—young British visionaries such as Danny Rampling, Paul Oakenfold, Nicky Holloway, Johnny Walker, and Trevor Fung imported the Balearic sound of Ibiza's legendary DJ Alfredo, in part spawning the UK's immensely pivotal early acid house movement. Somewhat closer to home, undeniable influence was shared by a handful of imaginative young freethinkers living within the Detroit suburbs.

Techno

In their DJ anthology *Last Night a DJ Saved My Life*, Bill Brewster and Frank Broughton wittily sum up one of techno's fundamental standards: "Its basic notion is this: if house is just disco played by microchips, what kind of noise would these machines make on their own." Whereas house music principally originated as a home-grown industry evolved from disco, techno serves as a type of source code describing a broader, international language. In opposition to house's adaptation to and evolution within a purposely designed environment, techno's abstract conceptualization reached beyond the physical and social constructs of its architects.

The narrative of the Belleville Three (after their high school)—Juan Atkins, Derrick May, and Kevin Saunderson—is a thing of techno legend. The trio grew up with an experience atypical of young, black Detroit teenagers in the '70s and '80s. Although they were raised within a relatively affluent, predominately white Detroit suburb, their incongruous, slightly dislocated experience of coming of age within Detroit's crumbling, post-industrial landscape led the three to venture clear, mentally and physically, of their surroundings in search of inspiration. A shared love of personal musical expansion eventually led to the discovery of synth-based European acts, such as Kraftwerk— long cited as a foundational element underpinning the stylistic developments of house, techno, hip-hop, and more.

Beyond their years, they realized that while Chicago's house music and New York's disco were propagated from within DJ culture, techno was necessarily conceptualized from the ground up—as musicians first. That is not to say that the club context of music did not have its effect. Family visits to New York allowed Saunderson to sneak into Levan's Paradise Garage and Mancuso's Loft. Simultaneously, May made regular trips to Chicago to immerse himself in the atmospheres of Knuckles' Power Plant and Hardy's Music Box. Taking this insight into the studio inspired the creation of the first true techno records. In 1985 as Model 500, Atkins unveiled "No UFO's"; as Rhythm Is Rhythm, May loosed "Strings of Life" in '87; while in '86, as Kreem, Saunderson released "Triangle of Love" and, of course, the insanely successful track, "Big Fun," in '88. Devoted to the end, they additionally launched their individual labels: Metroplex, Transmat, and KMS, respectively.

Techno's second coming birthed new artists, DJs, and entirely new techno subgenres. In the late '80s, Jeff Mills and "Mad" Mike Banks formed the pioneering Detroit-based Underground Resistance label collective, pushing edgier, industrialized techno. After some time in New York, Mills eventually moved to Chicago and in '92 launched his highly instrumental label, Axis, followed by a lineage of sub-labels. In '93, Rob Hood popularized minimal techno's terminology with the release of *Minimal Nation* on his own imprint, M-Plant. Simultaneously, a young Richie Hawtin swelled to embody techno's current evolution through the continual reinvention of his artistry, most commonly with his Plastikman alias, as well as historic labels Minus and Plus8, the latter of which he created with fellow Canadian, John Acquaviva. Further offspring emerged as exemplified by the staggering musical career of Carl Craig and others such as Blake Baxter, Kenny Larkin, Stacey Pullen, and of course the genius of Daniel Bell.

Figure 2.7 The Wizard, a.k.a. Jeff Mills.

Seemingly sharing house music's American destiny, techno was not faced with even remotely the same level of success as it was within Europe. More than anywhere else, techno encountered the widest acceptance inside Germany. Renowned Berlin techno institution Tresor opened its door in '91, while a few years before, Sven Väth launched his club, the Omen, a precursor to his massively successful Cocoon trademark. Releasing under Basic Channel, Maurizio, and more, Berlin-based Moritz von Oswald and Mark Ernestus more or less singlehandedly developed the dub techno genre in the early '90s (and opened the historic Hard Wax record shop in Berlin; www.hardwax.com). As a whole, Europe widely adopted this electronic explosion, exemplified through an influx of artists: Aphex Twin, Autechre, Peter Kuhlmann, Future Sound of London, the Black Dog, Dr. Motte (of Love Parade fame), Orbital, Speedy J, Surgeon, Regis, Female, Baby Ford, Mark Broom, Thomas Fehlman, CJ Bolland, Carl Cox—far too many to mention.

Akin to house, techno was permeated early on with an understanding that electronic music's fundamental gear requirements made music production a process for the everyman. Not surprisingly, the techno name insinuates a musical symbiosis with technology. From a performance perspective, techno boasts an exceptionally high percentage of performers embracing forward-thinking performance methods. Jeff Mills' technical rider requests a setup of no fewer than three Pioneer CDJ-1000s, two Technics 1200s, and a TR-909—pretty impressive, especially given that he has been performing this way for years. Richie Hawtin has progressed from his '99 release *Decks, FX & 909*, constantly incorporating new technologies into his performance setup in the persistent pursuit of artistic growth. Utilizing MIDI clock, he binds together a pair of laptops to seamlessly employ various software performance applications ranging from Ableton Live to Native Instruments' Traktor Pro and Maschine software, in conjunction with various MIDI controllers: NI's Traktor Kontrol X1 as well as his custom-built, MIDI-capable Allen & Heath Xone-series mixer.

Figure 2.8 Richie Hawtin performing "vinyl-free" with NI's Traktor and Maschine software.

Over the past decade or so, this techno frame of mind has spread at an exponential rate. Digital technologies and the Internet are allowing for the rapid cross-pollination of genres, sharing everything from performance techniques to what were once considered genre-exclusive characteristics.

Jungle and Drum 'n Bass

Nearly parallel to Detroit techno's second wave in the early '90s, the UK's underground DJ culture saw a visionary, urban community spawn its own brand of dynamic electronic dance music. Born in the UK from reggae roots, the distant Caribbean sound system culture suffused London's warehouse party circuit with an emphasis on dance music's quality and presence of percussion, yet specifically honing in on low- and sub-low-end properties while simultaneously speeding up the oft-sampled broken beats characteristic of late '80s and early '90s hip-hop.

Several sources claim credit for naming jungle; however, how the music was shaped remains more significant. Ingenious DJs Fabio and Grooverider experimented on crowds at their resident night, Rage, held within the London-based club, Heaven. At first, the duo took inspiration from Detroit's concurrent output, such as Derrick May and Kevin Saunderson; Chicago artists, such as Larry Heard; and New York artists, such as Joey Beltram, and mixed it with London's emergent breaks-based productions. As the crowds begged for the tougher stuff, turntable pitch faders were maxed out and 33s were played at 45 (turntable RPM). The result was the metamorphosis into a sound more closely associated with what jungle would become.

In '94 and '95, respectively, DJ producers such as Goldie and A Guy Called Gerald released jungle's first full-length albums. In congruence with California's hip-hop scene, over time jungle experienced a consistent influx of inner-city roughness that not only painted the musical input dark and aggressive, but also created a dividing line down the middle of the emergent scene. As no genre is complete without its drama and offshoots, DJs such as LTJ Bukem, Roni Size, and later Fabio were quick to associate themselves with their own brand of melodic-structured, jazz-inspired jungle, thereupon known as drum and bass. Thus, the UK had orchestrated its first homegrown musical genres in direct connection with DJ culture.

Figure 2.9 Pioneering force of jungle, A Guy Called Gerald.

From a DJ perspective, jungle adopted an assortment of performance methods motivated by everything from reggae and hip-hop to turntablism and the back alley warehouses of UK hardcore. Reggae and the scene's Caribbean roots not only leaned on the movement to remain dedicated to the sound system, but also transplanted the toaster to the stage as an MC. However, unlike U.S. hip-hop of the early '90s, jungle presented the MC as part and parcel of the musical emission. Vocalists often ported their mics through a series of effects processors, such as reverb, delay, and so on, in order to blanket the MC's atmospheric lyricism over the top of driving percussive beds. Turntablism made its way into the performance, often highlighted by the characteristic *rewind*: the DJ's, crowd's, or MC's call to stop the record in place and promptly spin the EP back to a particular phrase or to the beginning of the track. Sonically, one of the most distinctive properties that crossed over into everything from UK garage to dubstep and grime is the *bassdrop*: the dramatic silence before a track's explosion back into interwoven bass and percussion.

Almost in parallel to the splintering of jungle into drum 'n bass surfaced a well-dressed style of UK dance music that acquired house's soul and emotion. Restructured percussion was shuffled and meshed with pulsing low end to result in early UK garage.

UK Garage to Grime and Dubstep

For the most part, the shared similarities between UK and U.S. garage are in name alone. U.S. garage is predominately associated with the expressive, soulful house music played by legendary New York DJ Larry Levan and his club the Paradise Garage, from where the music takes its name, as well as New Jersey DJ Tony Humphries at his resident club Zanzibar. Whereas jungle and drum 'n bass, respectively, are often pigeonholed as too visceral or too cerebral, UK garage is more often than not composed with the mindset of a dance floor full of women. Swung percussion and pulsating half-tempo basslines interspersed with two shuffled kick drums per bar (unlike house's standard four) made UK garage's signature two-step groove easily approachable—hence why the mainstream recording industry dove in and corrupted it so early. Akin to jungle, UK garage DJs had the biggest impact on the maturation of their sound by pitching up a house EP's instrumental mix. The style's impact on DJ culture instantly became more interesting once it splintered.

Approximating hip-hop's foundling years, a preference for an EP's instrumental flip side naturally left room for two things: sonic experimentation and/or an MC. Dubstep and grime each represent relatively new, independent styles of dance music; however, their roots begin with UK garage, jungle, and drum 'n bass and profess influence from a broad musical spectrum. On some level, the differing factors are simple: Dubstep relinquishes the primary percussive signatures of UK garage and drum 'n bass and instead gives sub-bass the steering wheel, whereas grime generally maintains subtracted, dubstep-esque structures in order to make room for an MC's lyrical cadence.

Primarily credited around the millennium as the offspring of South London DJ producers, dubstep was coined as a genre by the promotions collective behind the London club night, Forward>>. Early defining sub-bass experimentation was more recently augmented with organic melodious elements and sound design, furnishing additional depth to the intrinsic low-end values. This attention to detail directly caught the interest of many modern techno DJs, fostering cross-pollination in part due to compatible time signatures—from remixes by techno nonpareil Ricardo Villalobos to the devotees of Berlin's Hard Wax crew and the Panorama Bar/Berghain/Ostgut DJs. The movement rapidly matured through the technical artistry of producers such as Kode9, Burial, Appleblim, Shackleton, Skream, Benga, and so on. Dubstep's huge leap in genre credibility was gained once the style was embraced by Radio 1 DJs, including the late John Peel and Mary Anne Hobbs.

Figure 2.10   Kode9, in shadow.

Flip the coin, and on the ground you will find grime. Originating within east London's Rinse FM pirate radio network around the millennium, grime artists took UK garage and dubstep's percussive beds and sparsely concocted them for an MC. In similar fashion to U.S. hip-hop more than two decades ago, grime MCs stepped away from the lyrical celebrations of their DJ selectors and placed themselves at center stage. Taking direct input from U.S. hip-hop, many grime artists find themselves caught between a thriving underground scene, consisting of collectives built through united solidarity, and the mainstream, with individualist ambition reaching for stardom generally reserved for hip-hop's "sellouts."

Preliminary crossover UK garage/grime artists such as So Solid Crew landed at the top of the UK pop charts. Grime's youth is also particularly evident through the age of its contributors; for example, Dizzee Rascal, arguably grime's most recognized artist, released his first hit in '03 at the age of 16. The Roll Deep crew, including Rascal, has also produced a handful of stars in the form of artists such as Wiley and Tinchy Stryder.

A particularly appealing aspect of both dubstep and grime's investment in DJ culture is that both maintain relatively high levels of vinyl-only output. In common with house, techno, and all subgenres of each, many artist-run boutique labels still press vinyl as either dubplates and/or as limited vinyl-only pressings. Additionally, grime and dubstep distinctively represent the multifaceted characteristics intrinsic to DJ culture's youth movement. The formative years of these intersecting UK-based and urban-fed genres have created an interesting narrative in DJ culture. Dubstep's relatively recent global explosion should generate an interesting set of circumstances for grime, because as grime attempts to keep pace, the innate competitive nature of MCs and their crews will hopefully create an intensely tireless environment of experimentation and inspired output.

To The Future

Who better to produce music for a dance floor than an individual who understands what rhythms people will dance to? A DJ is conscious that rhythm generates hypnotic undulations, melody toys with emotions, and frequency bathes dance floors in shifting magnitudes of shared sensation. In the past, these themes were largely understood by a DJ through the music of others—the postmodern process of creating new music out of existing music. For artists, the challenge for the future of DJing lies in expanding upon these concepts.

Over the last century, DJ culture's pioneers have built an industry that has continually rewarded experimentation. Now more than ever, the digitized music industry has provided DJs with an enormous resource of tools to expand upon performance and production. Because they are no longer constrained to turntables, vinyl, and a mixer, current laptops provide forward-thinking DJs with more than enough power to realize their musical ambitions.

The nonspecific nature of the contemporary DJ setup serves as a direct illustration of the modern performer straddling the stage and the studio. Powerful DJ-focused performance software shares hard drive space with studio-inclined digital audio workstations, virtual racks of synthesizers, hardware/software drum machine combinations, samplers, effects—and, of course, all of this rubs up against a DJ's music library. In combination, modern DJs come armed with a veritable sonic arsenal. ...

In the next chapter, you will find some foundational elements to help get your head around what is likely the best aspect of the stage and the studio: the gear!

3 Gear

Aside from music, perhaps the most exciting aspect of DJ culture is the seemingly never-ending wealth of new toys. Every year, music technology companies unleash a deluge of innovative new products or grow new limbs onto those that are already well established.

DJ culture's cornucopia of abundance has found itself snagged on the adage "spoiled for choice." The subsequent assortment of software, hardware, controllers, and hybrid mashups is not intended to be all-inclusive; rather, they are suggestions that cover a range of alternatives ranging from plug-and-play to those that require a significant time investment.

Computer Specifications

As you pull together your finances in preparation for some retail therapy, be sure to factor the potential cost of a new laptop into the equation. My experience has shown me that despite clearly listed system requirements, some customers opt for software purchases even though their computer does not match (or exceed) the prerequisites. If you already own a computer, it is paramount that you verify this information before spending any money. Because specifications are readily available to prospective buyers, software developers won't help you if your computer hardware is not up to par.

Caution: Be wary of system requirements. These are nothing but generalized guidelines under which software will launch and run. They do not take into account advanced use, so you may bump against the ceiling earlier than expected. On the flipside, the fastest, most powerful (read: expensive) computer on the market may not be the most cost-effective solution. Consider stepping one tier down and strategically placing the excess "saved" expense elsewhere—for example, in more RAM, a faster hard drive, a good audio interface, or that MIDI controller you've been eyeing.

Mac or PC?

Undoubtedly you have run into the Mac versus PC debate at some point. The unfortunate side effect is that misinformation abounds, and more often than not it is utterly inaccurate. Music software works equally well on either platform. In the likely event that you are using the laptop for more than just DJing, the choice becomes more about personal preference. There are dozens of applications in the audio and video worlds that are exclusive to either Windows or Mac OS X (though Boot Camp on the Mac runs Windows particularly well). Users on both sides of the fence have positive and negative experiences, so it is very important that you do your research prior to spending money on a laptop. Above all else, ensure that your purchase entitles you to a good warranty and a satisfaction (performance) guarantee inclusive of a return policy.

Few computers (even those sold as such) are prepared for professional audio applications right out of the box. As a suggestion, the Native Instruments Knowledge Base contains a handful of intelligible articles specifically focused on computer system optimization. Because computer operating systems change somewhat regularly, NI updates its databases in kind. You can find the Native Instruments Knowledge Base at www. native-instruments.com/knowledge.

Processor Speed

Computer makers wouldn't be doing their job if people didn't drool over that extra 0.33 GHz. Is it worth the $300 or so? Dwelling on it will drive you nuts, because six months later the ordeal will return full circle. When new computer hardware offers more power, software developers utilize that excess fuel to enhance their software—and so the cycle continues. Fortunately, there are plenty of other areas where that extra money is often more effective—areas that will outlive the benefits of a few extra plug-ins.

Memory

Random-access memory (RAM) is a form of computer information storage specifically designed for rapid access to particular types of data. To put this in perspective, an application such as Traktor temporarily deposits song data into RAM once a track has been loaded into a deck. This allows for immediate, gapless audio playback when cue points are used to jump to different positions within a track. Many new computers are sold with 2 GB of RAM, which is sufficient, but you should consider upping all the way to 4 GB (or more) for the simple reason that audio applications love their memory—not only is RAM relatively inexpensive, but it is also quite easy to install. Four gigabytes is a must if you plan on performing with some of the advanced setups explained in *Part 2* of this series of books.

Note: If upgrading laptop RAM feels slightly intimidating, take a couple of minutes and search for tutorial instructions on YouTube.

Connectivity

CPU speed is considered "sexy" in the computer world, but a laptop's connectivity is definitely...not sexy. Thus, it is often overlooked when shopping for laptops.

Controllers, hard drives, audio interfaces—these all require independent connections of varying types, so make sure that you factor in what else you plan to attach to your machine.

For example, it's a safe bet that even if you are unfamiliar with what a USB 2.0 connection is, at some point you have probably used one. Printers, computer keyboards/mice, MIDI controllers, soundcards, and even iPhones/iPads/iPods use USB to "talk" with your laptop. These days, most computers have at least one USB 2.0 port. On the other hand, be aware of the availability of FireWire connections. If you have a Mac, new laptops only offer FireWire 800 ports (older models offer FireWire 400), whereas Windows PCs may not provide a FireWire option at all. Definitely do a bit of preplanning with regard to your hardware connections.

Audio Interface (Soundcard)

As mentioned already, very few computers are purposely built for professional audio applications. The internal soundcard of a standard laptop is generally intended for multimedia usage: watching DVDs, listening to music, playing videogames, and so on. As a result, an internal soundcard's components and software drivers are insufficient in several critical aspects of DJ setups—namely, audio routing flexibility, connectivity, and sound quality. Although it may not feel like it, the professional audio market represents a tiny fraction of the millions upon millions of laptop users around the world. Therefore, "off the shelf" pro audio options are not of the highest priority for consumers and manufacturers.

Why Do I Need an Audio Interface?

One elementary characteristic of DJing is the ability to cue from two dedicated audio sources—the master channel, which is what the audience hears, and the monitor channel (also known as *pre-listen* or *cue*), which is what the DJ hears. As found on any standard club mixer, the monitor and master outputs each have their own discrete stereo gain control. Think of an audio interface as the heart of your software's audio signal flow; the device converts all incoming audio (Traktor or Serato's timecode vinyl, microphone inputs, and so on) from analog to digital (A-D) and all outgoing audio (from Traktor, Serato, Live, and so on) from digital to analog (D-A).

To clarify, remember that each stereo channel on a four-channel mixer offers specific input types, these generally being line-level (as for a CDJ: a CD-based turntable) and/or phono-level (as for a turntable). Generally, each channel on a four-channel mixer is set up to receive the outputs of a CDJ, a turntable, or...an audio interface (laptop).

Bearing this in mind, each stereo output (1/2, 3/4, and so on) of your audio interface connects to a line-level input on the back of any typical DJ mixer. For example, this is clearly labeled upon the rear of the Native Instruments Audio 8 DJ interface in Figure 3.1. Notice that each of the channels (CH) has an RCA output pair, totaling four stereo outputs. So, if each of the four Traktor decks represents four independent stereo outputs, then you would need a DJ mixer with four line-level inputs—one for each of the four decks. Phew…make sense now?

Figure 3.1 Notice the various connection types on the rear of the Audio 8 DJ.

What Audio Interface Is Best for Me?

The purchase of an audio interface is one of the most important investments you will make as a digital DJ. Make an informed choice here, and you stand to arm yourself with a device that will probably outlast a few computers. Thus, doing some research will pay off hugely down the road. There are several factors to consider once you begin shopping.

Note: If you are a vinyl purist, but you see yourself on the DVS/vinyl fence, consider using Traktor Scratch Pro or Serato's timecode control vinyl/CD. Your options are simple yet quite powerful, and you can still flip between real records and the DVS software.

Check out Traktor Scratch Pro (bundled with the Audio 8 DJ), Traktor Scratch Duo (bundled with the Audio 4 DJ), or one of the many Traktor Certified mixers. Alternatively, Rane/Serato's equivalent, the Rane SL1 or SL 3 interface, Sixty-Eight, TTM 57SL, or MP 4 mixers provide a somewhat similar experience. These bundles comprise the proprietary hardware/software combination necessary to control DVS software with timecode control vinyl. You can find detailed information at the respective manufacturer websites: traktorpro.com or serato.com.

Connectivity

The benefits that laptops provide in terms of convenience and portability come with certain sacrifices, most visibly in the form of connection options. The large majority of portable audio interfaces offer two ways to connect to your computer: USB 2.0 and FireWire. Be aware that USB 2.0 is the protocol used on the majority of MIDI control surfaces, on digital DJ applications, and also on many portable hard drives; however, if you venture away from the prepackaged DJ hardware/software combinations (such as

Traktor or Serato), you will find that the recording industry is mostly dominated by external FireWire audio interfaces. Therefore, you must ensure that you are not using up all of your laptop's USB and FireWire ports.

Outputs

As mentioned previously, the ability to pre-listen (cue) to tracks is critical to a DJ performance. Therefore, begin your search for a soundcard that supports a minimum of four independent audio channels (two stereo pairs): one for the cue output and one for the master output.

The number of outputs presents a favorable versatility for both experienced and beginning digital DJs. For example, if you have an audio interface with eight outputs (four stereo pairs), each output can be connected to independent inputs on a four-channel DJ mixer, adding the strengths of hardware mixing and flexibility between different stage setups. Further, advanced performance setups thrive with extra outputs when used for hardware effects sends or as autonomous signals from other software applications—for example, while running Traktor and Maschine simultaneously.

Although the bulk of DJ mixers make use of RCA channel inputs, this is not a trait shared across the audio interface market. A few soundcards, such as the Audio 8 DJ (refer to Figure 3.1), were specifically designed for the DJ market; therefore, they offer RCA connectivity instead of 1/4-inch.

Tip: Some words of advice: Always travel with a couple of RCA female to 1/4-inch male and 1/4-inch female to RCA male adapters.

Inputs

Once you leave the performance domain and enter that of production, inputs become a key factor when pricing out the right interface. Most travel-ready soundcards are compact and robust, so when you weigh input count against portability, inputs (and outputs) are often sacrificed. Nonetheless, if you are planning on recording multiple simultaneous sources in the future, this should be a serious consideration toward your final purchase.

On top of that, when it comes to inputs, connection type is generally more important than it is with outputs. For example, you will need an XLR input providing phantom power if you plan on using a condenser microphone in the studio. Further, some performers use XLR inputs onstage to address the crowd, for live MCs, or even to sample live audio for on-the-fly scratching and/or slicing to applications such as Ableton Live or Maschine.

Synthesizers, drum machines, and most other gear will require multiple 1/4-inch connections, whereas other devices may require further features, such as AES/EBU, S/PDIF, or ADAT Lightpipe. The interface in Figure 3.2, RME's Fireface 400, is extremely rugged, highly portable, and offers multiple input/output and MIDI options for traveling artists.

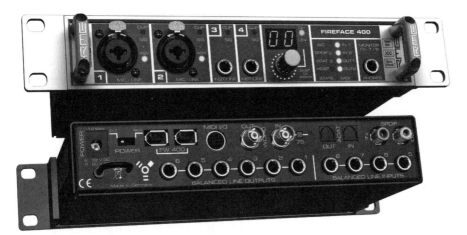

Figure 3.2 The RME Fireface 400 boasts pristine sound and offers an abundance of features for an interface of its size.

Don't worry too much if you do not recognize some of the input terminology. If you are just getting into the studio side of things, it isn't something that you need to be well versed on at this point.

Converters

Many audiophiles determine the overall worth of an audio interface through the characteristics of its *converters*. In loose terms, think of analog-to-digital (A-D) converters as a digital camera and digital-to-analog (D-A) converters as a photographic printer.

A-D converters capture the experience of the physical (analog) world—guitars, vocals, vinyl archiving—and translate it into the digital realm as a digital audio file of some form. Much like the quality of a camera lens, the quality of an A-D converter determines how accurately a recording (picture) is captured.

On the other hand, D-A converters reproduce the captured digital sound into a physical (analog) form. Similar to the caliber of components within photo printers, the grade of the D-A converter influences how precisely that sound (picture) is reproduced (printed) back into the analog domain.

Consider how the device will be used when evaluating converters. If you don't see yourself recording external sources, then all you should be concerned about is the quality of the D-A converters, or what your crowd hears. On the other hand, if you *do* see yourself recording external sources, keep the overall quality of both in mind when it comes time to make your purchase.

With audio interfaces, you will generally get what you pay for. Better components quickly drive up prices, so you could be looking at a range spanning a few hundred to several thousand dollars for a single piece of equipment. With regard to converters, the RME Fireface 400, shown back in Figure 3.2, is well regarded within the industry's range of portable audio interfaces. In addition, another device well worth considering is MOTU's UltraLite-mk3—it packs a powerful balance of features at a reasonable price. If you are looking to spend a bit less money, M-Audio manufactures a wide range of functional audio interfaces perfectly suited to the traveling performer.

MIDI

One of the most powerful features of modern digital DJ software is the ability to speak the computer music language of MIDI. Through MIDI, artists are able to assign a tactile overlay of software parameters onto expressive hardware control surfaces—allowing them to virtually reach into the application's feature set.

Furthermore, a five-pin MIDI input/output port is essential when considering an audio interface for advance performance and studio setups. One powerful feature that is often neglected is that some digital DJ software sends and receives MIDI clock timing information—to a drum machine, for example, or from another computer running Traktor, Ableton, or even instruments such as Maschine. This effectively syncs all of the slave equipment together to the same master tempo (bpm) and allows artists to perform with creative expression rather than worrying about beatmatching.

Drivers

Simply stated, an *audio driver* is the software side of an audio interface (or other external device) that determines the communication between the interface and the computer. Drivers automatically function in the background once a device is connected; minus the occasional updates, they require very little thought.

What is important to know about drivers is how they affect the *latency* of your music software. A simple definition of latency is the time it takes to convert analog audio to digital data and back. The more efficient the driver and the faster the computer processor, the faster the conversion rate and thus the lower the latency. Where this concerns digital DJs is best exemplified while using Traktor's timecode vinyl. When you are cueing up to drop the first downbeat, the time it takes between sliding the record forward and hearing the kick through the speakers is referred to as *latency*. The lower the value within Traktor's (or any other audio application's) preferences, the tighter the overall control.

Tip: If you experience unpleasant audio artifacts, such as clicks, pops, and/or dropouts, try raising your soundcard's buffer size. By increasing the audio buffer, you are giving your computer more headroom to efficiently manage all of the incoming/outgoing data streams. This adjustment setting is usually found within your DJ software's preferences page or through the soundcard's dedicated software setup panel.

On Windows PCs, most of the popular music software applications support the ASIO (Audio Stream Input/Output) drivers written years ago by Steinberg (developers of Cubase). Additionally, a vast number of audio interfaces also support the ASIO protocol to give PC users ultra low-latency performance. Mac users, on the other hand, are blessed with the highly efficient Apple-developed Core Audio.

Note: Windows PC users caught in a situation where connecting an audio interface is inconvenient (an airplane) should download the ASIO driver ASIO4ALL from www.asio4all.com. It's free and should serve as a temporary fix for troubles caused by standard Windows drivers.

The Software

At the heart of the digital DJ movement lie three groundbreaking models of software design. Two examples modernize a long-established DJ formula through innovative Digital Vinyl System (DVS) technology, while the other transplants an intuitive modular recording studio onto the stage.

Native Instruments: Traktor Scratch Pro

In 2000, Berlin-based Native Instruments began to release the first of many manifestations of the Traktor DJ brand. This seed, planted and developed over 10 years, has matured into one of the most powerful pieces of performance DJ software on the market. Along the way, Native Instruments has opened its ears to voices spanning DJ culture in order to refine Traktor and allow it to adopt exceedingly powerful features:

■ Traktor Pro's foundation is composed of four playback decks wrapped around the Beatgrid and Sync features, thus allowing DJs to transfer large chunks of time spent beatmatching over to time spent performing.

■ Further augment your performances with various configurations of the 28 independently assignable effects, ranging from the studio standards of delay and reverb to LFO-controlled filters, Beatmashers, and more. As you can see in Figure 3.3, Traktor also employs powerful EQ and filter sections modeled after industry-standard DJ mixers.

■ Ever empowering DJs, Traktor provides precise, quantized track looping utilizing seamless loop-adjustment points, fine-tunable and precisely synced to the master tempo without dropping a beat.

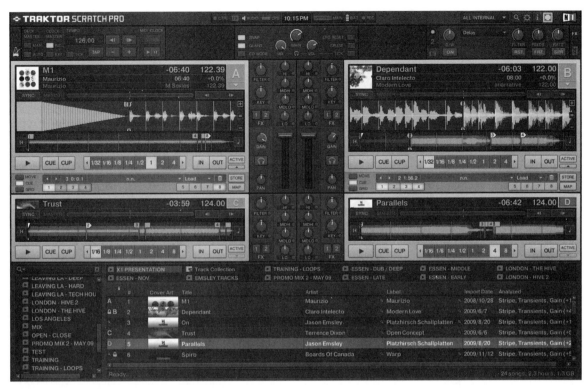

Figure 3.3 The Traktor Pro Interface.

- No doubt at some point in your life you have heard songs with annoying intros, amazing breakdowns, vocals, or even just a tiny section that would layer perfectly over another song in your collection. Virtually limitless, freely assignable cue points help mark (and avoid) these areas in the form of cue position pointers, loops, load markers (tracks load to specific start points), and so on.

- Can't find a song? Traktor's intelligent track browsing methodically filters tracks via keystroke entry. Use Crate Flick to scan through your music files by album cover; directly import your playlists from your iTunes library or create your own virtual record crates and assign them to one of 12 assignable Favorites playlists.

- Experience the tightest timecode control vinyl on the market. Traktor's control vinyl is embedded with a 2-kHz (2,000-Hz) carrier frequency, double that of the industry-standard 1 kHz (1,000 Hz).

- Versatile internal record features enable you to record live performances or archive your vinyl collection. Moreover, use an Internet connection to broadcast your performances over the SHOUTcast or Icecast streaming media services.

- Finally, and perhaps most importantly, comprehensive MIDI capability and advanced controller assignment hand software control over to DJs. Say farewell to the notorious stereotype of laptop performers seemingly just "checking their email."

If that wasn't enough, Traktor equips DJs with an exceptionally powerful element: MIDI clock! Herein lies the foundation of one of Traktor's greatest strengths.

Why should you care so much about integrating MIDI into your DJ setup? Here is an example: You and a friend can sync two laptops and literally double the sonic palette of your performances, all the while gaining the creative input, inspiration, and spontaneity created when sharing the stage with another performer. Then again, if your friends annoy you as much as mine do (despite my love for them), you are free to go it alone by syncing a second laptop running Traktor. Alternatively, you can also sync Traktor to your choice of drum machine, synthesizer, effects module, or Ableton Live.

Note: All of this sync talk requires a bit of explanation. Unless otherwise noted, whenever sync is mentioned, I am referring to the synchronized playback of two (or more) sound sources. For example, Traktor's Sync function locks the bpm of two or more Decks (tracks) to a master source. This source could be an individual Deck, Traktor's internal tempo clock, or an external MIDI clock source, such as a drum machine or another computer. This topic is thoroughly explained within the following chapters.

Serato Scratch Live

A few years after the early versions of Traktor hit the market, 2004 saw Rane, a Washington-based audio hardware manufacturer, partner up with Serato, a small audio software company founded in Auckland, New Zealand. Together the partnership unveiled another leading DVS bundle, Serato Scratch Live (or more commonly, Serato). Since the '80s, Rane has released numerous hardware solutions targeted at performing musicians, more recently focusing on the DJ market with its widely respected line of nightclub DJ mixers. Serato, on the other hand, established the standard for real-time audio stretching with its Pro Tools/Logic Pro–compatible plug-in, Pitch 'n Time. Who better to construct modern DVS technology than the masters of pitch themselves?

- Serato Scratch Live (SSL) proudly sets an example for what is likely the finest manufacturer/customer relationship on the digital DJ market. Attentive developers engage closely with an active user community to cultivate an environment of continuous software updates, fixes, and product enhancements. Best of all, updates are *always* free!

- Aimed at the "digital" vinyl purist, SSL, when connected to hardware such as Rane's Sixty-Eight DJ mixer, presents DJs with powerful, turntable-based control options over two, three, or four Decks.

- SSL DJs embrace powerful performance features ranging from the digital standards of cues and loops to the expressive SP-6 Sample Player. Expand upon traditional DJ performances with the ability to fire off up to six different MIDI-assignable audio sources on demand.

■ Scratch's astonishingly well-constructed Browser employs numerous paths to searching and organizing your music library. The inclusion of the Smart Crate concept creates an automatic rule-based organizational system that streamlines library organization via automatic criteria filters. On top of that, iTunes users gain immediate access to their (DRM-free) iTunes library, while album art offers visual cues over a vast collection of music.

■ DJ setups are never complete without effects. SSL provides a comprehensive and highly customizable array of serially connected FX plug-ins, as you can see in Figure 3.4. An intuitive, somewhat modular workflow lets performers specify the performance behaviors of MIDI-assignable effects devices.

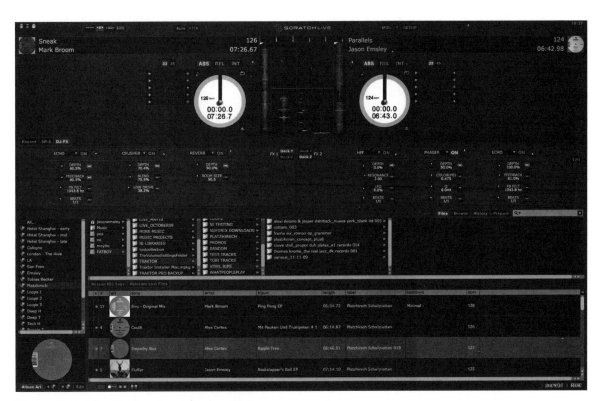

Figure 3.4 The Serato Scratch Live GUI.

■ With the lean toward vinyl-based DJing, it's no surprise that Serato built in a dedicated audio recorder equally suited for archiving a vinyl collection and recording mixes.

What is the most exciting thing about SSL's future? Back in 2008, Serato and Ableton announced a creative partnership that would reveal what the companies are calling the *Bridge*—essentially, the middle ground that lets performers blend the playback of Live's clips with the DVS technology of SSL. The creative potential of Bridge, released in September 2010, immediately after the writing of this book, seems infinitely promising. And speaking of Live...

Ableton Live

Emerging at the beginning of 2001, Live was introduced to the software music world by a group of like-minded individuals driven by the goal of harnessing an artist's experience between the stage and the studio. Robert Henke and Gerhard Behles (of Monolake fame) joined Bernd Roggendorf to create Ableton in 1999, and thus Live was spawned. Live's release began a metaphorical snowball effect within the music software world; constant workflow enhancements and new feature additions have made Live the go-to solution for hundreds of thousands of globally performing musicians and DJs.

- Ableton has upgraded Live's real-time pitch-shifting and time-stretching algorithms with multifaceted warp options to optimize the playback of various audio formats. Transient detection improves the drag-and-drop capability requisite for on-the-fly DJing. For those familiar with past versions of Live, the behavior of the Warp Markers has been changed such that it is now even easier to adjust an audio file's playback precision. This comes in particularly handy with music containing timing drifts, often experienced with recordings ripped from vinyl or any music from live musicians. This is less common with modern "machine-made" tunes, where at worst these tracks may only need one or two small adjustments.

- If you want to infuse a bit of variation into your music collection, apply Live's new Groove Engine to any audio or MIDI track to dramatically alter the overall feel of your DJ set. Try adding a bit of swing to a straight dance track and see how it alters the mood. Apply some dynamic changes, straighten out a loose rhythm section, or even apply some randomization for a touch of humanity. The best part of this feature is that each extracted groove is saved to the Groove Pool—a list of templates that can then be reapplied to other content within your Ableton set.

- Once you have cut up some loops and shaped them to your liking, try Live's Slice to New MIDI Track option. Rearrange the notes within the clip, modify parameters, reverse slices, or simply swap out a handful of samples with some of your own.

- When approaching Live as a DJ environment, do not forget that every channel is assignable to Live's Crossfader. This opens doors to scratch-style DJ artistry or smooth, transitional mixing. Notice the A and B assignments at the bottom of the channel faders in Figure 3.5.

- Performers who want to add a personal touch to their DJ sets have the option of performing with more than just preproduced tracks and loops. On top of the dozens of instruments and effects bundled with Live, masses of third-party Virtual Studio Technology (VST) or Audio Unit (AU) plug-ins are compatible with Live.

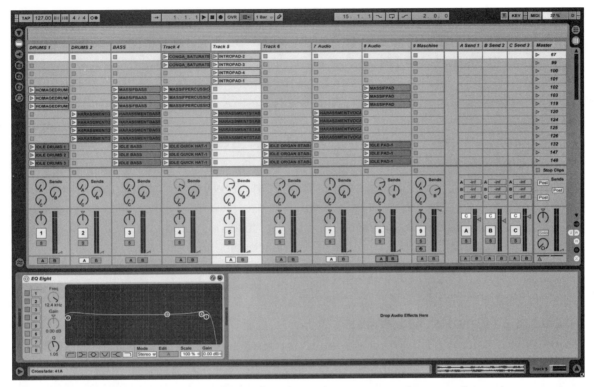

Figure 3.5 Live 8's Session view. Think of each track as representing one channel on any standard DJ mixer.

- Fully fleshed-out MIDI control is also at your disposal; extend Live's control potential with virtually any MIDI-capable controller. Parameter assignment is logical, fast, and directly integrated into the user interface to be handled on the fly. Further, use MIDI clock to sync software, such as Traktor, or any number of other hardware drum machines, synths, and effects units.

One interesting DJ aspect that is often overlooked is Live's unique viability as a potent effects rack. Send Live's inputs an audio signal from absolutely anywhere, and the signal-routing potential truly comes to life. Do not be discouraged if any of this sounds slightly confusing. Many of these concepts are explained within the following Live chapters (Chapters 10 through 12).

The Hybrids

One of the most curious trends in humanity at the moment is this fascination with hybridizing everything. In my lifetime, at least, I feel like it started with food: California's pan-Asian fusion cuisine or the creation of "health-Mex" food. Toyota popularized hybrid cars; breeders created hybrid dogs—labradoodles, puggles (a pug and a beagle...Google it), and so on. The ever-revamping music-technology industry has caught on and began the hardware hybridization of music software.

Much like labradoodles, these hardware/software combinations exemplify genuinely creative technological mating; however, instead of resulting in cutesy Hollywood pets, we get hardware appendages that allow for expressive control over their powerful software packages. This hybridization meshes well with current digital DJ setups and helps to remove the stigma that still taints mouse-driven music production and performance.

Note: My intent with this "Hybrids" section is to prime you for *Part 2* of this project—to introduce themes and to hint at the forward-thinking performance techniques that will be covered in *Part 2*. Because this book is concerned with the structural foundations of digital DJing, the following products step slightly beyond the scope of *Part 1*. Thus, I will only outline these hardware/software combos for now.

Native Instruments: Maschine

Taking the history of DJing into account, you can see why the launch of a groove production studio such as Maschine was so successful. The MPC-inspired hardware alone is a throwback to long-established styles of production and performance within DJ culture. This hardware provides creative access into an immensely powerful production environment benefitting any adventurous user willing to brave Maschine's logical learning curve. Layer percussion on top of preexisting tracks or compose entire productions from beginning to end—Maschine is a tool with undeniable potential. From a DJ's perspective, Maschine attacks on several fronts:

- Workflow speed is a substantial factor when weighing the purchase of a new piece of gear. As shown in Figure 3.6, the Maschine controller is intentionally laid out to expose critical features to a performer's fingertips while still providing multiple layers of depth to those who like to fiddle.

- Much of DJ culture spawned around percussive breaks that, by nature, contain rhythmic elements that make people want to shake their backsides. Incorporating Maschine into a contemporary DJ set allows performers to layer metrical imaginings over their entire music collection. In conjunction with software such as Traktor or Ableton, MIDI clock integration frees artists from the constraints of beat-matching and allows them to focus on a set's other performance aspects. Hit Record and freely drum along to add some live authenticity; quantize your recording output, so even if you're the opposite of sober, you still sound perfectly in control; or merely engage Maschine's Step Sequencer for ultra-precise beat programming. Figure 3.7 shows off Maschine's software side.

- No matter what style of music you play, the Maschine library provides DJs with more than 4 GB of genre-spanning samples. Samples can be stretched over eight

Figure 3.6 Maschine's hardware controller in all of its glory.

Figure 3.7 Maschine's software interface should be instantly familiar to anyone who has spent any time with Ableton or other loop-based audio environments.

banks as individual kits, each of which contains 16 sound slots (pads) as reflected upon the controller's layout.

■ What good would a sampler be without the ability to add custom samples? Users can effortlessly add and label their entire sample library. Still want to go deeper? The internal Sampler function allows exploratory artists to record any manner of incoming audio; for example, you could capture the output of a turntable, vocalist, or instrument—even the crowd—expand it across the 16 pads at the touch of a button, chop it up, hit Record, jam with the new sounds, and there you have it—improvisation!

■ How do you go about finding samples? As already mentioned, Maschine was designed to quickly capture inspiration. All tagged content is directly accessed through the Browser via the hardware LCDs or keyword searched within the software without having to stop the music.

■ If dry audio loops aren't really your thing, Maschine bundles a wide array of built-in effects. Flexible internal signal routing allows complex effect chaining for use on internal drum sounds or, much like Live, external sound sources.

■ To add to the previous point, Maschine provides one-touch automation recording. Think of the creative potential of automated filter modulations, reverb color, and so on played back in sequence with your drums. Note that these automated recordings are individually saved within each pattern; change patterns, and you change automation recordings as well!

■ In the spirit of creative freedom, Maschine was not designed as a proprietary hardware/software combo. If you are traveling, the Maschine software can be popped open on a laptop without the hardware connected. All edits and changes seamlessly translate over to the hardware the instant it is connected. Moreover, the Maschine hardware controller doubles as a highly versatile MIDI device—in other words, it can just as easily control Live, Traktor, or any other MIDI-capable software.

Tip: Try using one computer to run Traktor and Maschine simultaneously—one button combo switches the hardware to MIDI mode and back for instantaneous control over both applications. This self-contained, streamlined stage setup lets you instantaneously bounce back and forth between DJing with Traktor and jamming live with Maschine.

Native Instruments: Kore 2

The concept of the Kore 2 workstation was conceived around streamlining a performer's digital setup. Whether on the stage or in the studio, Kore 2 functions as an analog-styled tactile control interface, giving artists instant, no-fuss access to an entire library of VST or AU plug-in instruments and effects. Covering the entire scope of Kore's functionality would require its own dedicated book; however, you can see where it excels in the DJ realm through the following features:

■ Simply stated, if you are looking for a comprehensive "rack" for your software synthesizers, drum machines (Kore can host the Maschine plug-in), and effects, look no further. Not only does Kore host plug-ins, it can also be loaded as a plug-in itself within host applications such as Live. Load Kore upon one of Live's aux channels for direct control over an extraordinarily versatile effects unit.

Suppose you want to layer some classic Roland TR-909 drums and TB-303 acid lines over a track playing in Traktor or Live while causing chaos with your effects. If you're fortunate enough to own one (or both) of these timeless Roland gems, it is completely understandable if you are hesitant to bring it to a gig—Sod's Law dictates that partiers like to spill things (drinks, speaker stacks, and so on) at the most inconvenient times. Say hello to Kore 2....

Within minutes you can have Maschine (or any VST/AU 909 drum machine), your choice of 303 emulator plug-ins, as well as a rack of delays, reverbs, distortions, and so on ready and waiting for your tweaking. Using the Kore hardware, you can switch between a virtual rack of different instruments and effects with the press of a button, tweak filters and drum decays, modulate delays and reverbs, and mute and solo as needed. Meanwhile, every parameter is presented in clear text upon Kore's backlit LCD screen—in essence, as you can see in Figure 3.8, it is like having hands-on access to a carry-on-sized tabletop of studio hardware.

Figure 3.8 The controller looks all sweet and cuddly here, but trust me that the red backlighting looks sinister on a dark stage.

■ The concept of the Native Instuments KoreSound makes filtering and searching for sound and effect presets quick and logical. Construct your own rack configurations and save them as a KoreSound for instant, on-the-fly access within the middle of your performance. As you can see in Figure 3.9, Kore 2's mixer channels and my plug-in editors are all directly visible.

Figure 3.9 Kore 2 + Maschine + 303 emulator + effects = instant acieeed!

■ Combine Kore with Maschine's Step Sequencer to directly send sequenced melodies and rhythms or modulation data (think: effects) to any plug-in loaded within Kore's virtual rack.

■ Akin to Maschine, the Kore hardware and software can both be used independently of one another: the software for editing purposes and the hardware as an exceedingly versatile MIDI controller. Additionally, the hardware can be flipped from Kore control to MIDI mode and back, further amplifying the inspirational capacity of the device. Effortlessly switch from tweaking synths to controlling Live's playback functions, aux sends, and so on.

Note: Shortly after the release of Kore 2, Native Instruments began releasing themed library expansion bundles known as *Soundpacks*. Because Kore 2 utilizes the audio engines of all of NI's currently available products, Soundpacks provide the power of the Komplete library without the user having to own NI's individual products. Soundpacks such as Deep Freq, Deep Tranformations, or Deep Reconstructions instantly map their controls across the Kore controller and offer unique, otherworldly effect treatments to your DJ set.

Alternatively, powerful effects such as Reaktor-based (and aptly named) "The Finger" are affordable and do not require the full version of the Reaktor software. What makes The Finger particularly effective within DJ sets is the fact that while it is an effects unit, it can be "played" much like a live instrument to mash up sounds and remix tracks on the fly. Check out Warp recording artist Tim Exile's demonstration and explanation of the concepts behind his custom-designed instrument on the NI website.

Monome

Arguably, the Monome supports the most open-ended, contributory community of users and developers on the market. From the Monome's prototype in 2005 to commercial reality in 2006, Philadelphia-based Brian Crabtree and Kelli Cain have distilled the popular understanding of what a music controller should be. Monome, as a company, a device, and an idea, serves as a noteworthy case study into the delicate balance between form and function. The minimally designed control surfaces force performers to rethink the methodology of making music. A lack of faders, knobs, crossfaders, keyboards, and an on/off switch frees users from traditionalist methods and assumptions, while simultaneously rewarding discovery and experimentation.

Brian's explanation of the Monome concept sums up the theoretical approach of the community as a whole by saying, "The wonderful thing about this device is that it doesn't do anything really." Abstractly, this says enough. The concrete reality is that the Monome controller can be adapted for whatever situation is desired at any given time. It is likely the purest, most flexible, and most beautiful control device to date. As you can see in Figure 3.10, the various Monome controller models are absolutely gorgeous pieces of equipment.

Figure 3.10 Simplicity in form and function—with a Monome, you truly are performing on a piece of art.

Using the Open Sound Control (OSC) protocol, the Monome is able to speak to any number of MIDI-compatible applications, such as Ableton, through a simple OSC-to-MIDI converter. The controller's versatility becomes obvious when interfacing with applications such as the visual programming language Max/MSP. Ableton's recent partnership with the developers of Max/MSP, Cycling '74, has revealed yet another corridor for adventurous DJs to explore in the form of Max for Live. Effectively, the Max environment is accessible through Live much the same as inserting any other plug-in—albeit with a steeper learning curve underneath.

Note: Don't be frightened off by Max's learning curve. A large percentage of the Monome's user base also uses Live. With the recent addition of Max for Live, this community should grow exponentially, and as a result, the number of Monome-specific Max patches should increase as well. I highly advise checking out the Monome website (monome.org) for videos and further information on its implementation with Live.

The power of the Monome is held in its open-ended nature, which is where the device comes in quite handy for modern artists. For example, if you need a sequencer that performs in a specific manner, Max for Live will give you the tools to build one. If you need a sampler or any other type of audio-mangling device, you can construct that as well. Buttons can serve as shift functions—much like your computer keyboard—to access alternate "pages" or to change the Monome's playback behavior. Or, you can even simply use it to control clip, mute, solo, and other button-based Live functions.

Bear in mind that if Max isn't your thing, you don't have to go very deep. Only a tiny bit of reading stands in the way of playing. There are tons of Monome-community-member-made patches available that let you play synthesizers, drum machines, and so on in dozens of different ways that are just not possible with other controllers.

The Controllers

When the idea of the digital DJ first became a reality, the proverbial "line in the sand" was drawn across DJ culture. Over time, DJing evolved out of the obscure corners of warehouses and nightclubs and a living, breathing jukebox became the center of attention; DJing became a legitimate stage act, and DJs became performers.

At first, the introduction of laptops caused a backlash from fans and artists, in part because nobody wanted to go and see a stage act stand in front of his laptop and fiddle with a mouse. Most people get their fill of that at work every day. Fortunately, the development of specifically designed MIDI controllers helped legitimize the 'performance' side of digital DJing.

Consequently, Native Instruments and Ableton (with AKAI) have independently designed their own devices specifically aimed at steering their respective DJ software.

Native Instruments: Traktor Kontrol X1

Regardless of whether you perform with Traktor's control vinyl, the X1 simply can't be beat with regard to its wide-reaching scope of functionality and ease of use.

- When considering a controller for precision control, know that the X1 uses the Native Hardware Library (NHL) technology, providing nearly four times the control precision of MIDI. Further, bidirectional feedback between Traktor and the X1 informs DJs of parameter status, removing the need to look at the computer.

- Built upon a robust, Maschine-like chassis, the X1 (see Figure 3.11) sits flush against its sibling controller, thereby streamlining an advanced performance setup. Seating the X1 inside the optional protective casing places the controller at standard club mixer height, enabling unobstructed access to features such as playback, cue points, looping, effects, and so on.

Figure 3.11 The handiness of the X1 becomes obvious when reaching for your software controller suddenly feels logical.

- For DJs using all four Traktor decks, a second X1 can be "hot plugged" for immediate access to Traktor Decks C, D, and all of the related controls. There is no setup or configuration necessary.

■ Like the Maschine and Kore controllers, the X1 can be switched to MIDI mode to extend instant integration to any other MIDI-capable software.

Note: Serato users: Native Instruments created an X1 controller template expressly for SSL. In addition to preconfigured software controls, the X1 bundle includes an alternate, Serato-specific hardware controller overlay.

Akai Professional: APC20/APC40

If you use Ableton and want a controller with features conceived to reach inside of Live, the APC40 is your go-to gadget.

■ As you can see in Figure 3.12, the APC40 is more than just another standard digital DJ control surface. Rock-solid build quality should help put you at ease if (or I should say *when*) it gets knocked around in transit or onstage.

Figure 3.12 APC40: The physical manifestation of Ableton Live.

■ The remarkable Clip Launch Matrix opens access to clip status and control, scene launch, track selection, and so on while doubling as the Live set overview. DJs can instantly jump anywhere inside the Session View. Moreover, the Matrix buttons use three-color state-dependent backlights that display clip status feedback from within the Session Mixer.

- Exhaustive transport, track solo, mute, record status, as well as multifaceted device control functions lend well to the APC's versatility whether tweaking parameters in the studio or banging it out onstage.

- The strengths of plug-and-play functionality are augmented with the option to alter or entirely customize the APC's layout to suit your needs.

Note: If your Live set stretches across several tracks, the APC20 is a perfect companion to your APC40. Essentially, it extends all Live control outwards. The Session View Matrix can be used to launch clips or send MIDI notes or even as a step sequencer. Obviously, the faders are designed for track volumes, but they also double as send and pan level controls. If that's not enough, simply remap the layout to suit your needs. Further, six APCs can be linked to Live simultaneously, making Live easily one of the most adaptable performance platforms on the market.

Other Noteworthy Controllers

Let me point out that the preceding list of controllers is not intended to display the only viable solutions available to digital DJs. As mentioned earlier, each was chosen to represent a different approach. The massive number of DJs going digital has prompted an influx of MIDI controllers into the market. The following list represents some of the more versatile options.

Manufacturer	Model	Website
Faderfox	DJ3	www.faderfox.de
	DX3	
	DL3	
	FX3	
	FT3	
Allen & Heath	Xone:4D	www.xone.co.uk
Vestax	VCM-600	www.vestax.com
Novation	Launchpad	www.novationmusic.com
Korg	nanoSeries	www.korg.com

If none of the controllers listed above catches your interest, Swedish site www.digitaldj.se boasts an extraordinarily comprehensive list of "digital" DJ gear, ranging from CDJs to mixers and MIDI controllers of all types. If spreadsheet price points and feature sets aren't enough, links for each controller click through to a dedicated page containing YouTube product videos and PDF user documentation. It's a great one-stop resource if you are shopping for some new kit.

Traktor Certified versus Traktor Ready

NI's development of the Traktor Certified and Traktor Ready classification system was conceived as a guideline for DJs uncertain of Traktor's compatibility with specific hardware. Basically, the system falls into two camps:

- Traktor Certified mixers provide DJs with an all-inclusive mixer, MIDI-compatible DJ controller, and DVS system. These DJ tools are entirely integrated systems designed to run Traktor Scratch Pro with the timecode control vinyl and without the Audio 8 DJ interface. Each option comes with preassigned templates to easily assimilate the mixer into any DJ's setup.

- Traktor Ready mixers provide DJs with direct MIDI-controlled access over the Traktor Pro software. Although some double as audio interfaces through which to route Traktor's output, the Audio 8 DJ is still required to use Traktor's timecode control vinyl. As with the Traktor Certified line, each Traktor Ready option comes bundled with preassigned templates to easily incorporate these controllers into any DJ's setup.

Note: Many of the Traktor Ready/Traktor Certified devices also function well with Live as MIDI controllers or combined audio interface/MIDI controllers.

For the most up-to-date information on future developments on Traktor Certified and Traktor Ready mixers, check out the dedicated Traktor Certified/Traktor Ready sections on the Native Instruments website.

Other Hardware Considerations

If you are a fan of techno, it is likely that you are aware of the relatively well-known techno pioneers Juan Atkins, Kevin Saunderson, Derrick May, Eddie Fowlkes, Jeff Mills, Mike Banks, Richie Hawtin, and so on. More than 20 years ago, Atkins, Saunderson, May, and company were all beginning to incorporate Roland's TR-808 and TR-909 drum machines into their DJ sets. In fact, to this day Mills still uses two Technics 1200s, three Pioneer CDJ-1000s, and a 909 as part of his DJ setup. Hawtin released the seminal *Decks, EFX and 909* mix CD in 1999 on his record label, Minus, further embedding and expanding this concept into the forward-thinking DJ paradigm. (Check it out if you haven't heard it—required listening.)

There are a ton of sequenced synthesizers and drum machines that integrate nicely into an advanced DJ set, but here are a few that are particularly well suited:

Manufacturer	Model	Website
Elektron	Machinedrum SPS-1	www.elektron.se
	Monomachine SFX-60	
Korg	Electribe EMX1	www.korg.com
	Electribe ESX1	
Radikal Technologies	Spectralis 2	www.radikaltechnologies.com

iPhone/iPad

Like it or hate it, Apple's iUniverse perfectly suits the future of music software controllers. Digging for useful audio tools inside the iTunes Store is a bit of a nightmare at times—there is simply too much to sift through, and most music apps are essentially toys. I'm sorry, but I find it pretty irritating that I can find more than 10 vuvuzela apps in comparison to so few professional audio products.

An application like Korg's iElectribe emulation (as opposed to its hardware sibling mentioned a moment ago) is incredibly well made, and admittedly, it is fun for a bit. However, the design fits a hardware unit more effectively, and sadly, sync options are nonexistent. Of course, an abundance of musical instruments, mixing software, and simple DJ applications exist, but all they ultimately reveal is the iPad's infancy. The glass-full outlook: It's still early days for these devices.

Anyhow, for obvious reasons the iPad is a more practical controller than the iPhone, though there are some useful handheld audio apps. Of particular note are the multi-platform Hexler products.

Software developer Hexler has been busy constructing some truly revolutionary control software. SonicLife is a control application built around rules from what is known as *cellular automation*; essentially, it's an abstract sequencing application based on the mathematician John Conway's Game of Life.

For the purposes of this book, however, the application TouchOSC is slightly more relevant. Figure 3.13 shows one of what amounts to a nearly infinite number of possible TouchOSC layouts. I say "one of" because Hexler also offers the handy—and free—TouchOSC Editor. Exactly as it sounds, the Editor software lets users construct personalized layouts. You can create multiple customized pages of buttons, faders, XY controllers, control pots, and so on and quickly load them into the TouchOSC application.

To use TouchOSC with your laptop, download the free Osculator application from www.osculator.net. In simple terms, this software acts as a translator for the wirelessly transmitted OSC protocol, converting received data into MIDI messages. It's perfectly suited for digital DJ applications such as Traktor, Ableton Live, and Serato.

What is the best thing about this setup? No wires—yay! What's the potential downside? No WiFi hardware—boo! (There are workarounds for creating ad hoc networks. Again, Google is your friend!)

Given that the iPad's pricing structure starts just slightly above many high-end MIDI controllers, the device becomes a realistic option for both DJs and producers on and off the stage. Plus, consider the iPad's dozens upon dozens of additional benefits (or should I say *distractions*) when you're not performing! Check out what else Hexler has going on, including setup tutorials, at www.hexler.net.

Note: If you're interested in learning more about "iApps," check out G.W. Childs' *Making Music with Mobile Devices* (Course Technology PTR, 2010).

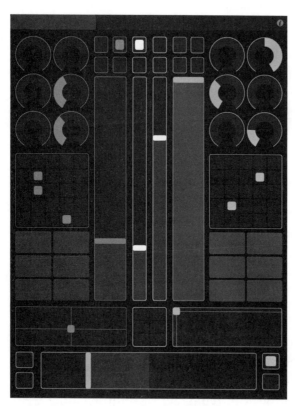

Figure 3.13 Hexler's TouchOSC: a prime example of where multitouch-based controllers are heading.

Note: Another option, called LiveControl, wires up Hexler's TouchOSC iPhone/iPad application as an Ableton Live "Remote" control surface. Although a bit of setup is involved, the LiveControl template is premapped to Live's features—in other words, you do not need to use the Osculator application to label each and every iPad button, knob, fader, and so on (which you would otherwise have to do without LiveControl).

For comparative purposes, the controller behaves somewhat like the APC40 in that feedback status between Live and LiveControl is bidirectional—that is, changes made within Live using a mouse (or another controller) are instantly reflected back to the iPad/iPhone and vice versa. Check out LiveControl at www.livecontrol.q3f.org.

Finally, if you are simply after an interesting approach to controlling Live's Clip Matrix, check out the iDevice-based application Griid, made by software developer Liine (liine.net). This simplistic software app utilizes the multitouch screens of the iDevices to creatively manipulate Live's clip playback. Ironically, two of the Liine's founders are techno stalwarts: Richie Hawtin and John Acquaviva.

Venturing into the world of open-ended controllers can be a little bit daunting at first. It usually requires a bit of DIY on the artist's end, so my advice is to approach the process with a bit of patience. One major plus is that the user communities are generally quite helpful—worst case, there is almost always a way to track down further information on the Internet.

As this topic is more aptly placed inside a category of advanced setup and performance techniques, further exploration will have to wait until *Part 2* of this project.

At this point, I hope that you understand the extent to which external hardware thrives when combined with the vast number of features modern DJ software provides. For the artist, hardware entirely reshapes the experience of DJing with Traktor, Serato, or Ableton; plus, crowds absolutely love it—as mentioned before, a DJ set is still a performance!

4 Finding, Organizing, and Storing Your Music

Traveling with vinyl these days has become both inconvenient and absurdly expensive. Some airlines still allow passengers two bags without extra cost— one carry-on and one check-in—while many other airlines charge for any baggage other than one carry-on. This presents obvious drawbacks to luggage-laden travelers, and it is only the beginning of the headache that traveling with records has become.

Don't get me wrong; I love my wax, and I still buy vinyl. In fact, I love it so much that I still travel to gigs with a bag of at least 100 records. However, I was recently forced to pay £90 GBP (approximately $140 USD at the time) to check my records. Bear in mind, that particular expense was for *one* leg of a return flight. To be sure, every profession has certain unavoidable expenditures. Sometimes this expense is part of a tour rider; sometimes it's out of pocket. Either way, the whole experience is infuriating.

Further, the wear and tear on some of my older records is making me rethink bringing them at all. On the upside, it's reassuring that recording technology has become so good that archiving vinyl at higher-than-CD quality is extremely easy and sounds fantastic.

Chalk up a point for digital DJing!

The New Crate Digging

While the remaining digital dust settles from the music industry's explosion into 1s and 0s, glimpses of a relatively stable future are beginning to take shape. Fans and DJs can find new music all over the Internet (legally or illegally). Musicians can independently and affordably record, distribute, and manage their careers from anywhere in the world. Moral and legal distractions aside, it has never been a better time for musicians and their fans to connect.

Legal access to music content continues to be a driving force behind hordes of budding online retailers. Inexpensive data storage and expanding Internet bandwidth have helped create the perfect breeding ground for digital media proliferation.

Back in June of 1999, Shawn Fanning fulfilled a popular desire with the launch of Napster, a file-sharing service that served as a catalyst for the deconstruction of the 20th century's music industry. The service popularized the concept of decentralized file sharing and created an inexorable ripple effect that, to some degree, spawned further peer-to-peer (P2P) technologies ranging from Kazaa to the BitTorrent protocol. More than anything else, what these sites emphasized was an increased consumer demand for artist content beyond traditional albums and singles; for example, live show recordings, live video, rare bootlegs, and unreleased songs. In response to rampant copyright infringements, numerous lawsuits were filed against illegal file-sharers over the last decade.

In 1976, the U.S. Copyright Act was modified to protect recorded sound sources—for example, recorded music. Prior to this, only *written* music could be protected. To many listeners of hip-hop and dance music, it's obvious that this barrier is widely ignored. Further, in 1998, the Digital Millennium Copyright Act (DMCA) was signed into existence; among other things, the DMCA makes the sidestepping of Digital Rights Management (DRM) protection illegal in addition to criminalizing the unauthorized digital distribution of protected works.

While public opinion on the morality of file sharing is still mixed, it is difficult to dispute that P2P networks had a definitive impact upon how digitized music is currently distributed. Amidst this perfect storm, innovative businesses were able to develop relatively happy mediums for labels, musicians, and fans. For digital performers today, this translates to the eased ability to pursue an art form that was purely conjecture 100 years ago; a combo of high and low art 70 years ago; isolated, specialist, and insular 30 years ago; and strictly analog as recently as 15 years ago.

For those old enough to remember crate digging in a record shop, it's sad to think that young DJs will miss out on such a formative sensory experience—developing relationships with record buyers; planning visits around release dates; cutting open, unsheathing, and holding a physical EP; the discourse between customers and customers, customers and employees, and employees amongst themselves; gauging one's respect (or lack of) quotient in the eyes of said employees; agreeing and disagreeing about music, gear, parties, and so on; but above anything else, making eye contact while doing it.

Thankfully, while the differences between DJing now and DJing then are fairly obvious, the end result is the same. The music is always there for those willing to dig a little bit deeper.

For the sake of the integrity of myself and this book, I will focus on a few of the *legal* businesses that have emerged from the chaos of the last decade—as mentioned earlier, the "perfect storm" that has allowed market forces to dream up some truly fantastic (and terrible) business models that were unimaginable 20 years ago.

The iTunes Music Store

On April 28, 2003, Apple launched the world's first successful mass-market online music retailer, in large part to drive sales of its iPod music hardware. Apple called it the iTunes Music Store. Upon opening, Apple offered more than 200,000 downloadable songs using a pricing model that would influence the future of online music retailers. Apple's efforts permanently changed popular listening habits and created all new expectations about how to "sync" one's digital life. More importantly, the iTunes Store proved that a future of legalized downloading is possible. At the time this book was written, the iTunes Store is thought to represent approximately 70 percent of the world's legally downloaded music. The largest advantage to buying music through iTunes is its user-friendly interface, as shown in Figure 4.1, and its exemplary search and recommendation functions.

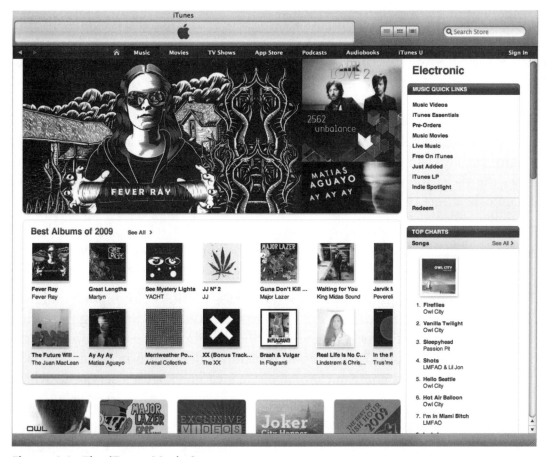

Figure 4.1 The iTunes Music Store.

Most popular music can be found within the iTunes Store; however, as you begin to diverge from mainstream styles of music, at some point you are probably going to have some trouble finding what you're after.

Note: An important factor for DJs to take into consideration is that as of April 2009, Apple removed the DRM protection from its entire catalog, which released the proprietary hardware/software combination between iPods and iTunes libraries. Prior to this, DRM protection upon iTunes-downloaded MPEG-4 (.m4p) files used the Fairplay Digital Rights Management technology, which prevented their use within third-party software DJ applications. What this means for today's digital DJs is that any music recently purchased through iTunes is open for use with virtually any music software or hardware.

Still, iTunes' most powerful aspect comes from the organizational features of the iTunes application itself. Like it or hate it, Apple has certainly pulled off the ability to mesh one's life into a single streamlined interface. With respect to DJs, playlist creation could not be any more straightforward: Create a new playlist, add some tracks, and you're finished. If you use Traktor or Serato, new iTunes playlists seamlessly integrate within the respective track browsers. If you receive a ton of promos, dump them into a defined playlist and sync it to your iWhatever. It's a great way to audition new music when you're in the car, at the gym, on the subway, and so on.

Beatport

When it comes to digging through larger online music shops, one disadvantage for DJs is that many retailers simply don't extend their catalogs into subgenre peripheries. Therein lies the niche for smaller, DJ-attentive music retailers, such as the electronic music–focused Beatport (www.beatport.com), shown in Figure 4.2.

In January 2004, Denver-based Beatport spawned from the vision of local DJ Eloy Lopez and was given breath through the savvy of CEO and founder Jonas Tempel. Since its inception, Beatport has become the go-to website for DJs around the world.

Retailers such as iTunes are primarily designed for mass-market consumption and thus do not offer the DJ-focused features that Beatport thrives on, from browsing through a label's back catalog, to details such as genre-specific categorizing or customized favorites (artists, labels, and so on). Furthermore, Beatport works hand in hand with DJs, labels, fans, and like-minded companies to facilitate customers with a service to which they will return.

Although browsing is critical to the overall customer experience, two of Beatport's greatest advantages are the format selection and delivery options. Customers are given the option of downloading their music in compressed MP3 or MP4 format or, with a slight extra expense, uncompressed WAV format. To streamline the download process, Beatport has developed a download manager application that allows users to customize the file-naming structure. It's fine-tunable down to the details of punctuation between artist names, labels, and so on. I am anal when it comes to music storage, so I

Figure 4.2 Beatport's DJ-focused user interface.

find features like this pretty useful. As you can see in Figure 4.3, I have chosen my delivery options to label my files as such:

Label_Artist(s)_Track Name_Mix Name

Other Essential Digs

The two previous examples are not the be-all-end-all of music shopping; they simply exist as solid examples of what customers should begin to expect. In the spirit of leaving no stone unturned, there are definitely more shops that are well worth checking out. It's also important to note that many record labels and artist collectives are beginning to launch their own web shops—definitely something to look out for.

Specialists: 1s, 0s, and Vinyl!

- **boomkat.com.** A UK-based specialist web retailer founded in "quality over quantity." Boomkat boasts an impressive collection of underground music spanning a wide array of electronic music subgenres and format options. The passionate staff takes the time to provide shoppers with well-written opinions and reviews, not just label-supplied press releases.

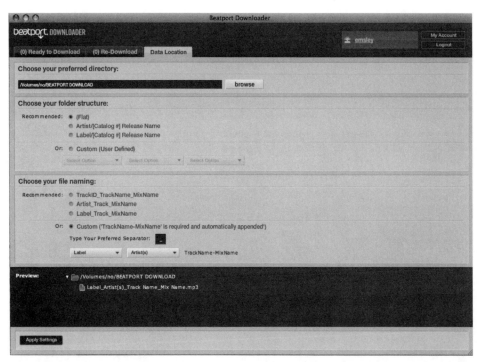

Figure 4.3 The Beatport Downloader: Beatport's standalone download manager application.

- **hardwax.com.** One of the last remaining bastions of vinyl purism. Absolutely peerless vinyl/CD retailer based in Berlin and founded by one of the members of the famed Basic Channel, Chain Reaction, and Maurizio dub techno imprints, Mark Ernestus. Hard Wax is a mecca for techno and house—especially so for rare vinyl, rereleases, and classics. Also sells incredible dubstep, reggae, dub, disco, and so on. Additionally, Hard Wax shares the building with the respected Dubplates & Mastering studio. (There is talk that Hard Wax is putting its foot into the digital download waters as well—fingers crossed!)

- **bleep.com.** Online music retail subsidiary of legendary UK-based Warp Records. Bleep offers music from more than 300 labels through a multiformat digital catalog, as well as CDs, vinyl, and other merchandise.

- **dustygroove.com.** Chicago-based online importer of rare vinyl ranging from jazz, funk, soul, and Latin to hip-hop. You can also find all of your turntable-based extras, such as needles, cleaning, and so on.

- **undergroundhiphop.com.** Boston-based online retailer specializing in underground hip-hop DJ culture. A must-visit for DJ gear, merchandise, a huge catalog of rare vinyl, CDs, and supplies for urban/graffiti artists.

Everything: Music and Gear

- **juno.co.uk.** As online retails shops go, Juno has everything that digital DJs require: dozens of musical genres available in vinyl, CDs, and multiformat music downloads. You can also order piles upon piles of various DJ kits. Vinyl junkies should definitely look out for Juno's seasonal sales—gems can be found at a fraction of the cost.

- **turntablelab.com.** Independent, DJ specialty store focused on equipment, music production hardware, software, and, of course, music sales—all pieced together and handpicked by a passionate staff focused on quality. Great source for merchandise and general DJ culture.

- **amazon.com.** It's Amazon, and it has everything; enough said. Amazon's recommendation system is great for finding some invaluable audio-related reading.

If You Know What You're After

- **discogs.com.** If you know what you're looking for, vinyl or CD-wise, Discogs is the place to find absolutely anything used. It's basically the eBay of music—but be prepared to pay a premium for the rare goods.

Streaming Tunes

Internet radio isn't exactly a new invention, but it has taken quite a while for usability to reach the levels that music lovers should expect. While the primary method and, therefore, limitations of streaming radio stations are fundamentally the same (you must have access to a stable Internet or mobile data connection), the companies that have made names for themselves have done so by taking a relatively new approach in the world of radio: They've made it bilateral.

Individual users affect the balance of what is played through the "airwaves." A process of individually chosen likes and dislikes creates a filter that effectively personalizes radio stations based on listening habits. Artists and record labels are given the opportunity to upload their creative output while click-through links allow listeners to purchase what they like—an incredible feature for DJs on their downtime.

Most of the larger services offer downloadable player applications that give listeners direct access to their user profile, streamlining the overall experience. Further, some offer subscription models furnishing a tiered system of options to paying members—on-demand track playback, playlists available offline, and even mobile phone–based clients.

Essentially, Internet radio stations have evolved into music-based social networking platforms. Users can develop online relationships with other members, which in effect creates a buzzing online community of music freaks with the ability to publicly share their vision of good music.

Each company takes a different approach and offers significantly more than I have described; however, I highly encourage you to check them out. Three that are particularly useful for DJs are:

- **soundcloud.com.** SoundCloud provides a meeting ground for DJs, producers, labels, licensing houses, fans, and so on. Create a profile (there are tiered membership levels/features) and upload DJ sets or releases. Send links directly to interested parties and adjust individualized privacy settings for visitors, friends, and colleagues. The SoundCloud music player itself is well thought out and allows the user community to leave time-based commentary. Users can also efficiently track their profile statistics—as SoundCloud says, view the who, what, when, which, and where of other members interacting with your profile. Overall, SoundCloud provides a highly functional outlet for the music industry while avoiding the obnoxious fluff of other social networks.

- **spotify.com.** Spotify is the definitive, subscription model–based Internet radio. For a monthly fee, users get access to thousands of albums through the Spotify application. Share music with other users and friends, build wide-ranging playlists, and learn a lot about music you have never heard before based on the sharing principles of collaborative playlists and the similar artists–recommendation system common in most digital music services. Although the content is actually streaming and requires a connection at some point, you can lock and access a playlist offline. This is particularly handy on its iPhone application. When you find tracks for your DJ sets, the click-through purchase feature is available for songs that you want to keep.

- **last.fm.** Last.fm is a community-based streaming radio service that lets you listen to radio on your terms. Download the Last.fm application, as shown in Figure 4.4, create your own profile, and build individualized radio stations (sort of like playlists) that select music based on likes and dislikes—a rating system that remembers preferential listening habits. If you run a search for so-and-so musician, the radio will then play other similar artist recommendations. Immediately access the playlists of friends and neighbors who have their own taste-making processes. Further, Last.fm also developed a mobile application for the iPhone/Android that is incredibly handy when you need to hear some new tunes. (I happen to have my Last.fm playing in the background as I type this.)

Other Resources

There is absolutely no way for the average person to stay 100 percent on top of music output at the moment. Sagging print media sales have resulted in the death of many great music magazines; however, some were able to adapt and resort to online content.

Figure 4.4 The straightforward interface of the Last.fm application.

Additionally, the blogosphere is hit or miss, though it still functions as a good resource once you find credible sources. Some notable online sites are:

- pitchfork.com
- xlr8r.com
- residentadvisor.net
- hypem.com
- urb.com
- thewire.co.uk
- factmag.com
- ugsmag.com

These are simply examples of a handful of sites that I frequent. Unsurprisingly, there are hundreds of online fanzines as well that cater to specific musical tastes and styles. If you need more, Google is your friend!

Hard Drives: The New Record Crate

It is pretty safe to say that most DJs, at some point, have been on one end or another of the "analog versus digital" chest-beating contest. Each camp maintains perfectly valid arguments, but at the end of the day the most important thing to remember is that this is supposed to be fun. There is a happy medium out there for everyone.

In the past, the logistics of storing and transporting music were primarily a factor of physical space, whereas today, hundreds of thousands of songs fit into your pocket. It seems that every six months data storage doubles in capacity while the enclosures halve in size—in fact, several feasible options now exist that are smaller than the average wallet. This is great news for portable setups; however, there are a few important points to note prior to purchasing a hard drive.

Do Your Research

External hard drives from a reputable manufacturer not only will increase the performance of your computer, but they also could potentially save you from an agonizing experience down the road. It is a common industry-wide practice to house audio data (music, samples, project files, and so on) upon a dedicated hard drive. The theory behind this practice is that streaming your audio off an external hard drive frees your computer's internal hard drive to do its business—in other words, running your operating system, applications, and so on.

A secondary advantage is that all of your data is consolidated into one location for efficient management and backup purposes. One indispensable piece of advice is of such value that it is only truly understood after disaster has struck: Back up your collection, and do it often!

Having fallen victim to hard-drive death, I cannot stress this enough. Make it a common practice to periodically back up your dedicated audio drive. If you're meticulous about your file management, all you have to do is clone this drive from time to time, and you can rest easy. This is doubly important if, beyond your music collection, the drive contains music project files, sample libraries, video, or anything else vital to your performance.

Speed

Pay close attention to the rotational speed of both internal and external hard drives once you start shopping around. As a specification represented in RPM, higher values yield better performance. This becomes critical if you are performing with multitrack applications such as Ableton Live, because it directly affects the playback of simultaneous tracks or clips.

Battery life is a massive bullet point for laptop manufacturers at the moment, and thus slower hard drives tend to get preinstalled because they require less energy to operate. Although you may see laptop and/or external hard drives displaying speeds of 4,200 to 5,400 RPM, the magic number to shoot for is 7,200 RPM. If necessary, special-order the faster option—it's worth the wait.

Increased competition has driven down internal hard drive prices, and laptop drives are relatively easy to replace. If you're unfamiliar with how this process works, definitely consult the computer manufacturer prior to attempting it yourself. There might be warranty issues involved, something you definitely do not want to gamble with. If the DIY approach is your thing, articles on this topic abound on the Internet, while YouTube is always a good reference point for visual learners.

Tip: As you add and delete files on any computer (Mac or PC), you begin to leave what can be loosely thought of as "holes" on your drive. Over time, these virtual holes make it more difficult for the hard drive to read information from disk, leading to poor performance. Therefore, it is a good idea to defrag your hard drive from time to time. PCs have this feature included with the Windows operating system; Mac users should use a third-party application such as DiskWarrior (alsoft.com/diskwarrior).

Note: There is a lot of recent hype around the new solid-state drive (SSD) technology. Reports show that they are faster, virtually silent, use comparatively less energy, and are apparently quite rugged, because they contain no moving parts. Currently, the SSD route is an insanely expensive option for much lower capacity and comparatively unproven performance within the audio industry. Although an attractive option for the future, as with all things great and new, it's often wise to wait until market forces crush down the prices and additional time has passed for industry-wide testing.

Connectivity

Give connectivity some thought before you purchase an external hard drive. In particular, take into consideration *how* you might connect additional devices to your laptop—for example, an audio interface, MIDI controllers, and so on.

The vast majority of laptops will have at least one USB 2.0 port. Many will offer multiple USB 2.0 ports as well as one or two FireWire ports. If you are a Mac user, be aware that Apple has abandoned FireWire 400 (1394a) for the faster FireWire 800 spec (1394b), and thus all new Apple computers will only have this option available. Don't worry if you have a device that only has a FireWire 400 connection, as FireWire 800 is backwards-compatible; this is easily accomplished with a FireWire 800 to 400 "bilingual" cable. Given the unavoidable limitations of laptop connectivity, hard drives are one area with a bit of connective flexibility. For example, some external hard drives are available with multiple connections on the same device, such as USB 2.0, FireWire 400, and FireWire 800.

I have had a handful of hard drive nightmares in the past; however, one particular manufacturer with whom I've had an exceptional experience is G-Technology. For DJs, its G-DRIVE mini (see Figure 4.5) is an attractive option that is the size of a wallet, is absolutely rock-solid, has an amazing warranty, and comes bundled with a tough leather case and high-quality cables. These drives are a bit pricey compared to the competition, but when you're concerned with the emotional and financial cost of losing data, in my eyes the extra expense is worth every extra penny.

Figure 4.5 The G-DRIVE mini Triple.

Final Thoughts

The primary purpose of this chapter has been to reframe the notion of the modern DJ and his record crate. Managing vinyl used to be a matter of physical handling and physical space. So, what do we do now that we can fit hundreds of thousands of songs in our pockets?

I hope to answer that question for you over the next few chapters....

5 Traktor Pro: Intro

From the early days of Digital Vinyl Systems (DVS), the laptop quickly became ubiquitous inside a DJ booth. Although vinyl remains DJ culture's nostalgic medium, a computer presents an artist with considerably more dynamic performance tools. As masses of established DJs go digital, DJ culture's youth is forming new understandings of what DJ performances are supposed to be.

The intention of this chapter is to expose the essentials of one DVS bundle in particular: Traktor Scratch Pro. Traktor is currently the strongest example of DVS technology's bright future, because it offers the most progressive feature array; an enormous, dedicated user base; helpful technical support/quality assurance resources; and, of course... software stability.

So, how did DVS software come about?

The Digital Vinyl System

In short, DVS applications embody the response from innovative music software companies to a digitizing music industry.

The foundations were laid once MP3-encoding technology was made public in 1995, at which point the new media format demanded a portable container. Thus, the first MP3 players hit the consumer market in 1998. That same year, Dutch developer, N2IT, fashioned a piece of music software that allowed consumers to emulate their DJ heroes with songs stored on their hard drive. They named it Final Scratch.

By the turn of the millennium, many international DJs had attained an almost mythical, god-like status, often reinforced with five-figure fees and jet-set lifestyles. With such widespread influence, it is hardly surprising to hear that 1999 saw music retailers sell more turntables than guitars.

When millennium doomsday theorists' predictions of universal implosion proved baseless, the human race rejoiced in their good fortune. Among mankind's other forward movements, 2000 saw two major software innovations birthed out of Germany's capital. Berlin-based developers Ableton and Native Instruments each independently released a software package that set industry precedents for capturing the artist's experience. While Ableton Live began primarily as a music production platform, it was later designed and adapted around the performing musician; with Traktor DJ, Native Instruments envisioned the true potential of a digital DJ performance.

Note: Because it doesn't technically fall under the definition of a DVS, Ableton Live is covered in later chapters.

Meanwhile, Apple's unimaginable grasp of form and function spawned the first-generation iPod in 2001, singlehandedly altering the public perception of music consumption for millions of people. The continued growth of the consumer DJ market saw Stanton release the Final Scratch bundle in 2002. The following year, Stanton paired with Native Instruments and produced the hardware/software combination of Traktor Final Scratch. Soon after, New Zealand–based Serato Audio Research joined the market with Serato Scratch Live in 2004, in partnership with famed Washington-based audio hardware manufacturer, Rane.

The end of 2006 saw the complete dissolution of the partnership between Stanton and Native Instruments, and in 2008, after countless version upgrades, product enhancements, and service updates, the release versions of Traktor Pro and Traktor Scratch Pro hit the market. After 10 years of adaptation, 2010 dawned with NI's diverse Traktor DJ line consisting of three hardware audio interfaces (the Audio 2, 4, and 8), multiple Traktor siblings (Traktor LE, Duo, Scratch Duo, Pro, and Scratch Pro), and a dedicated hardware controller (the Traktor Kontrol X1).

So, how does a DVS system actually work?

Each Traktor timecode vinyl/CD is manufactured with a constant 2-kHz carrier frequency. Traktor uses this audio signal to determine playback speed (bpm), playback direction (think: scratching), and playback positioning (needle-dropping within a track). If you want to hear what the timecode signal sounds like, plug your turntable/ CDJ directly into your DJ mixer (disregard the Audio 8 DJ connections for now), switch the channel input mode to Phono/Line, respectively, and press play on the device. If you adjust your turntable/CDJ pitch faders, you will hear the pitch of the carrier frequency rise and/or fall. This is how Traktor determines the playback speed.

The carrier frequency itself is a stereo audio file composed of two slightly phase-shifted sine waves. In Figure 5.1, I have loaded Traktor's timecode signal (downloadable to registered Traktor users) into Logic's Sample Editor. The compressions (peaks) and rarefactions (valleys) of the left and right channels are slightly uneven—or, said another way, they are *out of phase*. As you can see, the left channel (top) is approximately 1/4 phase ahead of the right channel (bottom). Though we can't hear the difference, Traktor certainly can, and thus the phase relations determine a Traktor Deck's directional playback—behavior that is essential to cueing and scratching.

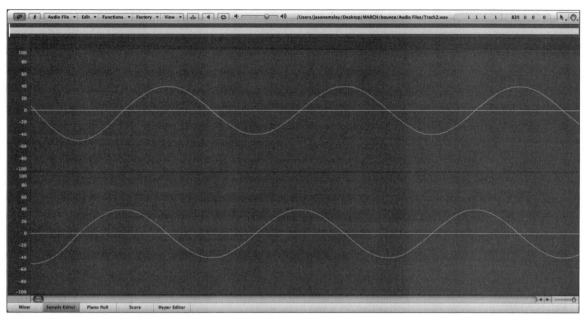

Figure 5.1 Traktor's timecode signal—up close.

Trying to explain playback positioning is a bit of a dead end, regrettably, because the full details fall into NI's proprietary info domain. In all likelihood it is a type of digital timestamp. Suffice it to say that data contained within the tiny boxes (visible up *very* close) embedded upon the timecode vinyl probably determine track playback position.

Is this information vital to retain? Not necessarily, but it never hurts to understand the inner workings of a system if you ever have to troubleshoot a problem. As you will see later, Traktor offers several status feedback reminders hinting at problems that may begin with the timecode signal's clarity.

Traktor Scratch Pro

More than a decade was spent shaping and polishing the Traktor lineage into its current state: Traktor Pro. As mentioned earlier, this process resulted in several Traktor blends, stratified according to differing technical requirements. With that said, the full Traktor Scratch Pro bundle is covered within this chapter, as it offers the extensive feature set required for the purposes of this book. The full package, as shown in Figure 5.2, comprises the requisite materials for using Traktor's control vinyl and/or CDs—specifically, the Audio 8 DJ interface (or alternatively, a Traktor Certified mixer).

Unless otherwise noted, all references to Traktor refer to an authorized copy of Traktor Scratch Pro. If you are unsure which version of Traktor best suits your needs, it would be best to check the version comparison chart on NI's website under the DJ products section.

Figure 5.2 The full Traktor Scratch Pro bundle.

Installation, Registration, and Updating

Software installation processes vary not only from developer to developer, but also between Mac and PC platforms as well as current operating system versions—for example, Mac OS X 10.5.x versus 10.6.x. Refer to the software documentation or the company's online knowledge database for specific information on software and driver installation, product authorization, troubleshooting, and, if necessary, technical support.

Once Traktor has been installed, activated, and updated, ensure that your computer is running the most recent hardware drivers for any/all audio interfaces and MIDI controllers that you plan on using. All Native Instruments software, along with drivers for the Audio 2, 4, 8 and Audio Kontrol 1, can be found within the Update section of the standalone Service Center application. You can find NI's Service Center here:

> OS X: Macintosh HD > Applications > Native Instruments > Service Center
>
> Windows: Program Files > Native Instruments > Service Center

The Setup Wizard

After the software is fully updated with the latest and greatest, the quickest way to get going is to use Traktor's Setup Wizard. By default, this dialog box should appear the first time Traktor is opened. Once you have completed the process, it will not appear again; however, for future reference, there are two ways to manually launch the Setup Wizard.

- Choose Start Setup Wizard from the OS X or Windows drop-down Help options located on the Application menu (not visible in full-screen mode).

■ Choose Setup Wizard found in the bottom-left corner of the Traktor Preferences window. Access Traktor's Preferences by clicking on the gear icon within the top-right corner, as shown in Figure 5.3.

Figure 5.3 Click to open Traktor's Preferences.

The purpose of the Setup Wizard is simple: It allows the user to automatically configure Traktor's audio signal routing, screen layout, and external MIDI controller mapping for future plug-and-play functionality. If you are using a USB or FireWire MIDI controller, select the manufacturer and the model in addition to whether you are using Traktor's control vinyl/CD.

Once you complete the process shown in Figure 5.4, Traktor should be ready to go. If your device is not listed, contact the controller manufacturer directly, as it may have a mapping file available. If the preconfigured layouts don't suit your style, I highly encourage you to remap the settings to suit your needs. Instructions on manual parameter assignment are in Chapter 8, "Traktor Pro: The Controller Manager."

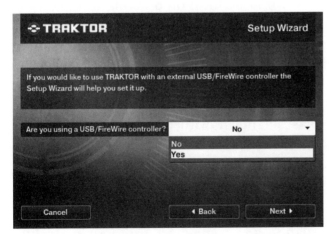

Figure 5.4 One of the Setup Wizard's unbelievably complicated questions.

Caution: Be aware that once you click the Setup Wizard's Finish button, all previous settings are overwritten. However, a backup of the current settings is copied to one of the following locations. If ever you need to revert to a previous setting, click Import from within Traktor's Preferences and navigate to the following location

- OS X: Macintosh HD > Users > (username) > Documents > Native Instruments > Traktor > Settings > Backup Settings

- XP: My Documents > Native Instruments > Traktor > Settings > Backup Settings

- Vista: Documents > Native Instruments > Traktor > Settings > Backup Settings

Note that the NI online user forum's DJ Area is incredibly useful when it comes to various controller mappings. If searching does not yield an answer, try creating a new thread. The forum is home to dozens of power users who are generally more than happy to lend a hand. You can find NI's online user forum at www.native-instruments. com/forum.

Manually Configuring Your Audio Setup

Even though Traktor's Setup Wizard streamlines the configuration process, situations will arise when a bit of flexibility is required. A busted soundcard, dodgy mixer inputs, bad cables, and so on are just a few examples of why it is critical to have a working knowledge of Traktor's audio routing versatility.

On any given club night, artists around the world perform on differing digital setups. When a DJ's only setup options involved CDJs, turntables, and a mixer, artist change-overs were, for the most part, seamless and straightforward. There was no pulling apart the DJ booth, no panicked cable yanking, no bumping into turntables or the artists using them (that last one is a lie), and no frenzied search for empty power sockets. I won't name the culprits, but I've seen a few epic performance and changeover disasters, all because one performer or another was unfamiliar with his setup. Don't get me wrong; everyone lives through a mischievous computer backstabbing at some point. However, you can avoid many situations with some old-fashioned product knowledge. Knowing how to set up your equipment is one of the most important requirements for performers—in fact, it's part of the job description.

Certain circumstances demand specific audio setup configurations; as such, Traktor was intentionally constructed with flexible routing options in mind. The following sections explain how and when to use them.

Internal Soundcard

I have mentioned this already, but as a general rule it is always best to steer clear of any laptop's built-in soundcard when using professional audio applications. Minus a few niche examples, computer manufacturers rarely have the pro-audio industry in mind when they are sourcing audio hardware parts. Rather, the internal soundcards are typically intended for multimedia usage: watching movies, listening to music, playing video games, and so on. Using the internal soundcard is absolutely fine when relaxing on the couch or stuffed into an airplane seat, but you won't be able to separate the monitor output channel (pre-listen or cue) from the master output channel (what the audience hears). If you want to get the most out of Traktor, an audio interface with at least two stereo outputs is a must.

Note: If you are using a Windows PC with the internal soundcard, please see the ASIO4ALL reference within the "Drivers" section of Chapter 3.

Hardware Configuration

1. Connect headphones or an audio cable to the laptop's mini-jack (headphones) output.

2. Verify that your laptop's volume is turned up. (Be careful of your ears.)

Software Configuration

1. Open the Traktor Preferences.

2. Under the Audio Setup tab, choose the built-in soundcard from the Audio Device drop-down menu. Leave the Sample Rate at the default of 44,100 Hz. Adjust the Audio Latency to about 30 milliseconds. (Low latency values translate to more responsive control but demand a fast computer.)

3. Under the Output Routing tab, choose Internal as the Mixing Mode.

4. Assign your soundcard outputs from the Output Monitor drop-down menu.

Note: While in Internal Mixing mode, you cannot hear Traktor's Beat Tick through the Output Master. It can only be sourced through the Output Monitor.

---

5. Click on the Close button to accept the settings.

Skip ahead to "Navigating the User Interface" once you have completed the steps listed above.

External Audio Interface: Internal Mixing

With an external, multichannel audio interface, you create options for how you can mix your tracks. Using Traktor's Internal Mixing features, DJs can utilize a mouse/keyboard configuration, a dedicated MIDI controller, or a combination of both to DJ without a huge number of extra hardware connections. Think of Internal Mixing as transplanting a traditional DJ mixer into your computer—EQ, volume, crossfading, cueing, and so on are handled within Traktor's "Internal" Mixer, but the actual audio is ultimately sent to the house system or speakers via your external audio interface.

Hardware Configuration

1. Connect the external audio interface to your computer.

2. Connect the primary outputs of the audio interface to powered speakers, an amplifier, or an empty line-level input channel on your DJ mixer, as depicted in Figure 5.5.

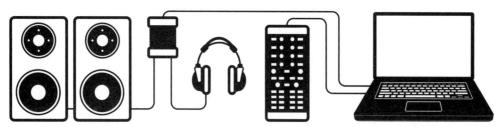

Figure 5.5 Routing for an external audio interface with Internal Mixing.

3. Connect your headphones to the secondary outputs of the external audio interface—for example, "headphones" (Output 7/8) on the front of the Audio 8 DJ.

Software Configuration

1. Open the Traktor Preferences.

2. Under the Audio Setup tab, choose the external audio interface from the Audio Device drop-down menu. Leave the Sample Rate at the default of 44,100 Hz. For now, adjust the Audio Latency to about 15 milliseconds. Once everything is up and running, try incrementally lowering this setting. Lower latency values translate to more responsive control but demand a fast computer. To adjust the latency on soundcards that use ASIO, click the Settings button nestled alongside Audio Latency.

3. Under the Output Routing tab, choose Internal as the Mixing Mode.

4. Set the Output Monitor to the secondary outputs of the external audio interface. Many audio interfaces offer a dedicated headphone monitor output.

5. Set the Output Master to the primary outputs of the external audio interface. This should reflect the same output used to connect the audio interface to powered speakers or an amplifier.

6. Click on the Close button to accept the settings.

Skip ahead to "Navigating the User Interface" once you have completed the steps listed here for your particular configuration.

External Audio Interface: External Mixing

Traktor's External Mixing mode is primarily designed for DJs who want to swap their decks for a modernized digital setup, yet still prefer the feel and performance of mixing tracks with high-end DJ mixers. With a setup such as this you can relinquish traditions of beatmatching and spend more time experimenting with the idea of Traktor-as-instrument rather than Traktor-as-jukebox. Emphasizing MIDI control, this configuration encourages you to creatively manipulate Traktor's internal effects, cue points, loops, and even MIDI-synced hardware, such as drum machines, synths, FX processors…even partner up and sync another computer running Traktor, Maschine, or Ableton Live.

Note: Be aware that Traktor does not maintain proprietary hardware requirements if you don't plan on using the timecode vinyl. This means that performers can design and customize each aspect of their DJ performance to suit changing needs. For example, if you produce as well as perform, a single higher-end interface, such as RME's Fireface 400, could serve as your one-stop workhorse between the studio and the stage.

Hardware Configuration

1. Connect the external audio interface to your computer.

2. Connect the primary stereo output of your audio interface, shown in Figure 5.6, to the applicable line or CD input of your DJ mixer.

3. Engage the line or CD input on the relevant mixer channel.

Figure 5.6 Routing for an external audio interface with External Mixing.

If you are using an audio interface with two or more stereo outputs, repeat Steps 2 and 3 for the remaining channels.

Software Configuration

1. Open the Traktor Preferences.

2. Under the Audio Setup tab, choose the external audio interface from the Audio Device drop-down menu. Leave the Sample Rate at the default of 44,100 Hz. For now, adjust the Audio Latency to about 15 milliseconds. Once everything is up and running, try incrementally lowering this setting. Lower latency values translate to more responsive control but demand a fast computer. To adjust the latency on soundcards that use ASIO, click the Settings button nested alongside Audio Latency.

3. Under the Output Routing tab, choose External as the Mixing Mode.

4. Set Output Channels A, B, C, and D to appropriate audio interface outputs—for example, assign Output Channel A to Out 1/2, Output Channel B to Out 3/4, and so on.

5. Click on the Close button to accept the settings.

These configuration options are entirely dependent upon the specifications of your audio interface. For example, the two stereo outputs of NI's Audio 4 DJ will allow external routing of Decks A and B only. Although it is not essential to have more than two stereo outputs, it does present Traktor with more routing flexibility.

External Audio Interface: The Audio 8 DJ and Traktor's Control Vinyl

Traktor Scratch Pro offers a digital solution to traditionalists who prefer the feel of vinyl, precise control over their music, turntablism, the ritual of beatmatching, the culture of DJing, and the desire to spin a mixture of digital music alongside their own vinyl collection.

This particular configuration (as well as that with Traktor's control CDs) requires the full Traktor Scratch Pro bundle; the control vinyl/CDs will not function without either the Audio 4/8 or a Traktor Certified mixer. This setup fits best with DJs who prefer the analog feel but welcome the advantages of a digitized performance setup.

Hardware Configuration

1. Connect the Audio 8 DJ to your computer's USB 2.0 port and route your setup according to the following, or as displayed in Figure 5.7.

2. Connect the multicore cable labeled Audio 8 DJ Output to the Audio 8 DJ Out 1/2' (CH. A).

Figure 5.7 Routing for the Audio 8 DJ and Traktor's control vinyl.

3. Connect the multicore cable labeled Audio 8 DJ Input to the Audio 8 DJ In 1/2 (CH. A).

4. Connect the multicore cable labeled Mixer TT/CD to the relevant Phono input channel on your DJ mixer. Use the mixer's Phono/Line switch to toggle between real vinyl (Phono) and Traktor's control vinyl (Line).

5. Connect the multicore cable labeled Mixer Line In to the relevant Line or CD input channel on your DJ mixer.

6. Connect your CDJ or turntable to the multicore cable labeled Player TT/CD.

7. Repeat Steps 2 through 6 for the next turntable.

Software Configuration

1. Open the Traktor Preferences.

2. Under the Audio Setup tab, choose the Audio 8 DJ interface from the Audio Device drop-down menu. Leave the Sample Rate at the default of 44,100 Hz. For now, adjust the Audio Latency to about 15 milliseconds. Once everything is up and running, try incrementally lowering this setting. Lower latency values translate to more responsive control but demand a fast computer. To adjust the Audio 8 DJ's latency value, click the Settings button nested alongside Audio Latency.

3. Under the Output Routing tab, choose External as the Mixing Mode. The Audio 8 DJ outputs should automatically pre-assign to their respective output channels. If they do not, use the drop-down menus to assign each Deck to its

respective output—for example, assign Output Channel A to Output 1/2, Output Channel B to Output 3/4, and so on.

4.   Click on the Close button to accept the settings.

Skip ahead to "Navigating the User Interface" once you have completed the steps listed here.

External Audio Interface: The Audio 8 DJ and Traktor's Control CDs

This is similar to Traktor's control vinyl, yet for any DJ who prefers the reliability, the precision, or simply the feel of CDJs.

Hardware Configuration

1.   Connect the Audio 8 DJ to your computer's USB 2.0 port and route your setup according to the following, or as displayed in Figure 5.8.

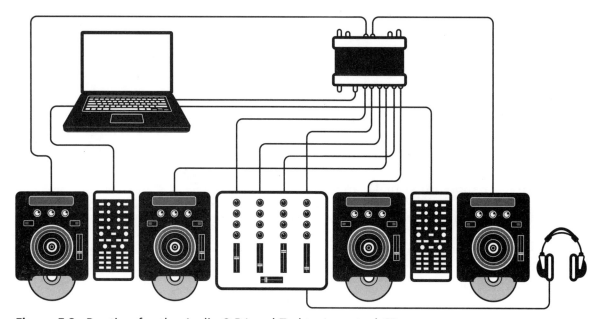

Figure 5.8 Routing for the Audio 8 DJ and Traktor's control CDs.

2.   Connect the multicore cable labeled Audio 8 DJ Output to the Audio 8 DJ Out 1/2 (CH. A).

3.   Connect the multicore cable labeled Audio 8 DJ Input to the Audio 8 DJ In 1/2 (CH. A).

4.   Connect the multicore cable labeled Mixer TT/CD to the relevant Line/CD input channel on your DJ mixer. Use the mixer's Phono (Line/CD)/Line switch

to toggle between real CDs and Traktor's control CDs. Refer to the following with regard to mixer configuration.

Caution: If you want to flip between real CDs and Traktor's control CDs, each individual DJ mixer channel must offer two Line inputs. As an example, some Pioneer mixers have a switch to reconfigure the Phono inputs as Line inputs; thus, each mixer channel would offer either two Line inputs or one Phono input and one Line input. If this is not an option, route the multicore cable Mixer TT/CD cable to an empty mixer channel's Line input. Do *not* use the Phono input with line-level (CD) signals. Doing so will boost an already amplified line-level signal into an extremely unpleasant and distorted mess.

---

5.   Connect the multicore cable labeled Mixer Line In to the relevant Line or CD input channel on your DJ mixer.

6.   Connect your CDJ or turntable to the multicore cable labeled Player TT/CD.

7.   Repeat Steps 2 through 6 for the next CDJ.

Software Configuration

1.   Open the Traktor Preferences.

2.   Under the Audio Setup tab, choose the Audio 8 DJ interface from the Audio Device drop-down menu. Leave the Sample Rate at the default of 44,100 Hz. For now, adjust the Audio Latency to about 15 milliseconds. Once everything is up and running, try incrementally lowering this setting. Lower latency values translate to more responsive control but demand a fast computer. To adjust the Audio 8 DJ's latency value, click the Settings button nested alongside Audio Latency.

3.   Under the Output Routing tab, choose External as the Mixing Mode. The Audio 8 DJ outputs should automatically pre-assign to their respective output channels. If they do not, use the drop-down menus to assign each Deck to its respective output—for example, assign Output Channel A to Output 1/2, Output Channel B to Output 3/4, and so on.

4.   Click on the Close button to accept the settings.

Navigating the User Interface

Very few things in life are more exasperating than having to work within a poorly designed graphical user interface (GUI). I'm sure that most people will agree that modern computer software should work *for* the end user, not the reverse. Unlike the symbiotic, evolving relationship between musicians and conventional instruments, such as violins, bass guitars, or drum sets, laptop artists are interfacing with a device more widely associated with Excel spreadsheets and email than with audible emotive textures. A computer's nonspecificity does have its advantages, but the aforementioned associations make the GUI concepts of familiarity and immediacy that much more important when artists adopt a laptop as their instrument.

Application Menu

Although the Application menu is actually part of the computer operating system rather than Traktor's full GUI, shown in Figure 5.9, it does offer a handful of helpful options. The menu provides direct access to various peripheral functions: Preferences, layouts, the user manual (RTFM!), or the Service Center.

Figure 5.9 The Traktor GUI.

Header

Shown in Figure 5.10, Traktor's Header section is designed to provide DJs with status feedback as well as instant access to Traktor's underbelly.

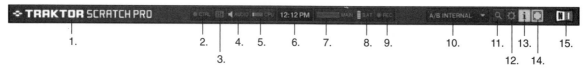

Figure 5.10 Locate important status information within Traktor's Header.

1. **Traktor logo.** Click to open Traktor's About window.

2. **MIDI (CTRL) indicator.** Flashes when receiving any incoming controller data.

3. **Controller State indicator.** Communicates the status of connected controllers.

    - **Blue.** All controllers are connected and configured properly.

    - **Orange.** There is a connection problem with port settings for at least one controller. For example, you may have additional unused mappings within the Controller Manager. Double-check the In-Port settings within the Controller Manager.

    - **Gray.** Traktor does not see any connected controllers. Double-check the In-Port settings within the Controller Manager.

4. **Audio indicator.** Displays audio interface status.

    - **Blue.** Audio interface connected and properly functioning.

    - **Red.** Either no audio interface is selected or there is a problem with the chosen device.

5. **CPU meter.** Indicates the Traktor audio engine's demand on the CPU. Percentages in excess of 80 percent or so will likely result in audio dropouts and/or unpleasant artifacts.

6. **Clock.** Direct from your system clock!

7. **Main (Master) Out.** Displays Traktor's combined audio output. Red indicates either signal compression (limiter *on* within Preferences) or clipping.

8. **Battery indicator.** Displays how much battery power remains.

    - **Blue.** Power cable connected.

    - **Red.** Power cable disconnected; running on battery power.

9. **Recording indicator.** Reflects audio recorder status. Red indicates enabled recording.

10. **Layout selector.** A drop-down menu of available screen layouts as configured within Traktor's Preferences under the Layout Manager tab.

11. **Maximize Browser button.** Expands the Traktor Browser to full screen.

12. **Preferences button.** Opens the Traktor Preferences.

13. **Tooltips button.** Enables information pop-ups when hovering the mouse over parameters.

14. **Fullscreen button.** Toggle Traktor between full-screen and windowed mode.

15. **NI logo.** Click to open Traktor's About window.

Global Section

Think of the Global section as a collection of outboard gear that Traktor swallowed. Ranging from tempo control and recording to effects racks and signal presence, this section is broken down into five distinct divisions.

The Master Panel
1. **Master Volume.** Control the combined output level of Traktor's internal signals from the Master Volume knob shown in Figure 5.11.

Figure 5.11   Traktor's Master Panel.

2. **Mouse Behavior selection.**
   - **Snap.** Cue points and loops snap to the closest grid marker.
   - **Quant.** Quantize function that allows seamless on-the-beat hot-cue jumping and loop manipulation.
   - **CD mode.** CDJ-inspired cueing stutter loop is engaged.

3. **Headphones Mix.** Adjusts the balance between the monitor and master output signals.

4. **Headphones Volume.** Controls the monitor output level for the headphone mix (only if a monitor output is assigned within the Preferences).

5. **LFO Reset.** Resets the global LFO (low-frequency oscillator) for all LFO-controlled effects.

6. **Cruise.** Activates the automatic playback of the currently selected playlist. (Also known as Autoplay.)

7. **Tick.** Sends the Beatgrid-synced beat tick to the monitor output. Use as a metronome or click track while setting Beatgrids. Cue must be engaged on the appropriate Deck in order to hear the signal.

The Master Clock Panel The Master Clock panel, shown in Figure 5.12, represents Traktor's virtual heart, because it provides the pulse for any and all timing information sent to

Figure 5.12   Traktor's Master Clock panel.

and from the application. Everything from internally syncing Traktor's Decks to slaving a drum machine to using Traktor's MIDI clock revolves around the Master Clock panel.

1. **Deck Master mode**
   - **Manual.** All Master Deck tempo and Sync functions are assigned by hand.
   - **Auto.** Traktor "intelligently" assigns one of the Decks as the master tempo source.

2. **Clock Master mode**
   - **Int.** The master tempo dictates the internal clock source to which Traktor's four Decks are synced.
   - **Ext.** The master tempo is determined from an external MIDI clock source.

3. **Master tempo parameters**
   - **Master Clock Tempo.** Displays the current master tempo and relevant offset (yellow phase meter).
   - **Tick.** Sends the Master Clock–synced beat tick to the monitor output.
   - **Tap.** Manually adjust the Master Clock by tapping in the tempo.
   - **Master Clock Pitch Bend.** Temporarily bump the Master Clock tempo up (>) or down (<).
   - **Master Clock Tempo Adjust.** Sequentially increase (+) or decrease (−) the Master Clock tempo.

4. **MIDI Clock**
   - **Sync.** Resets the MIDI Clock sync signal of any externally connected devices.
   - **MIDI Clock Start/Stop.** Activates/deactivates Traktor's MIDI Clock.

FX Panel Traktor's FX panel represents a versatile combination of effects routing potential, fully catering to and designed for inspired performance control. Four independent FX panels offer up to four potential sources of varied signal processing for each Traktor Deck.

Advanced Mode   Shown in Figures 5.13 and 5.14, each FX panel is loaded with a single effect type while offering a wide range of precise control parameters.

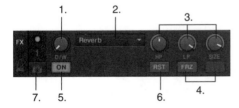

Figure 5.13 Advanced mode within FX Panel 1.

Figure 5.14 Advanced mode within FX Panels 1 and 3.

1. **Dry/Wet.** Controls the balance of clean (dry) to processed (wet) signals.

2. **FX Select.** A drop-down list of available effects. This list can be customized within the Traktor Preferences under the Effects tab.

3. **FX Parameter knobs.** Provides control over individual effect parameters.

4. **FX Parameter buttons.** Toggles between different effect parameters.

5. **FX On/Off.** Turns the relevant effect on or off.

6. **FX Reset.** Resets the effect parameters to the default snapshot state.

7. **Snapshot.** Saves the currently configured effect parameters as the default state.

Chained Mode   Load each FX panel with up to three effect types while offering a single depth control over a blend of designated parameters. Displayed in Figures 5.15 and 5.16, Advanced mode offers precise control, whereas Chained mode offers creative experimentation through a serially processed effects chain.

Figure 5.15 Chained mode within FX Panel 1.

Figure 5.16 Chained mode within FX Panels 1 and 3.

1. **Dry/Wet.** Controls the balance of clean (dry) to processed (wet) signals.

2. **FX Select.** A drop-down list of available effects. This list can be customized within the Traktor Preferences under the Effects tab.

3. **FX Amount.** Provides a single control knob over the depth of various predesignated parameters.

4. **FX On/Off.** Turns the relevant effect on or off.

5. **Snapshot.** Saves the currently configured effect parameters as the default state.

Audio Recorder When potential employees are applying for most jobs, one assumption is that they all submit some form of a CV or resume. When you're working as a DJ, promoters generally act the part of HR and do all of the hiring; thus, it makes sense that part of a DJ's CV includes recorded performances.

The DJ mix has been entrenched in DJ culture since the pioneers first transformed turntables into instruments. As such, mix demos have become the industry benchmark for every DJ's "voice." Until relatively recently, recording was generally accomplished via external recording devices—just one more piece of gear to lug around.

Traktor's Audio Recorder, shown in Figure 5.17, allows DJs to record laptop mixes without connecting a single cable, or entire stage performances through the house mixer. Further, the Audio Recorder provides the perfect solution to ripping your entire vinyl library into the Traktor collection.

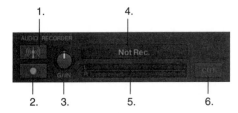

Figure 5.17   Use the Audio Recorder to capture your performances.

1. **Broadcasting On/Off.** Start/stop Traktor's broadcasting.

2. **Recording On/Off.** Start/stop recording.

3. **Input Gain.** Manually adjust the Audio Recorder input volume.

4. **File display.** Displays the length and file size of the current recording.

5. **Recording meter.** Audio Recorder volume meter.

6. **Cut.** Seamlessly trims a recording file into individual gapless recordings.

Decks

The turntable's digital progeny, Traktor's Decks, shown in Figure 5.18, are the advanced laptop equivalent of a traditional DJ's stage setup. Nearly all of the DJ staples have been re-created across Traktor's four Decks: from slip cueing and pitch bumping,

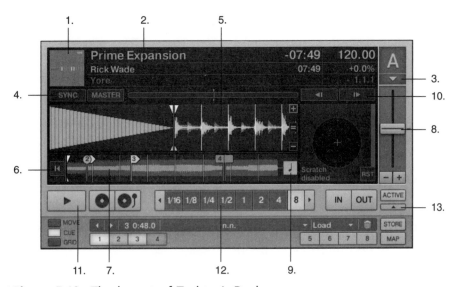

Figure 5.18   The layout of Traktor's Decks.

to the modern adaptations of looping, hot cues, auto-beatmatching, and instantaneous "needle dropping."

1. **Track Cover icon.** Displays the loaded track's album art.

2. **Track Info.** A display of track metadata: artists, title, and so on. Customize the Deck Heading display under the Deck Details tab within the Traktor Preferences.

3. **Deck mode.** Configures the input type for each Deck.

    -   **Internal Playback.** Traktor's Deck playback is controlled with an external control device.

    -   **Scratch Control.** Traktor's Deck playback is controlled with the control vinyl/CDs.

    -   **Audio Through.** Traktor's Deck acts as a line input for external devices: microphones, drum machines, and so on. Any input signal can be fed through Traktor's EQ or FX.

4. **Sync controls.**

    -   **Sync button.** Immediately syncs the loaded track to the master: another Deck, the internal Master Clock, or an external Master Clock.

    -   **Master button.** Sets the relevant Deck as the Master Clock tempo.

    -   **Phase meter.** Visual display of the sync offset between any playing Deck and the Master Deck or Master Clock.

    -   **Pitch Bend.** Temporarily bump the Deck tempo up (>) or down (<).

5. **Waveform.** Visual representation of the currently loaded track's playback position. Use the plus (+) and the minus (−) to zoom the track view in and out, respectively.

6. **Jump to Track Start.** Restarts the track from the beginning.

7. **Stripe display.** Visual representation of all cue point and loop assignments displayed across a zoomed-out view of the loaded track.

8. **Pitch fader.** Operates in the exact manner of a traditional turntable: Drag downward on the fader to speed up a track and upward to slow it down.

9. **Key Lock.** Engages the Key Lock feature.

10. **Pitch Adjust.** Incrementally bump the Deck's pitch up (+) or down (−). Right-click (Control-click) on the icons to set the Pitch Adjust precision.

11. **Transport controls.** Deck playback controls (dependent on Deck mode state).

    -   **Internal Playback.** Cue functions enabled.

    -   **Scratch Control.** Control Vinyl mode enabled.

    -   **Audio Through.** Function disabled.

12.   **Autoloop controls.** Sets automatic and manual loop points.

13.   **Open/Close Advanced Panels.** Show or hide the Advanced panels for parallel Decks.

Decks: Advanced Panels

Three pages comprise the Advanced panels, each of which is chosen from the left-hand side: the Move panel, the Cue panel, and the Grid panel. The Advanced panels epitomize modern track management and manipulation. Save and name various types of cue points; edit, move, manipulate, and store useful track loop sections; and manage Traktor's Beatgrids within an environment specifically designed for the combination of speed and efficiency.

Loop Move/Beatjump Panel

1.   **Move modes.** Switch between Beatjump, Loop, Loop In, and Loop Out modes.

2.   **Move sizes.** Determines the amount of each Beatjump or loop move in beats. A bidirectional yellow arrow is placed underneath the selected move size. The gray left/right arrow "bookends" shift the Move Size display to show further hidden options. xFine and Fine cater to precise movements.

3.   **Move buttons.** Enacts the chosen Move Mode function by Move Size amounts as displayed in Figure 5.19.

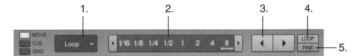

Figure 5.19 Traktor's Loop Move/Beatjump Advanced panel.

4.   **Loop mode.** Ties the Move button's actions to the active loop size. The active loop is affected based on the selected Move mode.

   ■   **Loop mode.** Clicking either Move button moves the looped section one full length forward or backward.

   ■   **Loop In/Out mode.** Clicking either Move button doubles or halves the loop in (left loop marker) or loop out (right loop marker) points.

5.   **Fine mode.** The selected Move mode is performed with extra precision.

Cue/Loop Management Panel

1.   **Next/Previous Cue/Loop Point.** Jump forward/backward through saved cue/loop points.

2.   **Cue Position display.** Displays the cue/loop point's temporal location within a track in the format mm:ss:ms (minutes:seconds:milliseconds).

3. **Cue Name display.** Click the downward-facing arrow to access the list of stored cue/loop points. Double-click the text to highlight/rename the cue/loop point.

4. **Cue Type.** Click the downward-facing arrow to choose or switch the cue/loop point type.

5. **Delete Cue.** Erases the currently selected cue/loop point.

6. **Store Cue.** Saves the currently selected cue/loop point. Each cue/loop point is sequentially mapped to the next available Hot Cue button. Although only eight hot cues are available, the total number of storable cue/loop points is virtually limitless.

7. **Map Hot Cue.** Once engaged, load a previously stored cue/loop and click any one of the eight hot cues shown in Figure 5.20 to store at that location.

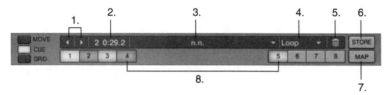

Figure 5.20 Traktor's Cue/Loop Management Advanced panel.

8. **Hot Cues.** Color-coded cue/loop point "favorites" that provide immediate loading of previously stored cue points (blue), fade-in/out points (orange), load points (yellow), grid markers (white), and loops (green). Clicking any empty (gray) hot-cue point will automatically store either the current cue point or the active loop.

Beatgrid Panel

1. **Move Beatgrid.** Slides the initial Beatmarker shown in Figure 5.21 (and thus, the entire Beatgrid) left or right.

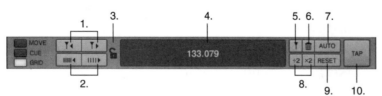

Figure 5.21 Traktor's Beatgrid Management Advanced panel.

2. **Adjust Beatgrid bpm.** Increase/decrease the Beatgrid's bpm.
    - Move the Beatgrid (shift left/right).
    - Adjust the Beatgrid bpm (compress/expand).

3. **Beatgrid Lock.** Locks the Beatgrid in place and disables all Beatgrid panel settings to prevent accidental changes.

4. **Tempo.** Displays Traktor's tempo estimation for the currently loaded track. Double-click to manually adjust the bpm.

5. **Set Grid Marker.** Sets a new or additional grid marker at the current playback position.

6. **Delete Grid Marker.** Erases the currently selected grid marker.

7. **Autogrid.** Automatically deletes all existing grid markers while simultaneously creating a new grid marker and estimating the bpm of the currently loaded track.

8. **Double/Halve Tempo.** Doubles or halves the loaded track's estimated bpm.

9. **Reset Tempo.** Resets the currently loaded track's bpm to the analyzed tempo.

10. **Tap Tempo.** Adjusts the Beatgrid bpm around successive button taps in tempo with the currently loaded track's playback.

The Mixer Section

The basic concept of any DJ mixer is simple: to manipulate various incoming audio signals and combine them into a single cohesive output. An evolution of elaborate studio mixing desks, DJ mixers were streamlined for performance, highlighting primary features such as EQ, filters, and volume controls to allow DJs to intuitively sculpt their music output.

Traktor's Mixer section, shown in Figure 5.22, takes these ideals as an influential foundation and develops them into an advanced framework for splicing music together. DJs can choose between EQs and filter slopes modeled after popular club mixers or lock a track's musical key to mix harmoniously and avoid turntable pitch effects.

Figure 5.22 Traktor's powerful Mixer section.

1. **Equalizer (EQ).** Separates the currently playing track's discrete audio frequency bands for smooth mixing and/or creative effect. You can choose different EQ models from Preferences > Mixer > EQ Selection.

2. **Channel fader.** Controls the relevant Deck's volume. The VU meter shows the Deck's prefader output level (in blue) and can be adjusted via the relevant channel's Gain knob.

3. **Filter.** Controls the relevant Deck's bipolar low-pass/high-pass filter. From the default 12 o'clock position, the low-pass (counterclockwise) and high-pass (clockwise) filters are engaged via the tiny on/off button nested directly alongside the Filter labeling. You can choose different filter models from the Filter Selection option within Traktor's Preferences under the Mixer tab.

4. **Key Lock.** Adjusts the key, or harmonic center, of the currently loaded track. Key Lock is engaged via the tiny on/off button nested directly alongside the Key labeling or by clicking on the quarter note from the Deck section nested directly alongside the currently loaded track's stripe.

5. **FX Insert buttons.** Clicking on one of the numbers inserts the relevant FX panel into the relevant Deck's signal. Be aware that disabling FX inserts completely cuts off the chosen effect, including any delay or reverb tails.

6. **Channel Gain.** Controls the relevant Deck's prefader gain. Choose Set Autogain When Loading Track to allow Traktor to determine the appropriate channel gain structure. This is set under the Mixer tab within the Traktor Preferences.

7. **Cue button (Pre-Listen/Monitor).** Click to pre-listen to the currently loaded track through Traktor's internal Mixer. Engage the Cue button to layer Traktor's beat tick over the relevant Deck's monitor output.

8. **Channel Pan button.** Adjust the volume output balance (left/right) for the relevant Deck across the stereo field.

Crossfader

To some degree, a crossfader is like a volume channel flipped on its side; the difference is that it is a specific class of fader that controls the balance between two volume outputs—for example, Deck A and Deck B. Generally, when a crossfader rests in the middle position, both Decks will play simultaneously. Drag the crossfader to the left, and the track playing on Deck B will fade out as Deck A continues playback; drag the fader to the right, and the track playing on Deck A will fade out as the track playing on Deck B slowly fades back in. Many MIDI controllers on the market have built-in crossfaders that emulate that of a traditional DJ mixer—perfect for scratch DJs gone digital;

in other words, "controllerism." When enabled within the Preferences, Traktor's Crossfader will appear as in Figure 5.23.

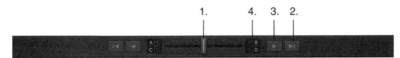

Figure 5.23 Use Traktor's Crossfader to blend deck outputs.

1. **Crossfader.** Controls the output balance levels between the currently assigned Decks.

2. **Auto-Crossfade button.** Clicking either button initiates an automatic transition from one Deck to the next. Clicking it again will stop the transition. Auto-Crossfade speed is configured under Preferences > Mixer > Crossfade.

3. **Manual Crossfade button.** Click to incrementally adjust the Crossfader or click and hold for a continuous transition. Adjust the accuracy by right-clicking (Control-clicking) on either Manual Crossfade button.

4. **Deck Assignment buttons.** Click to assign/unassign the Decks from Crossfader control.

Browser

Functionally serving as Traktor's record crate, the Browser is like a filing cabinet for the music files on your hard drive. The album art you can see in Figure 5.24 helps maintain vinyl's crate-digging nostalgia, expedited through transparent track access, customized playlists, and other useful track-organizing features. All track information edits to, among other things, artist and release names, label, bpm, track key, ratings, and so on, and expanding to cue points, Beatgrids, and loops are all directly embedded into file metadata via the Traktor Browser. You never have to worry about losing your customized collection data.

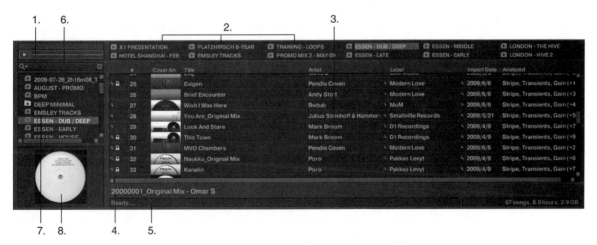

Figure 5.24 Use Traktor's Browser to dig through your track collection.

1. **Preview Player.** Prior to loading tracks into a Deck, or to audition certain songs, drag and drop directly onto the player or click a track's Preview Player icon (magnifying glass) from the Browser List.

    ■ **Internal Mixing mode.** Preview Player output is sourced from the monitor output: Preferences > Output Routing > Output Monitor.

    ■ **External Mixing mode.** Preview Player output is sourced from the output preview: Preferences > Output Routing > Output Preview.

2. **Favorites playlists.** Provide immediate access to specifically chosen favorite playlists.

3. **Track List.** Displays the track results contained within the Browser Tree's currently selected source—for example, playlist, search field, iTunes, and so on.

4. **Track Info.** Displays the artist and track name for the song that is currently highlighted within the Track List.

5. **Status Bar.** Displays Traktor feedback information, such as track analyzation progress and error messages.

6. **Track Search field.** Provides an "intelligent," real-time search engine that filters down results with each keystroke.

7. **Browser Tree.** Provides a tiered organizational structure of the various sources through which to access your music. Any folder, or *node*, with a small plus (+) icon contains further subfolders.

    ■ **Track collection.** Contains all imported tracks within your Traktor collection. Subfolders automatically sort all tracks (via track metadata) into four specific categories: Artists, Releases, Labels, and Genres.

    ■ **Playlists.** Contains all available playlists and playlist folders.

    ■ **Explorer.** Browse the file structures of any internal or external hard drives for tracks that may not have been imported into Traktor's collection.

    ■ **Archive.** Located immediately under the Explorer icon, the Archive icon tracks and records a playlist of Traktor's playback history. Each playlist is time-stamped with the Traktor session date and provides additional information columns offering start time, duration, and Deck playback history.

    ■ **Audio Recordings.** Provides a list of every recording made with Traktor's Audio Recorder.

    ■ **iTunes.** Provides instant access to all iTunes playlists.

    ■ **History.** A playlist that provides the current session's playback history. After every session, the History playlist is stored, or archived, under the Archive icon mentioned a moment ago.

8. **Cover Art.** Displays the cover art embedded within the metadata of the track currently selected within the Track List.

This chapter was written with a dual purpose. One goal was to provide you with a reference-focused breakdown of Traktor's most critical features. The other was to demonstrate the versatility that allows these features to easily integrate with the needs and wants of stylistically different DJs. You are highly encouraged to flip back to this chapter from time to time to refresh your memory. You never know—you may have missed something important!

6 | Traktor Pro: Getting Started

If you found the previous chapter a little bit dry, please wake up. It's time to start fiddling about!

Your Music Collection and the Traktor Browser

Bearing in mind music's overwhelming availability, it's hardly surprising that the success of a digital DJ application is partially balanced on its organizational features. As an example, consider the image of a DJ turning around, rifling through his vinyl, physically earmarking a handful of "maybes," and then cueing and dropping the mix just at the right moment. How can a software company capture this experience? DJs have historically sought the shortest distance between two points, so why not ask them?

Native Instruments did precisely this, and the artist/developer discourse yielded the Traktor Browser. While playlists are nothing new, Traktor's Browser implements playlist functions in a modernized way that presents several obvious advantages over a bag full of vinyl. With the click of a mouse button, you can categorically reshuffle hundreds of tracks around artist name, track name, genre, and so on. Album art provides visual reference points across a vast track collection. You can also spread tracks across several customized playlists and then export them to portable folders outside Traktor. Further, when a night goes well, History playlists archive your set for future reference. Options are the theme here.

Loading Your Music

It's a safe bet that you have at least a few music files on your computer, so let's get them loaded. From an organizational standpoint, you can store your music files virtually anywhere. All it takes is telling Traktor where to look for them. Structured folder trees, iTunes playlists—it doesn't really matter. As a word of caution: Organization will reduce your risk of developing a serious headache later. *Think of a formula and stick with it!* Now, with regard to your music, be aware that Traktor supports nearly all of the major (non-DRM) digital audio formats.

Note: If you use iTunes playlists to organize your music, those playlists are seamlessly mirrored within the Traktor Browser. However, bear in mind that in order to store Traktor-related data (cue points, loops, and so on) or to edit track metadata, you must import tracks into the Traktor Browser. You will find instructions on how to do this further along in this chapter.

Note: Traktor's supported formats are MP3, non-DRM M4A (AAC), WAV, AIFF, non-DRM WMA, FLAC, and OGG Vorbis.

Note: PC: Windows Media Player must be installed if you plan to use WMA files.

OS X: QuickTime must be installed if you plan to use M4A (AAC) files.

Importing Your Music Folders

Considering the number of ways that people store music files on their hard drives, Traktor's Collection Import was designed to be flexible. Whether music files are managed through custom file structures, managed within Apple's iTunes, or simply dumped into a random desktop folder, Traktor will find them. Automate the import process or manage it manually; it's up to you. Here's how.

1. Open Traktor's Preferences and click on Data Location. You can see the Data Location Preferences window in Figure 6.1.

   Directories displays the locations on your hard drive of the Traktor root folder (where all Traktor's collection information is stored) and the iTunes Music Library.xml file (from which Traktor reads your iTunes data). You can consolidate both on an external hard drive, but be sure to connect the hard drive when you start Traktor, or you will get missing-file error messages when loading tracks. Click the ...! button on the right-hand side if you ever need to choose a new file path.

   Music Folders, on the other hand, allows you to add your own additional files from an external hard drive or, for example, a file on your desktop used for promo downloads. On both OS X and Windows, you will notice that the computer's user music folder is also listed—for example, Music or My Music.

   Click Add at the bottom of the list and browse to any parent (topmost) folder holding your music.

2. Click OK or Choose.

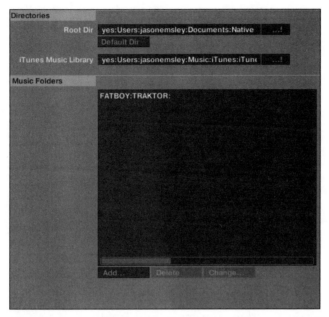

Figure 6.1 Designate the locations of your music files. FATBOY is my external HD.

3. Repeat the process to add any or all remaining music folders.

4. Close Preferences.

5. Right-click (Control-click) on Track Collection, as I have done in Figure 6.2, within the Traktor Browser Tree and choose Import Music Folders. All tracks contained within locations listed under Music Folders should now populate the Browser List.

Note: For example, I have a folder on my external hard drive called Traktor. Inside that folder I have a series of subfolders, which in turn have further subfolders. All you have to do is add the topmost folder in the tree—in my case, I would choose Traktor so that everything underneath that file gets imported. You do *not* need to add individual subfolders.

Importing Your iTunes Playlists

1. Click on the iTunes CD icon in Traktor's Browser Tree.

2. Navigate to the desired iTunes playlist.

3. Right-click (Control-click) the playlist and choose Import to Playlists.

4. Repeat for all subsequent playlists.

Figure 6.2 Choose Import Music Folders to bring your music into Traktor.

Alternative iTunes Import Options

■ Drag and drop an iTunes playlist onto the Playlist icon within Traktor's Browser Tree.

■ Drag and drop an iTunes playlist onto any Favorites slot.

■ Right-click (Control-click) on the iTunes icon and choose Import to Collection to import your entire iTunes library into Traktor.

Caution: Traktor's iTunes access is a strictly read-only view—hence the limited functions, such as editing track metadata. You must add tracks to the track collection before you can make edits.

Even Further Import Options

■ Drag and drop any folders from the OS X Finder or Windows Explorer directly onto the Track Collection icon within Traktor's Browser Tree. Directly drag and drop tracks onto any of the Traktor Decks, playlists, and so on.

■ Drag and drop folders from Traktor's Explorer icon onto the track collection, favorites, or playlists. Directly drag and drop tracks onto any of the Traktor Decks, playlists, and so on.

■ Right-click (Control-click) on any folder under Traktor's Explorer icon and choose Import to Collection, Playlists, or, most importantly, Add to Music Folders. The latter will add the chosen directory to your Music Folders list described a moment ago, within the Preferences under Data Location.

Importing from Serato

NI's border patrol recently made it easy to migrate from Serato to Traktor. With the release of the Traktor SSL Database Importer (a bit of a mouthful), NI created a platform that allows (former) Serato DJs to effortlessly prep their data for direct import into the Traktor Browser.

As you can see in Figure 6.3, Traktor's collection is prepped to receive Serato music libraries from the SSL database, crates, or folders. The most important part about this import process is that DJs do not lose cue points, loops, and/or metadata that was created and saved within the Serato database—all of that information is directly converted over.

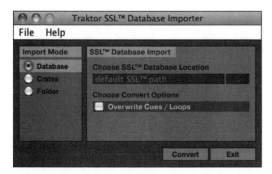

Figure 6.3 Use the SSL Database Importer to seamlessly migrate your Serato crates into the Traktor Browser.

Simply import the newly created Traktor .nml file, and you should be good to go. Painless crossover!

Creating Your Own Playlists

A few years ago, I was on the phone with a Traktor user who was complaining about his trouble maintaining a collection of more than 300,000 tracks. I'm sure we can agree that he paid for every single one of those songs…right? Anyhow, I held my tongue, let him finish ranting, and proceeded to explain the concept of Traktor's playlists and Playlist folders. It was as if the heavens opened up and poured holy light all over his DJ pulpit.…

Legalities aside, our friend obviously maintains quite a large music library. Navigating a track collection that large would be extremely tedious without some form of organizational filter, which is where Traktor's playlists come in.

There are a few different procedures through which playlists can be created:

Procedure 1:

1.   Right-click (Control-click) on the Playlist icon within Traktor's Browser Tree.

2. Choose Create Playlist, as shown in Figure 6.4.

Figure 6.4 Click Create Playlist to begin organizing your Traktor collection.

3. Enter a name for the new playlist.

4. Click OK.

5. The new playlist will appear alphabetically under the Playlist icon.

Procedure 2:

1. Click on either the track collection or an individual playlist within Traktor's Browser Tree.

2. Choose one or multiple tracks within the Browser List.

3. Drag and drop the highlighted tracks onto the Playlist icon within the Browser Tree.

4. Enter a name for the new playlist.

5. Click OK.

6. The new playlist will appear alphabetically under the Playlist icon.

Procedure 3:

1. Open an OS X Finder or Windows Explorer window.

2. Drag and drop any music folder onto the Playlist icon within Traktor's Browser Tree.

3. Enter a name for the new playlist.

4. Click OK.

5. The new playlist will appear alphabetically under the Playlist icon.

Creating Playlist Folders

Over time, the number of playlists that you create might get a bit unwieldy. Creating a few Playlist folders will help pare down the total number of playlists into manageable categories.

1. Right-click (Control-click) on the Playlist icon within Traktor's Browser Tree.

2. Choose Create Playlist Folder.

3. Enter a name for the new Playlist folder.

4. Click OK.

5. The new Playlist folder will appear alphabetically under the Playlist icon with a tiny plus (+) over the icon. Clicking the plus icon will expand/contract the folder.

6. As when creating playlists, either drag and drop some playlists, highlighted tracks, or folders from the OS X Finder or Windows Explorer into the folder or right-click (Control-click) on the Playlist folder itself and choose Create Playlist. You can even create more Playlist folders to create a deep subdirectory of categorization.

Sorting Playlists

Anyone who has played out with vinyl knows that earmarking a handful of "maybes" is many a DJ's organizational M.O. at a gig. Traktor's digital equivalent begins with categorical playlist sorting.

Organizing Playlist Sort Order

1. Click on any column heading to alphabetically sort the playlist by that category—for example, clicking on Title will rearrange the playlist by title.

2. Click the column heading again to invert the playlist sort order.

3. Click on the # icon to reset the playlist to its original state.

Manually Organizing Playlist Sort Order

1. Click on the # column to reset the playlist sort order.

2. Click and drag tracks to the desired position within the Browser List. The orange line dictates where the tracks will be dropped. If you have not reset the original sort order, you will notice that the pointer is crossed out, preventing order changes.

Consolidating (Saving) Playlist Sort Order

1. Click on any column heading within Traktor's Browser List to sort the playlist by that category.

2. Right-click (Control-click) on the playlist within Traktor's Browser Tree. Choose Consolidate to save the playlist sort order as the permanent setting.

The Favorites Playlist

If playlists and Playlist folders start to get out of control, create a handful of readily accessible, go-to virtual record crates…also known as favorites, as shown in Figure 6.5. If you do not see the Favorites menu, ensure that Show Playlist Favorites is checked under Preferences > Browser Details.

Figure 6.5 Using favorites significantly speeds up track searching.

Assigning Favorites

1. Click on any playlist within Traktor's Browser Tree.

2. Drag the playlist to any Favorites slot. You can replace any preexisting favorite by dropping the playlist on top of it.

3. The Favorite slot can now be immediately accessed by mouse-click, hot key, or MIDI assignment. You can also directly access favorites by using the function keys on your computer's keyboard. (Be aware that laptops often have an additional function modifier key—for example, Fn or similar.)

Note: Right-clicking (Control-clicking) on any favorites playlist will provide the same drop-down list as right-clicking from Traktor's Browser Tree.

The Preparation Playlist

You can create any number of playlists in anticipation of a gig; however, most dance floors require performers to adapt—something that often separates a good DJ from a great one. A DJ knowing his tunes certainly factors in here, but quick access for the appropriate moment is essential. Specifically emulating vinyl earmarking, Traktor's preparation playlist was designed to efficiently sort out music on the fly. To create a preparation playlist:

1. Click on any playlist within Traktor's Browser Tree. (It may be helpful to create a new playlist specifically for this purpose.)

2. Right-click (Control-click) on the playlist and choose Preparation. Consider dragging the preparation playlist over to a Favorites slot as well.

3. The selected playlist's icon will change, and small diamonds (think: angled vinyl sleeves) will appear beside tracks within the Browser Lists's Track Icon column, shown in Figure 6.6. This denotes the track as earmarked and is displayed throughout Traktor's collection as a reminder.

Figure 6.6 The diamond icon marks a track that has been "earmarked" within the preparation playlist.

4. While browsing, right-click on any track and choose either Append to Preparation List or Append as Next to Preparation List. Append as Next will drop the selected song into the preparation playlist immediately following the last track played.

5. If you like to begin every set fresh, right-click (Control-click) the preparation playlist within the Browser Tree and choose Clear Playlist.

Tip: Assign the preparation playlist Append functions to a MIDI controller or hotkeys to seamlessly integrate the process into your workflow.

The History Playlist

If a gig goes particularly well, you may want to keep and/or share what you played, including the order in which you played it. Although the History playlist resets every time Traktor closes, a separate playlist is created and archived for each Traktor session. As mentioned previously, you can find all archived Traktor History playlists from within Traktor's Browser Tree, under Explorer > Archive.

Some useful History playlist functions:

- Import previous History playlists to access old sets.

- Export previously imported History playlists, including all tracks.

- Export clearly labeled track listings in HTML format for printing/sharing via Save as Webpage.

Exporting Playlists

If you want to move a playlist to another computer, share it with a partner, or create a mobile playlist on a USB drive, perform the following:

1. Right-click (Control-click) on any playlist from the Browser Tree or the favorites and choose Export Playlist.

2. Change the playlist title, if desired, within the dialog box shown in Figure 6.7.

Figure 6.7 Use this window to customize the exporting of your playlists.

3. Click on the ... to choose the playlist destination.

4. If you want to create a mobile playlist, check the option to Copy Tracks to Destination. The files are directly copied—in other words, the destination file remains the same format as the source.

5. Double-check for the newly created folder at the destination. You should find the (Playlist Name).nml file located within the folder, as well as all tracks contained within the playlist.

Importing Playlists

Similar to importing tracks into Traktor, you can import playlists in many ways.

Procedure 1:

1. Click on the Explorer icon within Traktor's Browser Tree.

2. Locate the relevant playlist.

3. Perform any of the following steps:
    - Drag and drop the playlist onto the track collection within Traktor's Browser Tree.
    - Drag and drop the playlist onto any Playlist folder within Traktor's Browser Tree to add tracks to the existing playlist.
    - Drag and drop the playlist onto any favorites slots.
    - Right-click (Control-click) on the playlist and choose Import to Playlists or Import to Collection.

Procedure 2:

1. Locate the (Playlist Name).nml file within the OS X Finder or Windows Explorer.

2. Drag and drop the playlist file onto the track collection or Playlist icon within Traktor's Browser Tree or onto a Favorites slot.

Procedure 3:

1. Right-click (Control-click) on the Playlist icon within Traktor's Browser Tree.

2. Choose Import Playlist (.nml file) or Import Playlist Directory (folder of .nml files).

3. Click Open to import the playlist and all relevant tracks.

Other Playlist Functions

Right-clicking (Control-clicking) on any playlist within Traktor's Browser Tree will pop open a drop-down list of useful track collection management options, as shown in Figure 6.8.

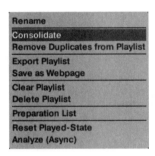

Figure 6.8 A list of playlist management options.

■ **Rename.** Assigns a new name to the chosen playlist.

■ **Remove Duplicates from Playlist.** Eliminates any duplicated tracks from the chosen playlist.

■ **Clear Playlist.** Removes all tracks from the chosen playlist.

■ **Delete Playlist.** Deletes the chosen playlist (does not delete tracks from the track collection).

■ **Reset Played-State.** Removes any or all track icons from the Browser List Icon column.

■ **Analyze (Async).** Analyzes all tracks within the chosen playlist.

Maintaining and Navigating Your Music Collection

It can be difficult to keep thousands upon thousands of tracks in order (not to mention in mind). Playlists do offer a systematic process, such as that found within the iTunes application, but the iTunes application and its playlist model are not designed for the sometimes manic environment of a DJ performance. Mercifully, NI considered this when designing Traktor's Browser.

Now that your Traktor collection is organized into at least a few playlists, it's time to run through how to navigate and maintain all of this stuff.

Editing Track Information (Metadata)

The biggest problem I have with a digital music library is its intangibility. There is something to be said for physically handling vinyl and/or CDs. However, I have to admit that it's pretty tough to beat the gains I have achieved with regard to customization. Instead of messing up my wax with a permanent marker, I can now make comments, rate, and edit my digitized files without defacing the vinyl they were ripped from. Within Traktor, there are a few different ways to edit track data.

Using Inline Editing (Edit Visible Metadata)

1. Click on any track in the Traktor's Browser List.

2. Double-click on any info field—for example, Title, as I have done in Figure 6.9.

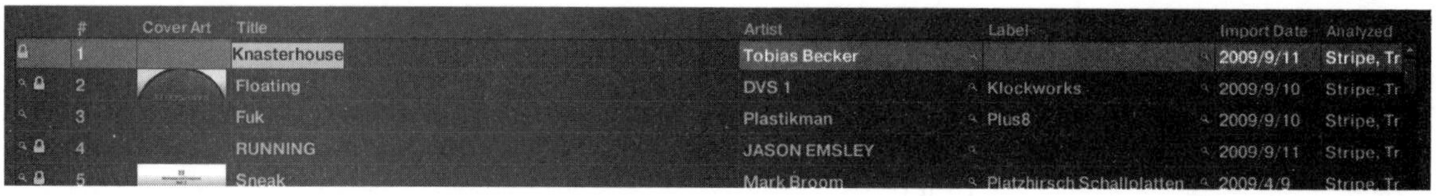

Figure 6.9 Editing inline track data.

3. Type in your changes when you see the cursor appear.

4. Press Enter to accept changes or Esc to cancel any changes.

Using the Edit Dialog (Edit All Metadata)

1. Select a track (or multiple tracks for group edits) within Traktor's Browser List.

2. Right-click (Control-click) and choose Edit. The Edit dialog will appear, as shown in Figure 6.10.

Figure 6.10 Use the Edit dialog to manage various track metadata.

3. Edit any relevant track information. If you're editing multiple tracks, notice Previous, Next, and Sel. All in the bottom-left corner. Previous and Next flip through the tracks one by one, while Sel. All applies any changes to all selected tracks. The check box displays shared information—that is, if the Artist box is unchecked, the Artist tag is not shared across all of the selected tracks.

4. Click the downward-facing arrows on the right of the text entry fields to choose a previously assigned category.

5. Click Restore to revert track information to its previously stored data.

6. Click Apply or OK to accept any changes.

7. Click Cancel to exit without making any changes.

Deleting Tracks

Invariably, we all need to remove some garbage from our music libraries at some point or another. Traktor offers a few different ways to do so.

Deleting from the Traktor Collection

1. Select a track (or multiple tracks) under Track Collection within Traktor's Browser List.

2. Right-click (Control-click) and choose Delete.

3. Choose one of the delete options shown in Figure 6.11.

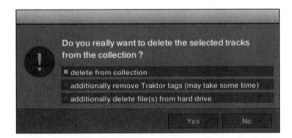

Figure 6.11 When you need to bin those promos.

- **Delete from Collection.** Chosen tracks will be deleted from the Traktor collection only.

- **Additionally Remove Traktor Tags.** Chosen tracks will be deleted from the Traktor collection, and any Traktor-specific tags will be removed—for example, cue points, loops, and so on.

- **Additionally Delete File(s) from the Hard Drive.** Chosen tracks will be deleted from Traktor and erased from the hard drive.

Caution: Pay close attention to the Delete mode you have chosen. If you accidentally delete a file from your hard drive, it's gone for good.

Deleting from the Traktor Playlists

1. Select a track (or multiple tracks) from any playlist within Traktor's Browser List.

2. Right-click (Control-click) and choose Delete. (Delete from Collection behaves as stated in the previous section.)

3. Confirm by clicking Yes or cancel by clicking No.

Track Icons

Traktor's track icons provide visual status feedback over the track collection—a helpful feature when things get busy. See Figure 6.12.

Figure 6.12 Traktor's track icons.

- A, B, C, and D locate a track within a Deck.

- The check mark signifies that a track has already been played.

- The lock icon signifies a track with a set/locked Beatgrid.

- An exclamation point (not shown) signifies that the track is missing from the expected location.

Adding Cover Art

One of my favorite aspects of Traktor's Browser is the simple aesthetic of album or EP cover art. While flying through the Traktor Browser, I find that visual beacons prove more efficient than text—especially with regard to new music I'm not familiar with by name.

First, ensure that Traktor is displaying cover art from at least one of three locations.

- Preferences > Browser Details > Cover Art (should be checked). Figure 6.13 shows two of Traktor's three cover art sections.

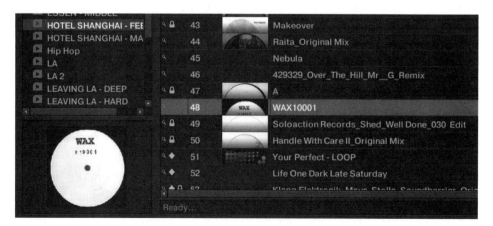

Figure 6.13 Use cover art as a visual marker within your music collection.

- Preferences > Deck Details > Deck Heading > Show Cover Art (should be checked).

- Right-click (Control-click) on any header within the Browser List—for example, Title—and choose Cover Art. You can click and drag the placement of the cover art filter along the Browser List header.

If any of your tracks is missing cover art, you can use Discogs to find it (www.discogs. com). Once art is downloaded, loading JPEG images is straightforward.

1. Right-click (Control-click) on any track (or group of tracks) from within Traktor's Browser List.

2. Choose Import Cover, as shown in Figure 6.14.

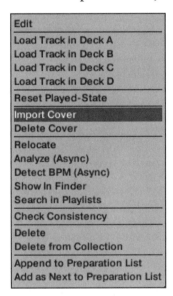

Figure 6.14 Adding cover art to your music.

3. Navigate the OS X Finder or Windows Explorer dialog to your image file.

4. Select the file and choose Open. The image file will now be embedded into the file's metadata.

If you accidentally add the wrong image file or simply want to discard cover art from a file (or files), perform the following:

1. Right-click (Control-click) on any track (or group of tracks) from within Traktor's Browser List.

2. Choose Delete Cover.

Caution: If you maintain your music library through iTunes, remember that Traktor's iTunes node is read-only—music must be imported into the Traktor collection before you can make tag edits.

On the other side, tag edits made within the Traktor collection will not be recognized properly within iTunes without a few extra steps. Said simply: If you use iTunes, in order to avoid headaches, only edit your tag metadata inside the iTunes application before importing it into the Traktor collection.

If you do not see your iTunes editing reflected within Traktor, get into the habit of running a manual consistency check: Right-click on Track Collection and choose Check Consistency. (You can automate this process from Preferences > File Management > Show Consistency Check Report On Startup.)

Crate Digging (Searching)

No matter how well you organize your Traktor collection, there are situations when browsing isn't fast enough. Say hello to Traktor's "intelligent" incremental search functions.

To begin a search:

1. Click in the Search field or press Command+F (OS X) or Ctrl+F (Windows).

2. Type in a few characters of an artist, track, label, and so on. As you can see, I have done this in Figure 6.15.

Figure 6.15 Use Traktor's Search function to quickly find your music. Yay, I can spell my name!

3. Each letter you type will narrow search results based on the text entered.

4. Pressing Tab will return Traktor to hot-key control for the currently selected playlist, allowing you to browse through the search results.

Additional Search field controls include:

- Pressing Enter will extend the Search field text to cover the entire track collection.

- Pressing Esc will cancel text entry.

- The Search field text will remain in place and effective until cleared. In other words, if you search "Britney Spears" in Playlist A and switch from Playlist A to B, once you navigate back to Playlist A, your search results for good ol' Britney will remain in place until you cancel the search by pressing Esc or clicking on the X directly to the right of the text.

Note: Hot-key assignments do not work when using the Search field.

To refine your search:

1. Click on the small magnifying glass on the left-hand side of the Search field.

2. Choose one of the search criteria from the drop-down list. All subsequent text entry will apply only to the chosen criteria.

Other search functions:

- Click on the miniature magnifying glass on the right-hand side of particular criteria within Traktor's Browser List—for example, within the Artist or Label field. For example, if you click on the magnifying glass directly alongside Artist, the artist name will appear within the Browser Tree Search field, and the entire collection will be searched for that artist. Note that the search will be restricted to the column criteria (or file-tag data) that are searched—that is, if you search for Artist, the Artist filter will be applied within the Browser Tree's Search field drop-down, as explained previously.

- Right-click (Control-click) on any track within Traktor's Browser List and choose Show in Playlists. This search function brings up a dialog box describing the various playlist locations of the chosen track. Double-clicking one of the results opens that particular playlist within the Browser List.

- Right-click (Control-click) on any track within Traktor's Browser List and choose Show in Finder/Explorer. This search function opens the OS X Finder/Windows Explorer and displays the file location on your hard drive.

Collection Maintenance

If you twitch when thinking about manually maintaining thousands of tracks, note that Traktor provides upkeep features specifically designed to keep you on the level. Therein lies Traktor's exhaustive status report, known as the consistency check.

1. Right-click (Control-click) on Track Collection within Traktor's Browser Tree, as I have done in Figure 6.16.

2. Choose Check Consistency.

The consistency check primarily resolves three things, shown clearly in Figure 6.17.

Relocating Missing Tracks

1. Click the Relocate button at the bottom of the Consistency Check window.

2. Point the OS X Finder or Windows Explorer dialog to the location of the missing tracks and choose Open.

3. If many tracks are missing, or you do not remember where the files are stored, simply choose higher up the folder tree—for example, selecting your entire hard drive scans its entirety. This may take time, but if the track exists, Traktor will find it.

Figure 6.16 Use Check Consistency as the first step in troubleshooting your music library.

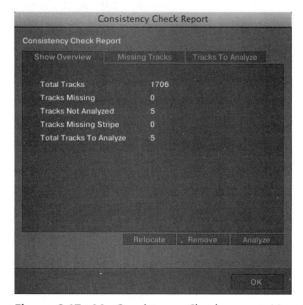

Figure 6.17 My Consistency Check report. Yep, I failed....

Note: Cancelling the Relocate process does not damage the track collection.

Removing Missing Tracks

Click the Remove button at the bottom of the Consistency Check window. All tracks reported as missing will be removed from the Traktor collection.

Analyzing Tracks

Click the Analyze button at the bottom of the Consistency Check window. All unanalyzed tracks will be put through Traktor's analyzation process. With a large number of tracks, this can take quite a long time. However, analyzation is a background process and does not interrupt your DJing.

Analysis

With respect to all of the collection maintenance functions on offer, the analysis process is unquestionably the most indispensable to Traktor's overall performance. During a scan, specific track data is analyzed in order to gather the following information.

- **Bpm estimate.** Determines a track's recorded tempo and creates the Beatmarker/Beatgrid. If you want this done automatically (you do), ensure that Set Beat-Grid When Detecting BPM is checked from Preferences > File Management > BPM Detection Range.

- **Gain Value.** Measures properties of a track's perceived loudness to automatically adjust a Deck's Gain knob output to 0 dBFS (full scale). To ensure Autogain is set automatically, check Preferences > Mixer > Level > Set Autogain When Loading Track.

- **Stripe.** Creates the visual overview of an entire track directly underneath a Deck's Waveform display. If you cannot see the stripe, reanalyze the track.

Automating Collection Management

If your collection has a regular inflow/outflow of tracks, you might want to automate at least one part of your collection management. Open Traktor's Preferences and click on the File Management tab. Figure 6.18 shows the File Management heading within which you will notice the following options.

Figure 6.18 Check any of these options to automate portions of your collection management.

- **Import Music Folders at Startup.** Imports any new track additions from the directories listed under Music Folders within the Data Location section of the Preferences.

- **Determine Track-Time Automatically (Before Analysis).** Traktor determines track length before a track has been analyzed.

- **Analyze New Tracks on Collection Load/Import.** When the track collection is loaded, Traktor analyzes any or all newly added tracks in the background.

- **Analyze New Tracks When Loading into Deck.** New tracks dropped onto any Deck are analyzed in the background. A useful feature when dragging tracks directly into Traktor from the OS X Finder or Windows Explorer.

- **Show Consistency Check Report on Startup.** Traktor launches directly into the consistency check process as described earlier.

Creating, Customizing, and Saving Your Traktor Profile

The more time spent with Traktor, the more obvious personal workflow patterns become. Even though Traktor employs a handful of fundamentally static industry-standard design choices, most features can be configured to complement any DJ's personal touch. All GUI layout, effect, collection, controller, and audio device settings are unique to your Traktor profile. Cue points, loop points, Beatgrids, artist and release info, and so on are all embedded in audio file metadata. With a button click, you can import your personalized Traktor fingerprint onto another computer—or, more importantly, you can revive it should fate ever decide that it's time to euthanize your laptop.

Layout Appearance

Although the overall theme and positioning of Traktor's GUI cannot be drastically changed, you can show/hide specific sections of the layout and generally optimize them to fit different performance styles. For example, many scratch DJs prefer a less cluttered workspace, so they strip back Traktor's GUI to the barest minimum, as shown in Figure 6.19.

Figure 6.19 Minimize your options if you want to reduce screen clutter.

On the other hand, performers utilizing Traktor's breadth of features often need immediate reference points to control effects, loops, and so on. Figure 6.20 shows Traktor with all of the major features readily visible. Given a laptop screen's relative "real estate" limitations, you may notice that using an expanded view swallows the Browser. Try clicking the Maximize Browser button (see Figure 6.21) and see what happens. Like most features in Traktor, this, too, is hotkey or MIDI-assignable. (Refer to the control tutorial examples further on.)

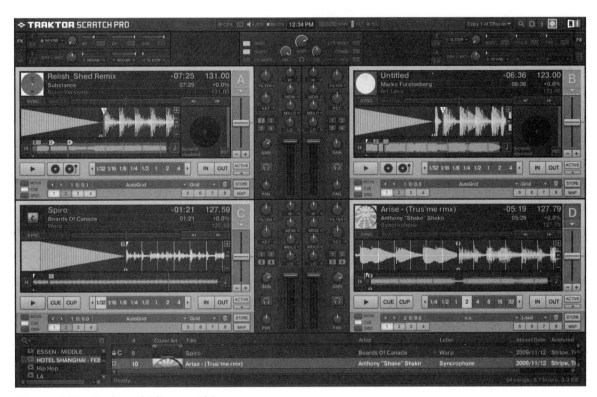

Figure 6.20 Traktor hiding nothing.

Figure 6.21 Click to fully expand the Traktor Browser.

Bear in mind that these are only two of several layout customization possibilities. You can create layout arrangements sitting somewhere between these two examples for specific situations—instantaneously choose from the Layout Selector drop-down menu, map to hotkeys, or map them to your external control device.

To optimize Traktor's appearance, open the Preferences and click on the Layout Manager tab. You should see the screen displayed in Figure 6.22. For the most part, the descriptions are relatively straightforward. Nonetheless, let's try customizing one now.

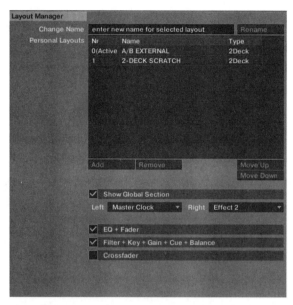

Figure 6.22 Define your customized Traktor layouts from here.

1. Click Add and choose, for example, TPro Ext. Mixer – 4Deck. You'll notice a new profile has been added within the personal layouts. Click on it.

2. Double-click within the Change Name dialog box, enter a name for your personal layout, and click the Rename button to the right. Note that the number of the listing will reflect the order in which your personal layout will appear when cycling through your customized views. Click the Move Up/Down buttons to adjust the arrangement of your layouts.

3. For this example, ensure that all of the check boxes are checked and decide whether you want the global section to display the FX, the Master Clock, or the Audio Recorder.

Tip: If your layout has a visible Global section, consider duplicating it within the Preferences and configuring two global states—one showing FX and one showing the Master Clock and Audio Recorder.

---

4. Click on the Deck Details tab. Check and uncheck the various options a few times and note how they affect the GUI. Choose Full under Deck Size A & B and Deck Size C & D to view the expanded Decks. Check the Adv. Controls check box for both pairs of Decks and ensure that Cue is chosen from the dropdown boxes directly below the Adv. Controls, very simply labeled A, B and C, D. Finally, if you are using the Traktor's control vinyl/CDs, check the relevant Scratch Panels options.

5. Check the box labeled Show Cover Art under Deck Heading. Along with track data, Traktor's Decks will now show the currently loaded track's cover art.

6. You can configure the Traktor Deck Heading to show up to nine different types of information related to the currently loaded track's metadata. Load a track after organizing a few categories to view how collection data is displayed.

7. Check both options from under the Pitch Controls heading to view the Phase meter and the Pitch fader.

8. Finally, click on the Browser Details tab and briefly note the various options. Ensure that all are checked.

Now that your Traktor interface is fully loaded, take a few minutes to go back through the previous steps. The previous configuration is one that I use; understandably, you'll probably have your own process in mind. Repeat Steps 1 and 2 a few times so that you have a handful of varied layouts and then go through Steps 2 through 8 again and alter the configuration for different performance scenarios.

The .TSI File

Traktor's .TSI file is an abbreviation for Traktor Settings Information; it's a file that saves all of the composite details pertaining to your personalized Traktor settings. You can import and export these personalized settings as needed, as you can see in Figures 6.23 and 6.24.

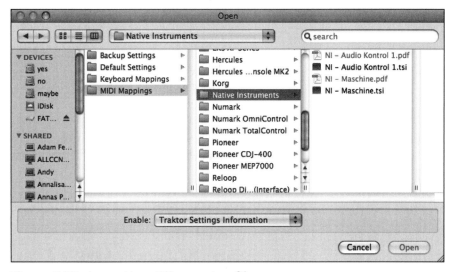

Figure 6.23 Importing .TSI mapping files.

Import/Export Settings

■ Keyboard mappings

■ Controller mappings

Figure 6.24 And exporting .TSI mapping files.

- GUI layout

- File load and write paths

- Favorites

- Broadcasting

- Audio device settings

- MIDI Clock settings

- Effect settings

- Other Preferences and settings

The Traktor Root Folder

As you invest more time into your Traktor collection, make habitual backups of your Traktor root folder—the consolidated folder of information that provides a database for your Traktor fingerprint.

- The entire Traktor profile: collection data and backups, settings, MIDI mappings, and hot keys.

- A personalized, portable Traktor workspace that can be duplicated onto another computer. This can be incredibly valuable when you're DJing with a partner, as both stage setups will then be identical.

- Separate Traktor collections on the same computer. For example, when I train my clients on Traktor, I have a separate, dedicated Traktor collection specifically designed for training purposes.

You can find Traktor's root folder here:

■ OS X: Macintosh HD > Users > (username) > Documents > Native Instruments > Traktor

■ PC: (My) Documents > Native Instruments > Traktor

Tip: Copy the Traktor folder somewhere safe. You'll be happy you did on the off chance that your hard drive blows up.

To reassign the Traktor root folder:

1. Open the Traktor Preferences and click on the Data Location tab.

2. Click on the ...! button on the right-hand side of Root Dir.

3. Point the OS X Finder or Windows Explorer to the new location of the Traktor root folder.

4. To go back to the original location, click Default Dir.

Maintaining Multiple Collections

As an example, let's say that you want to maintain Traktor's collection between two computers: your studio machine, where you do all your collection management (cues, loops, playlists, and so on), and your laptop, with which you perform. To successfully accomplish this, you will need an external hard drive to house all of your data.

Studio computer:

1. Connect the external hard drive to your studio computer.

2. Copy your music library to the external hard drive. For example, if you keep all of your tracks under a folder called Music, drag and drop this file into a logical location on the connected hard drive.

3. Copy the Traktor root folder to the external hard drive. (Unless otherwise specified, it will be under User > Documents > Native Instruments > Traktor.)

4. Launch Traktor and open the Preferences.

5. Select the Data Location tab and click Add.

6. Point the OS X Finder or Windows Explorer to the location of the folder containing your music and select Choose.

Laptop:

1. Connect the external hard drive to your laptop.

2. Launch Traktor and open the Preferences.

3. Select the Data Location tab and click on the ...! button on the right-hand side of the Root Dir, as shown in Figure 6.25.

Figure 6.25 Redefining Traktor's root folder.

4. Point the OS X Finder or Windows Explorer to the Traktor root folder on the external hard drive and select Choose. You should be prompted to restart Traktor.

5. Run a consistency check to verify that Traktor has located your Traktor collection properly.

In the end, the aim of this chapter was to reveal Traktor's organizational capabilities—a process so well executed that it sets the bar for how a digital DJ crate should function. Equipped with this chapter's fundamental information, we can now move on to the enjoyable stuff: performance.

7 Traktor Pro: Loading, Playing, Mixing, and Syncing

At this point, you should have an understanding of Traktor's foundations: setup configuration, the GUI, layouts, playlists, preparation, collection maintenance, and so on. It's fairly easy to see how the DJ culture's proliferation influenced Traktor's appearance and workflow patterns. As soon as you load and start mixing some tracks, you will see just how digital software lets DJs expand beyond hardware limitations.

Hopefully, you've been breaking up the reading with a bit of your own Traktor noodling. If not, it's that time....

Intro to Loading Tracks

Traktor provides several straightforward methods to load music into the four Decks. Select a track within the Browser List using your mouse or the up/down keys on your computer keyboard and then perform one of the following:

- Click and drag a track from the Browser List to Deck A, B, C, or D.

- Press Ctrl+< or > on the computer keyboard to load the track into Deck A or B, respectively.

- Right-click (Control-click) on any track within the Browser List and choose Load Track into Deck A, B, C, or D.

Tip: You can easily assign Deck Load to any external MIDI control device under Preferences > Controller Manager. For more information, check the Controller Manager section further along.

When navigating from the Browser to the Decks and back becomes second nature, you may want to look into some of Traktor's Deck Loading configurations. The various playback and loading functions, as shown in Figure 7.1, are adjusted within the Preferences to augment as well as streamline your workflow. Open Preferences > Loading > Loading.

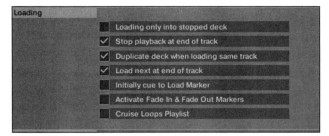

Figure 7.1 Check/uncheck these options to customize Traktor's Deck Loading behavior.

Loading controls:

- **Loading Only into Stopped Deck.** Check the check box if you want a safeguard against accidentally replacing the currently playing track mid-playback (only slightly embarrassing!). If you are using the control vinyl/CDs, this feature can be a little bit irritating, because you have to stop the turntable/CDJ every time you want to load a new track. This is not the best option if you prefer to pre-listen to your tracks on the fly from the control vinyl/CDs.

- **Stop Playing at End of Track.** Track ends. Playback ends.

- **Duplicate Deck When Loading Same Track.** Check the check box if you want the Deck Duplicate function to load the duplicate track from precisely the same position as within the currently playing Deck. Leave it unchecked if you want a duplicate track to load from the beginning or to a load cue point.

- **Load Next at End of Track.** The next track in the playlist is loaded when the currently playing track ends.

Intro to Playing and Mixing Tracks Internally

These intro sections are deliberately constructed to get you DJing with Traktor as quickly as possible, as well as to demonstrate Traktor's instinctive internal mixing workflow. While running through each of the steps, use Figure 7.2 as a quick reference for the controls mentioned. Amidst the following walkthrough, test out a few of the different EQ models found at Preferences > Mixer > EQ Selection > EQ Type, as well as the two filter types located at Preferences > Mixer > EQ Selection > Filter Selection.

If you plan on mixing Traktor's output from an external DJ mixer, it may still be a good idea to familiarize yourself with these facilities should you find yourself in a situation where a mixer isn't available, such as on an airplane.

1.   Load a track into Deck A, lower the Channel fader, and press the Play button.

2.   Click around on the stripe and the Waveform display to get a feel for how the mouse affects each section.

3.   Click Deck A's Cue button to pre-listen to the track.

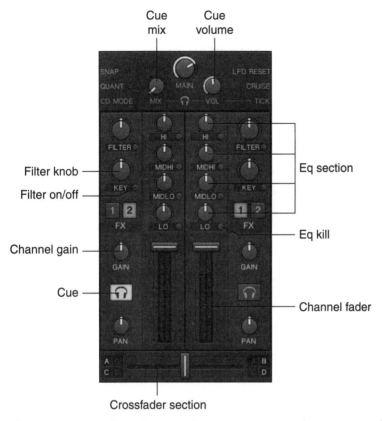

Figure 7.2   Use the Mixer section to test out Traktor's powerful internal mixing features.

4. Adjust the headphone mix/headphone volume from the Master panel.

5. Adjust the Mixer section's Gain knob and notice how it affects the prefader VU meter.

6. Raise Deck A's Channel fader to send signal to the master.

7. Adjust the EQ knobs and test the EQ kills.

8. Turn on the filters and sweep through the low-pass and high-pass ranges.

9. Load a track into Deck B, lower the Channel fader, and press the Play button.

10. Click on Deck B's Cue button to pre-listen to the track.

11. Adjust the Gain knob so that the VU meter matches Deck A.

12. Raise Deck B's Channel fader to send signal to the master and blend the signals.

13. Adjust the EQ knobs and drag the Crossfader back and forth.

14. Experiment with the other Deck and Mixer features while listening to what does what.

Note: If you have Traktor hooked up to an external mixer, all pre-listening should be done through the hardware mixer's cue functions.

Depending on your mixing style, you might run into a performance situation in which you want to start each individual mix from scratch. In Figure 7.3 you can see the Deck Reset controls found here: Preferences > Loading > Resetting Controls.

Figure 7.3 Defining Deck Reset functions.

- **Reset All Deck Controls When Loading a Track.** Loading a track reverts Deck controls to their default state.

- **Reset All Mixer Controls When Loading a Track.** Loading a track reverts Mixer controls to their default state.

Intro to Syncing Tracks

Traktor's Sync function exemplifies one of Traktor's most hotly disputed features. Basically, Sync automates the traditional beatmatching process to allow artists to focus their attention on other aspects of their performance. Think about it: Gather all the minutes spent beatmatching, and what are you left with? Time...

Digital DJs see this extra time gained as creative potential. Like it or hate it, the Sync function embodies a progressive concept through which digital DJing is developing and diversifying.

Acting as Traktor's heart, the Master Clock panel (see Figure 7.4) exhibits top-level control over the Sync function. Subdivided into two parts, the actual sync behavior is either controlled by the Deck Master or by the Clock Master, each of which determines specific playback conditions.

Figure 7.4 Use this panel to establish Traktor's Deck Sync behavior.

Deck Master Manual

- The Master Clock tempo is determined by a manually chosen source—that is, by clicking the Master button at the top of the desired Deck.

■ The Master Clock tempo displays that of the Master Deck.

Caution: If you stop the current Master Deck, ensure that you reassign a new master. If you were to change the tempo of the stopped Master Deck and then press Play, all of the Intermediate Synced Decks would jump up/down in tempo, following the Master tempo.

Deck Master Auto

■ The Master Clock tempo, and therefore status, is automatically assigned to the track with the longest uninterrupted playtime.

■ Once the current Master Deck is stopped, another master is immediately assigned via the same criteria.

■ All synced tracks follow the Master Deck's Pitch fader.

■ The Master Clock tempo displays that of the Master Deck.

Caution: Quick pitch-fader movements within the Master Deck cause all other Decks to lose their sync status. Use gradual movements.

Clock Master Internal

■ Traktor's internal Master Clock creates a stable Master tempo source—the go-to setting when DJing with a four-Deck setup without the control vinyl/CDs. Entirely hand over beatmatching responsibility to Traktor's Master Clock.

■ All Deck Sync functions follow the tempo settings assigned within the Master Clock tempo field.

■ Used when sending MIDI Clock to external sources—for example, drum machines, another computer running Traktor, Ableton Live, and so on.

■ All Deck Master buttons are all grayed out.

Master Clock Parameters	
Master Clock Bend	Momentary pitch-bend function. Temporarily bumps the tempo up/down.
Master Clock Tempo	Click the (+) or (−) to adjust the overall Master Clock tempo up/down.
Tap	Manually tap in (or adjust) the desired Master Clock tempo.

Clock Master External

- Traktor receives master tempo from an external source—for example, drum machines, another computer running Traktor, Ableton Live, and so on.

- All tempo changes must be enacted from the master tempo (external) source.

- All Deck Sync functions follow the incoming MIDI timing information.

Confused? The single best way to understand these settings is to test each of them out. Although there are subtle differences between each mode, they each serve a specific purpose. To help you understand Traktor's powerful Sync function, let's do a quick run-through of internal syncing.

1. Check Int within the Master Clock area of the Global section.

2. Load and play tracks into both Deck A and Deck B. Note the cyclical shifting of the Phase meter's yellow bar on the Slave (non-Master) Deck.

3. Click and hold the Pitch Bend buttons on either Deck and notice how the Phase meter adjusts accordingly. Alternatively, click and drag the Phase meter's yellow bar to bring the phase back in sync.

4. Press the Sync button on both Decks (yellow = active). Each Phase meter's yellow bar should hold steady in the center. Figures 7.5 through 7.7 show the Phase meter in various states.

5. Notice that the Deck playback never drops out of time. Try slowly adjusting the Master Clock tempo by clicking the (+) and (−) buttons and notice how the synced Decks follow accordingly. Additionally, double-click on the Tempo field and try entering a new bpm.

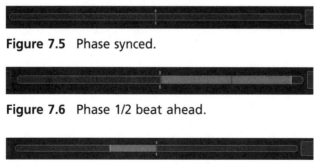

Figure 7.5 Phase synced.

Figure 7.6 Phase 1/2 beat ahead.

Figure 7.7 Phase 1/4 beat behind.

As you can see, Traktor's Sync feature allows DJs to reconsider the significance of beatmatching within their performances. If you head down this route, be aware of the visual status feedback signals presented by the state of the Sync button.

Sync State	Status	Icon
Off	The Sync function is not engaged. If Sync will not engage, it is most likely because a Beatgrid is missing from one of the loaded tracks or the Deck is set to Scratch mode.	SYNC
On	The Sync function is engaged, and the Deck is following the master tempo source.	SYNC
Verify	This "intermediate" Sync state is informing that: • The synced Deck is currently selected as the Master Deck. • The Master Deck has not started playback. • A loop shorter than one beat is active; the Deck cannot sync or act as master. • The bpm differential between the two tracks is larger than the current pitch range allows. Adjust the settings in Preferences > Transport > Pitch.	SYNC

Intro to Playing and Mixing Tracks with Timecode Vinyl/CDs

For DJs who prefer the hands-on precision of vinyl or CD mixing, Traktor's DVS technology exhibits the best features of the analog/digital pedigree. To ensure that the control vinyl is playing nicely with the connected hardware, NI has devised Traktor's Calibration process to help narrow down potential conflicts. In short, Calibration analyzes the clarity of the timecode signal to determine whether you are using the timecode vinyl or CD, as well as verifying the presence of the left and right audio channels.

Turntables in particular are often host to any number of unpredictable complications. For one, most nightclubs do not take good care of their equipment. You should always carry your own needles/cartridges, because a snag with either can lead to missing channels, leaving Traktor unhappy. Moreover, other possible annoyances reveal themselves through bent tonearms, damaged RCA cables, faulty grounding leads, and so on.

Don't let this scare you off the control vinyl route. It is simply something Traktor users should be aware of. Thankfully, Calibration provides DJs with useful feedback to help troubleshoot unexpected situations; missing channels, dusty needles, skipping control vinyl/CD, incorrect input modes, and improper tonearm weighting are but a few examples. Much of this information can be gleaned from the Scope or Vinyl view, shown in Figures 7.8 and 7.9. To begin Traktor's Calibration process:

Figure 7.8 Scope view displays timecode clarity as well as potential complications. Click the RST button to begin the Calibration process.

Figure 7.9 Vinyl view. Also known as Sticker view. The current timecode position is displayed.

1. Choose the appropriate Input mode (Timecode Vinyl or Timecode CD/Line) on the front of the Audio 8 DJ interface or, as you can see in Figure 7.10, from the drop-down menu under Preferences > Timecode Setup > Timecode Input Mode.

Figure 7.10 Choose the Audio 8 DJ's Input mode from here.

2. Ensure that the Traktor Scratch hardware is set up via the instructions listed earlier in this chapter. If you do not see the Scratch panels within the Traktor Decks, enable the Scratch Panels check box from Preferences > Deck Details > Deck Style > Scratch Panels.

3. Click directly on the Scratch panel so that the Scope view is showing.

4. Ensure that the Deck mode is set to Scratch Control on Decks A and B.

5. Click the RST (Calibrate) button upon each Deck's Scratch panel to start the Calibration process. They should say Waiting.

6. Choose a Tracking mode for each deck.
    ■ **Absolute mode.** Timecode vinyl/CD provides "needle drop" performance—in other words, the track within Traktor's Deck will cue precisely to the playback position of the turntable needle or CD seek function on the timecode vinyl/CD.

- **Relative mode.** Timecode vinyl/CD provides control pitch only—in other words, Traktor's timecode vinyl/CDs will not control playback position.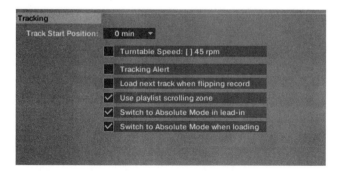

7. Play the timecode vinyl/CDs. Switch between Absolute and Relative modes to get a feeling for how they differ.

Caution: If you are using CDJs, make absolutely sure that any master tempo functions are turned off within the CDJ's settings. Traktor's control vinyl/CDs are frequency dependent, and thus any "coloring" of the 2-kHz carrier signal will cause tempo problems with Traktor's playback.

When Should I Calibrate?

Obviously, calibration isn't necessary if you are not using the timecode vinyl/CDs; however, when using Traktor Scratch's external control media, ensure that you calibrate the Decks in each of the following circumstances:

- Every time you launch Traktor or change the hardware configuration.

- Every time you change Traktor's Input mode.

- Every time you switch between "real" vinyl/CDs and the control vinyl/CDs.

Tip: If you are scratching with Traktor's Key Lock function engaged, open Preferences > Transport > Key Lock and enable Scratch mode and HiQ to get the best results.

Additional Timecode Configurations

When using Traktor's control vinyl/CDs, familiarize yourself with some of the mediums' extra behaviors (see Figure 7.11). For example, the Absolute Mode settings give you one less button to assign/press every time Traktor switches to Relative mode. (If you use looping, which you will, this will be a lot.) Scrolling a playlist with the record/

Figure 7.11 Double-check the additional timecode behaviors.

CD is quite useful—nearly as much as getting warned that dust is distorting the time-code signal fidelity (think: warehouse party!).

- **Track Start Position.** Move the positioning of a track's lead-in farther along in the record's Playback section.

- **Turntable Speed.** Check the check box if you like the feel of spinning at 45 RPM.

- **Tracking Alert.** Red flashing will prompt you that the clarity of the timecode signal is bad. Generally caused by dust or a dropped channel.

- **Load Next Track When Flipping Record.** Flipping the timecode vinyl loads the next track in collection/playlist.

- **Use Playlist Scrolling Zone.** Allows manual collection/playlist browsing with the end segment of the timecode vinyl and Track 3 of the timecode CD. Stopping the vinyl/CD loads the highlighted track into the Focus Deck.

- **Switch to Absolute Mode in Lead-In.** Needle-dropping on the intro sections of the vinyl/CD will automatically set the Deck to Absolute mode.

- **Switch to Absolute Mode When Loading.** Loading any track automatically switches the relevant Deck to Absolute mode.

Note: Traktor's Sync feature will not function while using the Traktor's control vinyl. Think of it this way: Using Scratch Control (external control) means that you are syncing your Decks manually—in other words, beatmatching via manual pitch-fader adjustments on your turntables/CDJs.

Mouse Control

Although using a mouse/keyboard combination doesn't really fall in line with the theme of this book, they are entirely necessary during preparation or traveling or while playing around on the couch.

There are three fundamental methods of manipulating Traktor with a computer mouse.

- Click and hold any fader/knob. Drag the mouse vertically for coarse adjustments and horizontally for precise adjustments. Double-click any fader/knob to revert to its default.

- Hover over any fader/knob and use the mouse wheel.

- Hover over a fader/knob and click the plus/minus buttons. Hold down the Plus/Minus buttons to adjust in succession.

Track Control

Even if a computer mouse is not the ideal Traktor controller, it is wholly indispensable during preparation of the Traktor collection; for example, setting and editing cue points, positioning loops, mapping out hot cues, and especially while configuring Beatgrids—all of which will be explained in depth shortly.

Navigate to Preferences > Transport > Mouse Control.

- **Vinyl mode.** Using the mouse pointer on the waveform emulates fingers on a vinyl record.
    - Click and hold upon the waveform, and the Deck grinds to a halt. Release, and playback revs up again.
    - Click and drag the waveform to imitate scratching.
    - Click and "throw" to emulate a vinyl backspin!

- **Snap mode.** Using the mouse pointer on the waveform emulates cue point behavior.
    - Click upon the waveform, and the Deck will jump to the relevant beat and stop playback.
    - Click and hold upon the waveform in a stopped Deck. Playback behaves like the Cue button—that is, the track plays until the mouse button is released.
    - Right-click upon the waveform in a stopped Deck. Playback behaves like the Cup button—that is, the track begins playback from the point that is clicked.

Note: Don't confuse the mouse control Snap mode with the Master panel Snap mode. The latter applies only to cue point and loop behavior. When it is engaged, setting cue/loop points snaps to the closest beat on the Beatgrid.

Mouse Sensitivity

Right-click (Control-click) on any fader/knob +/− buttons to access a drop-down menu of parameter adjustment options. The self-explanatory choices (see Figure 7.12) of Min, Fine, Default, Coarse, and Switch dictate how the +/− buttons will respond to mouse clicks.

Figure 7.12 Choose an option to define how the mouse behaves with the + and − parameter controls.

Advanced Mouse Control

Although a mouse cannot replicate the control depth of an external device, the "ghost pointer" is one particularly useful feature. For example, with the ghost pointer you can quickly cut or boost an EQ frequency at the click of a button. In effect, this process yields results much more quickly than manually clicking and dragging a parameter each time you wish to make changes. To use the ghost pointer, refer to the following:

Two-button mouse:

1. Right-click and hold any fader/knob. You should see a gray ghost pointer, shown faintly in Figure 7.13, if you move the mouse.

Figure 7.13 The ghost pointer shows up slightly faint.

2. Manipulate the ghost pointer—for example, drag an EQ or FX knob counterclockwise.

3. While holding the right mouse button, left-click a few times and notice the behavior of the knob's state.

4. Still holding the right mouse button, left-click and hold and then release the right mouse button to keep the ghost pointer's position.

One-button mouse or trackpad:

1. Control-click and hold any fader/knob. You should see a gray ghost pointer if you move the mouse.

2. While holding, manipulate the ghost pointer—for example, drag an EQ or FX knob counterclockwise.

3. Release the Control button and click away at new ghost pointer positions. The parameter should jump between two values.

4. Drag the ghost pointer to the desired location, hold Control, and release the mouse button.

Preparation and Performance

One particularly difficult challenge faced by music software developers is how to ride the fine line spanning beginner allure and professional performance. How does a manufacturer embrace the "easy button" without damaging an application's credibility as a pro product? The answer is simple: within intelligent software design that adapts to the user's artistic process, not vice versa.

Something that Native Instruments nailed on the head is that its DJ products appeal to any skill level. On one hand, a DJ application needs to meet plug-and-play expectations for DJs who just want to mix two records together. On the other hand, veteran performers should find that advanced customization options are both immediate and intuitive. After all, powerful results manifest through logical processes.

Beatgrids, Cue Points, and Loops

If the Master Clock symbolizes Traktor's heart, the Beatgrid is the nervous system. Functionally, a grid marker is a type of cue point, but it's also much more than that. Grid markers and their Beatgrids direct Traktor's internal playback and Sync functions: looping, Deck sync, Beatjumps, Traktor's tempo-based FX, and so on.

Working with Beatgrids

In most cases, Traktor's automated tempo estimation sets Beatgrids relatively well, especially when working with music that has steady, machine-generated tempo—for example, virtually all 4/4 electronic dance music. As a word of advice: Get in the habit of double-checking your Beatgrids whenever you import/analyze new music into the collection. Although the process may seem complicated at first, Beatgridding a track will only take a matter of seconds once you get the hang of it.

Adjusting Beatgrids

1. Set Traktor's mouse control to Snap. This will adjust mouse behavior so that movements directly "snap" to the Beatgrid markers within the Waveform display. Adjust mouse control from Preferences > Transport > Mouse Control > Snap.

2. Select the Grid panel from within the Advanced panels.

3. Load any analyzed track from Traktor's Browser List into Deck A. Again, you should be able to visually verify that a track has been analyzed if the waveform appears within the Deck's Stripe display. If the waveform doesn't appear, analyze the track from the Browser List.

4. Click on the Tick button from the Master panel.

5. Click on the Cue button from Deck A's Mixer section.

6. Click on the (+) button from the Waveform display to zoom in on the track.

7. Press Play on Deck A. You should now hear the beat tick overlaying the track. The beat tick pulses every time a grid marker passes the current playback position. If the beat tick is too faint in comparison to the track volume, slightly lower the track gain to balance the difference.

    In addition, you can visually verify the Beatgrid's placement over a track's downbeats; just remember to trust your ears.

8. If the Beatgrid matches the track tempo, they should be playing perfectly in sync.

9. Move farther ahead in the track by clicking within the Stripe display. Do this in a few different locations. If the beat tick still matches the track tempo, you're finished. If not, proceed to the next step.

10. Click on the Jump to Track Start button (see Figure 7.14) and find the first grid marker. By default, the first grid marker gets assigned to Hotcue 1.

Figure 7.14 Jump to Track Start button.

11. Verify that the grid marker sits on the first downbeat (most often a kickdrum, as shown in Figure 7.15). If it does not, there are three primary ways to adjust the location.

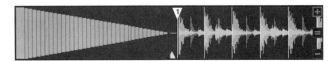

Figure 7.15 A grid marker situated directly on the first downbeat.

- Click the Move Grid Fwd/Bwd buttons to slide the grid marker (and the whole Beatgrid) along the track's waveform. A left-click will slide the grid marker in fine increments. A right-click (Control-click) will slide the grid marker in coarse increments. Hold the mouse button for continuous movement.

- Click on the Delete Gridmarker button shown in Figure 7.16. Use the mouse to find the initial attack of track's first downbeat. Click the Set Gridmarker button, shown in Figure 7.17, to set the initial grid marker and establish the Beatgrid.

Figure 7.16 Delete Gridmarker button.

Figure 7.17 Set Gridmarker button.

- Click the Reset Gridmarker or Auto Grid button (see Figure 7.18). Note that this may not work properly if Traktor's automatic grid marker was not correctly set to begin with.

Figure 7.18 Auto and Reset buttons.

12. Press Play on Deck A and verify the Beatgrid by clicking through the Stripe display.

13. If the track continues to drift away from the beat tick and/or the estimated track bpm readout is not an integer, you need to make adjustments to the BPM Inc/Dec—that is, the compression/expansion of the entire Beatgrid.

14. Click the BPM Inc/Dec buttons to compress/expand the Beatgrid, thus changing the tempo of the entire Beatgrid. A left-click adjusts the bpm in fine increments. A right-click (Control-click) adjusts the bpm in coarse increments. Hold down the mouse button for continuous adjustment.

15. Finally, verify the Beatgrid one last time by clicking through the Stripe display. If the beat tick and the track play back in sync, click the Lock button from the Grid panel so that no accidental changes are made.

Figure 7.19 An example of a perfect Beatgrid.

Figure 7.20 An example of an incorrect Beatgrid.

This process should quickly become second nature, at which point you will fly through dozens of tracks in a matter of minutes. As a suggestion, don't solely rely on the beat tick to match up the grid markers. Load a track that you are sure has a 100-percent accurate Beatgrid (a reference track, if you will) into a "reference" Deck, sync it to the

Master Clock tempo, and use the reference track in combination with the Tick function to fine-tune Beatgrid positioning. Once again, trust your ears!

Note: Check the "Mixing in Sync: Phrases, Beats, and Bars" section later in this chapter for further information on how to optimize your mixing through Traktor's visual Phrase/Bar/Beat display.

Working with Cue Points

If you are unfamiliar with the concept of cue points, think of them as bookmarks positioned within your tracks. Traktor offers a few different types of these bookmarks as place markers, each with its own distinct purpose. Nearly all cue-point functions are handled through either the Deck Transport section or the Cue Panel subsection of a Deck's Advanced panels. Essentially, cue-point status breaks down into two main categories: temporary or saved.

In Figure 7.21, the blue upward-facing arrow found within the Waveform and Stripe display represents Traktor's temporary cue point (*current cue point* in the manual): an on-the-fly cue position controlled from each Deck's transport controls. Labeled Cue, Cup, and In/Out, each control is intended for instant auditioning, playback positioning, prepping saved cue-point positions, and so on.

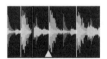

Figure 7.21 Traktor's temporary (current) cue point.

Saved cue points, on the other hand, offer a virtually unlimited number of bookmarks at your disposal. You can save numerous track positions—intros, breakdowns, vocal sections, and so on. Once you determine a handful of cue points, up to eight are mapped to MIDI-assignable hot cues.

For example, you could map eight different hot cues to a MIDI MPC-styled groovebox (think: NI's Maschine), with each hot cue marking, for example, a capellas, drum hits, notes, and so on. Effectively, you are transforming Traktor's Decks into an improvised phrase sampler. Moreover, DJs with a bit of production experience can create, edit, or design short "tracks" containing specifically selected sounds (think: alarm sirens, vocal cuts, random FX, and so on).

The different types of temporary cue points found within Traktor are:

Button	Stopped Deck	Playing Deck
CUE	Clicking sets a temporary cue point and auditions the current playback position. Clicking and holding engages playback until release. Releasing jumps back to temporary cue position.	Clicking jumps the playback position to the temporary cue position and stops Deck playback.
CUP	Clicking engages playback and sets a temporary cue point from that location. Clicking and holding sets a temporary cue point and begins playback upon release.	Clicking jumps the playback position to the temporary cue position without stopping playback.
IN	Sets a temporary cue-in point at the current playback position.	Sets a temporary cue-in point at the current playback position.
OUT	Sets a second, temporary cue-out point at the current playback position and engages manual looping.	Sets a second, temporary cue-out point at the current playback position and engages manual looping.

Note: The functions of loop in and loop out points are covered within the Loops section further along in this chapter.

The different types of "storable" cue points found within Traktor are:

Cue Point Variety	Description	Marker
Cue	Used to mark a specific reference point within a track—for example, a breakdown, vocals, the bass drop, and so on.	
Fade-In/ Out	Used to automate the Cue/Play functions between two Decks (think: bathroom break).	
Load	Immediately loads a track to a specified start point. Load cue points are incredibly useful to cut out extended intros.	

Cue Point Variety	Description	Marker
Grid	The first grid marker—also the first hot cue. Use it to jump to the beginning of a track.	
Loop	Stored loop in/out points for a stored, predefined loop.	

Storing Cue Points

1. Click on the Cue panel from within the Advanced panels.

2. Load an analyzed track into Deck A.

3. Find the desired location and press the In button from the transport controls.

4. You should see the temporary cue point jump to your current playback position.

5. Click the Store button, shown in Figure 7.22. If any hot-cue slots are empty, the cue point will automatically assign to the next available location.

Figure 7.22 Store button.

6. If desired, double-click within the Cue Name section shown in Figure 7.23 and type a description for the cue point.

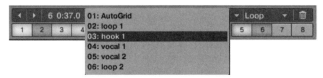

Figure 7.23 Use this drop-down menu to name cue points or select cues not assigned to one of the hot-cue buttons.

7. To change cue point types, click the Cue Type drop-down menu, shown in Figure 7.24, and select an option.

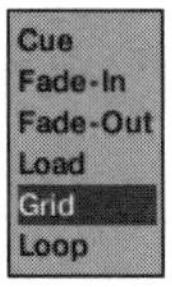

Figure 7.24 Choose a cue point type from the drop-down list.

Setting Hot Cues

1. Ensure that Snap is engaged from within the Master panel to ensure that the hot cue snaps to the Beatgrid.

2. Ensure that Snap is engaged from Preferences > Transport > Mouse Control to ensure that mouse clicks within the Waveform display instantly snap the cue position to the Beatgrid.

3. Click any empty (gray) hot-cue button, shown in Figure 7.25, from 2 through 8. (The 1 button is generally reserved for the initial grid marker.)

Figure 7.25 Click any unassigned hot-cue slot to store a new cue point or loop.

4. Change the cue type as needed.

Tip: If you like the loop or autoloop currently playing, click any empty hot cue to store the current loop for future use.

Remapping Hot Cues As you work with hot cue–mapped cue points, loops, and so on, you might run into situations where you want to replace existing hot cues with new ones or simply rearrange those that are already assigned.

1. Within the Deck's Advanced panel, select the relevant cue point via the Previous/Next Cue Point arrow, the drop-down Cue Name List, or the pertinent hot-cue button.

2. Click the Map button in Figure 7.26, located on the right-hand side of the Cue Advanced panel.

Figure 7.26 Use the Map button to organize your hot cues.

3. Click the new hot-cue button. Alternatively, mapping to an occupied hot cue will overwrite it.

Using Load Cue Points Load cues offer DJs a powerful tool over their track-loading behavior. Taking influence from hip-hop's needle dropping, load cues instruct tracks to load into a Deck cued up at a virtual "sticker" that marks the perfect point to drop in a track. Moreover, load cues are particularly useful in cutting out extended intros or other unusable sections. If you are using the timecode vinyl/CDs, try mixing in Relative mode after setting load cues across a handful of songs. The speed at which you can bang through tracks is mind-blowing.

1. Check the Initially Cue to Load Markers box from within Preferences > Loading.

2. Follow the steps for storing cue points.

3. Click on the drop-down Cue Type list and choose Load to reassign the cue point's behavior.

Using Fade-In/Out Cue Points In situations where some automated DJing is needed, fade-in/out cue points activate Traktor's self-mixing functions whereby two parallel Decks—A/B or C/D—automatically mix in and out of one another. Position fade cue points anywhere within a track, and they tell Traktor's internal engine when to start mixing in and when to start mixing out.

1. Ensure that the Fade-In/Out check box is checked from Preferences > Loading > Activate Fade-In & Fade-Out Markers.

2. Load a track into Deck A.

3. Navigate to a point near the end of the track and press the Cue button from the transport controls.

4. Click the Store button.

5. Click the Cue Type drop-down menu and choose Fade-Out.

6. Load a track into Deck B.

7. Navigate to a point near the beginning of the track and press the Cue button from the transport controls.

8. Click the Store button.

9. Click the Cue Type drop-down menu and choose Fade-In.

10. Click the Sync button on the Slave Deck (or on both Decks if the Clock Master is set to Internal).

11. Press Play on Deck A so that the song starts playing somewhere before the fade-out cue point. When Deck A's playback position passes the fade-out marker, Deck B will start synced playback.

Using Cruise Mode While fade-in/out cue points instruct Traktor where to automate track mixing, Cruise mode goes one step further. Enabling Cruise mode automates the playback of an entire playlist—for example, once a track is mixed out on Deck A and the Volume fader hits the 0 mark, the next track is automatically loaded from the currently selected playlist, and automixing continues. If all tracks have properly configured Beatgrids, enabling Sync on both Decks will ensure that Traktor not only mixes the playlist automatically, but also mixes the relevant tracks in sync.

1. Determine the Auto Crossfade Time setting and, as shown in Figure 7.27, whether you want the transition smooth or sharp, located within Preferences > Mixer. A higher value equals a slower/smoother transition.

Figure 7.27 Adjust these sliders to determine the auto crossfade behavior.

2. Select the desired playlist. When every track within the playlist has been played, if you want playback to automatically jump back to the beginning, check Cruise Loops Playlist from Preferences > Loading.

3. Load an analyzed track into Deck A.

4. Click Play on Deck A and raise the Volume fader (otherwise Cruise mode cannot be engaged).

5. Click the Cruise button from the Master panel. Once engaged, as in Figure 7.28, the next track within the playlist will be loaded into the parallel Deck—for example, Deck B.

Figure 7.28 Cruise button engaged.

Deleting Cue Points

1. Within a Deck's Advanced panel, select the relevant cue point via the Previous/Next Cue Point arrow, the drop-down Cue Name List, or the pertinent hot-cue button.

2. Click the Delete Cue button, represented by the trashcan icon.

Working with Loops

Repetition in music predates the modern understandings of loop-based production by several generations. With foundations ranging from sonic experimentation to religious ritual, cultures from around the world claim a vast history of musical traditions conceived around repetitive rhythmic structures. Properly employed, these looped rhythms, textures, chants, and so on can have pleasantly hypnotic effects on listeners. (Speaking of hypnotic looping, as I write this section I am listening to Jeff Mills' 2005 *Contact Special* album—a must-have for techno fans.)

Traktor's Loop section explicitly encourages this type of creative experimentation. Beatgrids ensure the seamless quantization of spontaneous on-the-fly looping. Spread this across four Decks, and DJs can blend snippets of tracks together to form entirely new cut-and-paste compositions.

There are a few different ways to initiate Traktor's looping functions. Loops can be instantaneously dropped at specific beat lengths, or they can be set outside this quantized framework to achieve unexpected results. The following examples illustrate a few different approaches.

Setting Auto Loops

1. Navigate to the desired loop location.

2. Find the desired loop length (in beats) within the Auto Loop Control menu displayed in Figure 7.29. Be aware that screen resolution determines the extent of the listed loop lengths. Click the bordering left/right arrows to reveal hidden loop lengths ranging between 1/32 to 32 beats.

Figure 7.29 Select any number to set the length (in beats) of your autoloop.

3. Click the loop length within the Auto Loop Control menu. The Loop Control value and the Active button (shown in Figure 7.30) will both highlight, signifying an activated loop. Green loop start/end markers within the Waveform and Stripe displays represent the loop length.

Figure 7.30 Active button.

4. Click Store to save the autoloop to the next free hot-cue slot.

5. Click on Cue Name if you want to name the stored loop.

Setting Manual Loops

1. Navigate to the desired loop-in location and click the In button from the transport controls.

2. Navigate to the desired loop-out location and click the Out button from the transport controls.

3. Click Store to save the manual loop as the next free hot cue.

4. Click on Cue Name if you want to name the stored loop.

Automatically Changing Loop Lengths

1. Click on any Auto Loop value to engage the Loop function.

2. While Auto Loop is engaged, click on any other value to instantly shift the loop length.

Manually Changing Loop Lengths

1. Initiate the playback of either an auto or a manual loop.

2. Select the Move Advanced panel.

3. Click the Move Mode drop-down list (see Figure 7.31) and choose either Loop In or Loop Out. The names are fairly straightforward. Loop In moves the loop start point; Loop Out moves the loop end point.

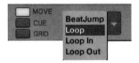

Figure 7.31 Choose Traktor's Cue/Loop Move behavior from this drop-down menu.

4. Select a value from the Move Size control (nearly identical to the Auto Loop directly above) by which to resize the loop-in/out points. Fine and xFine adjust loop points by small and ultra-small amounts, respectively.

5. Use the Cue Move BWD/FWD arrows to resize the loop-in/out points (see Figure 7.32).

Figure 7.32 Cue Move BWD/FWD arrows.

Moving the Entire Loop

1. Initiate the playback of either an auto or a manual loop.

2. Select the Move Advanced panel.

3. Click the Move Mode drop-down list and choose Loop.

4. Select a value from the Move Size control (nearly identical to the Auto Loop directly above) based on how far you want to move the entire loop. Fine and xFine adjust the loop location by small and ultra-small amounts, respectively.

5. Use the Cue Move BWD/FWD arrows to move the entire loop in either direction. With the Loop button selected from the right-hand side of the Move panel, the entire loop is moved by the value of the currently active loop.

Deactivating Loops

- Click on the currently highlighted (yellow) autoloop to deactivate looping.

- Click on the currently highlighted (yellow) Active button to deactivate looping.

Beatjumping

If you drop a track too late or too early, you need to jump elsewhere inside a track, you want to fabricate beatbox-styled stutter effects, or anything in between, Beatjumping lets you "jump" the current playback position 100-percent quantized to the Master Clock tempo.

1. Select the Move Advanced panel.

2. Click the Move Mode drop-down list and choose Beatjump.

3. Select a value from the Move Size control (nearly identical to the Auto Loop directly above) based on how far you want to jump within the track. Fine and xFine adjust loop location by small and ultra-small amounts, respectively.

4. Use the Cue Move BWD/FWD arrows to jump the current playback position backward/forward by the selected amount.

Intro to Effects (FX)

To me, the most fascinating characteristic of studio effects is their ability to create entirely new textures from existent sounds. A liberal application of effects can swell an atonal hi-hat into an oscillating bed of icy noise; transplant a vocalist into impossibly cavernous spaces; distort lifeless drum loops into angular, rhythmic pulses—even a simple filter sweep can surge a wave of anticipation across a packed dance floor.

With Traktor's effects, NI managed to find a happy medium between the studio and the stage. Studio-inspired effect units retain their "tweakability," while form-factor optimization supports performance immediacy.

You can patch 28 effects across two or four effects banks via direct insert. Alternatively, use a DJ mixer's FX send channels to send the outside world directly into Traktor's FX panels—for example, mics, vinyl, synths, guitars, drum machine, and so on. At some point you will probably hear the conservative studio adage "A little bit goes a long way." Well, a lot goes a long way, too.

Configuring the FX Panels

If you don't have any practical experience with effects of any kind, the best way to understand what effects do to a sound is through experimentation. Apply some effects to a track that you know well—this way, you will instantly hear how the original sound is getting altered. However, before we move on to making weird noises, it is helpful to understand the options offered by Traktor's FX panels.

1. Open Preferences > Effects. Your options will appear as shown in Figure 7.33.

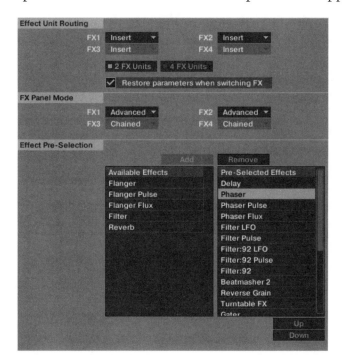

Figure 7.33 Use this dialog to customize your FX settings.

2. Under Effect Unit Routing, choose Insert or Send FX and either two or four effects units.

3. Whether you check Restore Parameters When Switching FX largely depends on your controller type. For example, if you are using a traditional MIDI fader/knob (sends values 0 to 127), the values it sends are absolutely positioned—thus, when you switch effects, the Snapshot parameters will probably be different than the positioning of your MIDI fader/knob. In this situation, moving a hardware knob will cause the software parameter to jump to the hardware position, sounding drastically out of place. In this case, leave the box unchecked. Don't worry if this is confusing; quickly test it out, and you should hear the difference.

4. Under FX Panel Mode, select either Advanced or Chained Mode.

5. Under Effect Pre-Selection, separate the list of preselected effects (visible within the FX Panel drop-down menus) from the list of available effects (removed from the FX Panel drop-down menus). Double-click names within the relevant list or highlight a selection and choose Add/Remove to define what effects you will or won't use.

6. Use the Up/Down buttons to establish a sort order for the FX Panel drop-down menus.

Advanced FX Mode

As mentioned previously, Advanced FX mode provides precise control over multiple parameters of one selected effect (see Figure 7.34 and Figure 7.35). For performance efficiency, all Advanced FX mode effects share the Dry/Wet knob and Rst (Reset) parameters—in other words, if you map the controls to an external device, the behavior is the same for all of the available effects.

Figure 7.34 Advanced mode (one effect unit per FX panel).

Figure 7.35 Advanced mode (two effect units per FX panel).

Chained Mode

Within Chained FX mode, each FX panel (see Figure 7.36 and Figure 7.37) allows up to three effect types while offering a single depth knob controlling a blend of designated parameters. While Advanced FX mode offers precise control, Chained FX mode encourages creative experimentation through a serially processed effects chain.

Figure 7.36 Chained mode (one effect unit per FX panel).

Figure 7.37 Chained mode (two effect units per FX panel).

Insert versus Send Effects

The primary difference between insert and send effects is fairly straightforward.

■ **Insert effect.** Clicking the 1-4 FX On buttons redirects a Deck's signal through the relevant FX panel. The percentage of the signal that passes through untouched is controlled by the dry (no effect)/wet (effect) signal. The result is then mixed with the output of the other Decks and passed through to the master output.

- **Send effect.** The Send option transforms Traktor into a hardware FX unit—in other words, rather than only internally blending signals, audio is received into Traktor from an external mixer's send channel. For example, Traktor is able to receive audio from an external source—vocalists, drum machines, Traktor's own output, and so on.

Configuring Send Effects

Due to the nature of the signal routing, Traktor can only utilize send effects while set to External Mixing mode—in other words, the computer must be connected to a multi-channel audio card that is in turn connected to the send/return sources of an external hardware mixer.

1. Open Preferences > Output Routing.

2. Set the Mixing mode to External.

3. Set the output send shown in Figure 7.38 to the output channel that will route the dry/wet (effect) signal from Traktor back to the FX return of the hardware mixer.

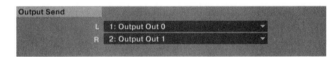

Figure 7.38 Use this drop-down menu to set your send FX outputs.

4. Switch to Preferences > Input Routing.

5. Set the input send to the input channel that will receive the signal from the hardware mixer's FX send. The input you see in Figure 7.39 is immediately sent to Traktor's FX panel.

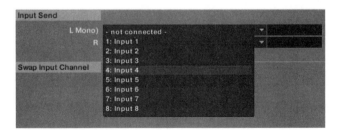

Figure 7.39 Use this drop-down menu to set your send FX inputs.

6. Switch to Preferences > Effects.

7. Change the relevant effect unit routing to Send.

8. Try sending Traktor some signal from the hardware mixer's FX send and experiment with the effects. If you cannot hear anything, verify the FX send/return hardware settings upon the mixer itself.

Using Traktor's Effects

Earlier, I mentioned something about testing effects on a track you are familiar with. Load that track into Deck A and step through the following:

1. Click on the FX tab within the upper-left or upper-right corner of the Global section to show the relevant FX panel.

2. Choose any effect from the Effect Select drop-down menu.

3. Click the FX Unit On button.

4. Click the corresponding FX insert button from the Mixer section to insert the effect into the signal flow and then begin tweaking the various parameters.

5. Apply Steps 1 through 4 in any combination across all four FX units. Note that all four FX units can be applied to one Deck, all Decks, or any configuration in between.

6. Additionally, go back to the Effects Preferences and test out the drastic differences between the Advanced and Chained modes.

Note: Keep the differences between FX inserts and FX On/Off states in mind while you are performing. If you are using effects with decay tails—for example, delays or reverbs—deactivating the FX insert from the Mixer section will completely cut off any remnant effect. Obviously, you can use this to creative effect; however, if you want to let the effect tails fade out naturally, use the FX On/Off button instead.

Saving FX Presets

As you narrow down a selection of effects to use on a regular basis, saving a default state (snapshot) for each effect will help to optimize your performance. For example, one useful default state keeps each effect unit turned on, sets each parameter to a value that sounds good out of the gate, and keeps the wet/dry balance to 0 percent. This way, each time you switch effect types (or click the RST button), the effect will bounce back to its default with a 0-percent wet/dry balance—all you have to do is adjust the wet/dry mix (the effect's on/off button is already defaulted to on), and the effect will begin from an instantly usable point. Further, a snapshot with a 0-percent wet/dry mix will erase the chance of jumping from, for example, a reverb (which will get cut off) to a distortion (which may sound awful if unintended).

1. Choose an effect type from the FX Select drop-down menu.

2. Engage the effect from any Deck so that you can hear the effected signal (FX 1 On, and so on).

3. Tweak the effect parameters until you hear a sound that works.

4. Turn the Dry/Wet parameter to 0, but leave the effect turned On.

5. Click the small Camera icon, shown in Figure 7.40, to save the current effect state as a default snapshot.

Figure 7.40 Save the current effect state as a default snapshot.

Traktor (Pro)ficiency

The DJ market tends to shy away from the word *complexity*—perhaps understandably so. Thankfully, a great thing about Traktor is that it's an application that lets DJs jump in anywhere along the learning curve. Yes, there is a logical "button-mashing" process that every Traktor user goes through. But, it's definitely a great way to learn: Button-press = noise, "Whooaaaa!" Knob-twist = weirder noise, "Ooohhh!"

Whenever I host training sessions at my studio, I truly enjoy the moment when my client takes over and applies his or her personal style onto the application that I'm teaching. That's the point when the entire process morphs from memorizing button functions into shaping a customized workflow.

Understanding Quantization

If you are new to DJing and/or music production, you may be unfamiliar with the concept of quantization. For the purposes of defining quantization in relation to this chapter, note that most music production software bends tracks, loops, and so on around predefined temporal fractions. For example, in 4/4 electronic dance music such as techno or house, this is often exemplified by the "four-to-the-floor" structure consistent with four kick drums per bar—each kick signifying one beat.

Within music production software, quantization is often (though not always) applied to the recording input of MIDI note information. For example, strike a key on a MIDI keyboard, and quantization acts to "magnetically" snap MIDI notes to the nearest marker within a predefined grid—the higher the grid resolution, the higher the recording accuracy. Basically, the idea is to clean up imprecise timing from the live playback of keyboards, percussion, and so on.

With regard to Traktor, quantization refers to playback synchronicity in reference to Traktor's beat-based Beatgrid. In practice, this is particularly useful when moving through cue points or hot cues, working with loops, or simply jumping around within a track. Timing is kept entirely synchronized through each jump, even with the Deck Sync function turned off.

One thing to be aware of before jumping around within a track is that you should consider what the crowd is hearing. Unintentionally moving from an audibly complex section to an intro drum loop can sound pretty terrible. To engage the Quantize function, simply click on Quant within the Global section's Master panel.

Mixing in Sync: Phrases, Beats, and Bars

When you are playing songs that follow a "traditional" song structure, certain sections of tracks tend to mix together more smoothly than others. Taking an example from electronic dance music again, some type of audible shift usually occurs every 4, 8, 16, or 32 bars. Subtle, emotive, or obnoxious—whatever form it takes is usually fairly obvious within a track's progression.

Simply stated, a musical phrase can be seen as a unit of music exhibiting some form of definitive structural completeness. Commonly, phrases can be distinguished from one another by varying intensity—for example, the addition, subtraction, or shifting of percussion, vocals, bassline, crash cymbals, snare rolls, and so on. In combination, these phrases contribute to the commonly understood "pop music" song structure of intro, verse, chorus, verse, chorus, bridge, verse, outro—or some combination of the like.

Now, the importance of mixing within these boundaries is entirely subjective, but within some styles of DJing it makes perfect sense to match phrases. But remember, as much as mixing within these borders fits, it can also just as easily be tossed out the window for creative effect.

As an example, load a track into Deck A and duplicate it (or a remix of it) within Deck B. Play both tracks with a one beat offset in between. Now try that with all four Decks playing the same track a beat apart. Yet one more example of Traktor refreshing old vinyl-DJ staples…

To mix within this framework, there are a couple of considerations that will help everything run smoothly.

- Navigate to Preferences > Deck Details > Deck Heading and choose Beats somewhere within one of the rows. Notice that the beats appear within the Deck display in the format of x.x.x (Phrase.Bar.Beat). As you can see in Figures 7.41 and 7.42, the Beats option I have chosen in the bottom-right of the Deck Details Preferences are reflected in the Traktor GUI Deck Details.

Figure 7.41 Configure your Deck Details here.

Figure 7.42 View your Deck Details here.

- Navigate to Preferences > Transport > Beat Counter (see Figure 7.43) and adjust the Bars per Phrase slider as desired. As an example, 16 bars per phrase will count up from 1.1.1 to 1.16.4 before progressing to 2.1.1.

Figure 7.43 Adjust the slider to configure how many bars per phrase are shown in the Deck Details.

- Ensure that you establish your grid marker on the first downbeat of the track. Doing so will guarantee a proper readout within the Deck Display, allowing you to drop tracks at the right moment. If the grid marker is set properly, cueing to the track's first downbeat should show 1.1.1 within the Deck Display.

Mixing in Key

Simply stated, the DJ technique of harmonic mixing is finding a creative blend between two or more tracks that have a relationship of the same key, a relative key, sharing harmonic space within the Circle of Fifths, and so on. Music itself is composed of organized sounds falling somewhere within the frequency range of human hearing, generally between 20 Hz and 20 kHz. Where does Traktor fall into this equation?

Traktor provides DJs with tools to blend and manipulate musical frequencies into new and interesting, cohesive compositions.

Tip: If harmonic mixing piques your interest, I highly suggest checking out the application Mixed In Key. In short, the software scans audio files for both bpm and key information to aid DJs in their quest against key clashes. You can find more information here: www.mixedinkey.com.

Key Lock Key correction is Traktor's cornerstone of harmonic mixing. In short, key correction uses a powerful time-stretching algorithm to protect the original musical properties of your tracks despite changes in bpm. For example, if you struggle with the clichéd "Mickey Mouse" effect when pitching music up too far, Key Lock is your friend.

Engage Key Lock in one of two ways: Either click on the quarter note on the right-hand side of the Deck's Stripe display, as shown in Figure 7.44, or click on the tiny Key knob on/off button directly below the Filter, as shown in Figure 7.45. Further, navigate to Preferences > Transport > Key Lock and adjust the self-explanatory settings based upon your hardware setup.

Figure 7.44   Click on the quarter-note button.

Figure 7.45   Click on the on/off button below the Key knob.

Obviously, you can use Key Lock if you want to maintain the music's originally recorded sound. However, be aware that you can also apply key correction to situations in which you want to adjust a track to fit with other music you are playing. Each integer adjustment up or down changes the track's key by one semitone.

EQ

Using the imagery of Traktor as a toolbox, the kit's metaphorical wrenches can be found in the frequency bands of Traktor's EQ section. Think of EQ as the DJ's means of delicately plying or forcefully wrenching an audio file's frequency range into submission. Generating anticipation by briefly cutting the bass is one example of a DJ staple used for years on end. Simultaneously cutting the bass from Track A and slamming in the bass of Track B is another. Manipulating mids and highs causes tracks to smoothly glide together, and in situations where two tracks have an uneven balance of loudness levels, EQ is there to fix the problems on the fly. Essentially, DJ EQs provide performance-optimized controls to balance and mix the frequencies of two or more tracks.

Traktor provides DJs with four different EQ models: Allen & Heath's Xone:92, Pioneer's DJM-600, Ecler's Nuo 4, and the Traktor-born Classic EQ. Choose one of the EQ types from the drop-down list shown in Figure 7.46 from Preferences > Mixer > EQ Selection.

Figure 7.46 Use this drop-down to select your preferred EQ model.

Note: If you cannot see the Traktor EQs, navigate to Preferences > Layout Manager and check the check box labeled EQ + Fader. This will expose Traktor's Mixer section within your currently selected layout.

Almost in contradiction with the potent expression it enables, EQ is an extremely straightforward function to use. Each knob exhibits volume control over a particular range of frequencies, also known as *bands*. Manipulating the EQ knob clockwise or counterclockwise will respectively boost or cut any audio signal falling within its designated frequency range.

All of Traktor's EQ models are three-band parametric EQs, except for the Xone model, which (if you are familiar with the Xone:92) offers slightly more precise control with its four-band EQ section. Finally, pay particular attention to the little buttons on the right-hand side of each knob. Clicking any of these buttons completely cuts that frequency range out of the audio stream. This is particularly useful when assigned to MIDI controllers with a shortage of knobs or an abundance of buttons.

Filters

Whereas EQs generally cater to precise tweaking through boosting and cutting specific frequency ranges, filters are designed for somewhat more drastic manipulation, such as removing a wide range of frequencies. Under Preferences > Mixer > Filter Selection, you will find two of Traktor's Filter options: Xone and Ladder. Again, the Xone filter is modeled after the filter built into the Xone:92 DJ mixer. On the other hand, the Ladder filter is based on an old-school (ahem) filter model influenced by a particular style of electronic audio circuitry, such as those found within the famed Robert Moog filters.

Most filters are characterized by two controls: cutoff and resonance. Filter cutoff is relatively self-explanatory; it is the point within a frequency range at which a sound is attenuated. On the other hand, filter resonance is commonly understood as a parameter used to boost the volume of a narrow band of frequencies at and immediately around the cutoff frequency. This sound is clearly heard in the wet squelching and squealing of Roland's TB-303 synthesizer, acid house, acid techno, acid trance (see a theme?), and so on.

Strangely, NI decided to leave resonance controls off of Traktor's filters, instead opting for a fixed resonance setting and a single, bipolar Cutoff Frequency knob. Click the small button shown in Figure 7.47 to turn on the filter. From the neutral, center position (off), twist the filter clockwise for the high-pass/low-cut filter. Conversely, twist the

Figure 7.47   To use the Filter On/Off, click the tiny button immediately to the right of the Filter text.

filter counterclockwise for the low-pass/high-cut filter. Alternate between the two filter models—you can hear how specifically resonance affects a cutoff frequency more clearly with the Ladder filter.

Additional Deck Settings

Given the extent of Traktor's features, visual status feedback becomes increasingly more important as DJ sets progress. Figure 7.48 displays useful Deck behaviors, such as track-end warnings, minute markers, and the transient view of the Channels options, combined together to orient DJs to current playback conditions. Check Preferences > Global View Options > Decks.

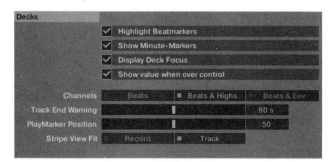

Figure 7.48   You can configure additional Deck behaviors from this dialog.

At this point, you should have a fairly solid grasp on how Traktor functions within the performance context. NI spent a load of time contemplating how to optimize a digital DJ environment to suit the needs of all types of performers—something that becomes quite evident from the moment you start fiddling around with Traktor's GUI. In the next chapter, we'll take a look at how to match Traktor's performance features to your specific hardware control needs.

8 Traktor Pro: The Controller Manager

I hope that by now you have a strong grasp on how all of Traktor's constituent parts play together. Building on this foundation, you should be able to quickly coax sounds out of Traktor that are simply unattainable within the confines of a traditional DJ performance. We began this process with a mouse and a keyboard, but as I have mentioned, these devices are often counterintuitive to an artist's creative process—not to mention that they have stigmatized digital DJs for years.

Fortunately (or unfortunately, depending on how you look at it), there is a silly number of DJ-specified MIDI controllers on the market; choosing which way to go is often a difficult decision. Product marketing, word of mouth, Internet forums, salesmen, and so on all present biased opinions. But at the end of the day, the perfect controller is a matter of personal preference—there are just as many reasons to control Traktor with a MIDI keyboard as there are to control it with a MIDI mixer. Do your research and bear in mind that Traktor should be configured to *your* specifications. Envision how you would like to control each section and the features that comprise it, and factor those mental mappings into your purchasing decision.

So, in the spirit of examining the bigger picture, let's drive the car instead of playing with the engine.

Intro to Controller Assignments

Most popular DJ-focused MIDI controllers have a .TSI mapping file either included within the Traktor installation support files or provided directly through the hardware manufacturers themselves. For the least amount of fuss, use Traktor's Setup Wizard to automatically load controller templates.

Alternatively, click on Preferences > Import to bring up a dialog box pointing to the preinstalled .TSI files of various manufacturers. Again, these files are fine as a starting point; however, you will probably want to make changes as you hone your workflow. Once you get the hang of it, Traktor's Controller Manager (see Figure 8.1) makes this process relatively painless.

Try to think of Traktor's mapping files as "pages" for each controller. Once you try mapping out a customized control scheme, be aware that Traktor offers more than 200

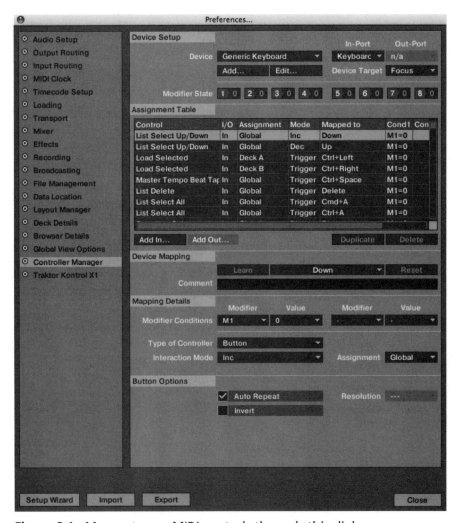

Figure 8.1 Map out your MIDI controls through this dialog.

controller parameters. Some of these you will use constantly; others you may never touch. One useful thing about creating multiple control mappings for a single controller is that you could, for example, create one for preparation: setting and storing hot cues, cue points, and loops or adjusting your Beatgrids. Of course, you would then want to create one specifically for performance: transport controls, effects, autolooping, and so on.

Assigning Controls

Possibly one of Traktor's most challenging qualities is the somewhat open-ended nature of the Controller Manager. Although it presents the advantages of countless control possibilities, it is all too easy to get lost in the midst of configuring the Holy Grail of layouts. For me, the most effective way of learning these types of applications is to systematically work through little milestones. Start with something small, consider what you want to accomplish, and then break it down into its components.

For example, you will probably use your MIDI controller to operate Traktor's Play function. Determine what controls are relevant and construct your controller mapping from the ground up. It often helps to sketch an outline of some form, especially once your controller mappings become more complex.

First things first, ensure that your MIDI controller is connected to your computer before proceeding.

Creating a New Control Device

The first thing we need to do is define a new control device within Traktor's Controller Manager.

1. Navigate to Preferences > Controller Manager.

2. Under Device Setup click on Add and choose Generic MIDI. This will create a new, empty controller .TSI mapping.

3. Click on In-Port and choose the name of your controller from the drop-down menu. As you can see in Figure 8.2, I have chosen my Maschine controller for this example. If you are using a standardized MIDI device that only offers a five-pin DIN MIDI connection (no USB/FireWire—like the previous generation of Faderfox MIDI controllers), you will need to choose the In-Port of your MIDI interface—for example, the Audio 8 DJ MIDI input.

Figure 8.2 All connected MIDI-capable gear should show up within the In-Ports menu.

4. Leave the Out-Port and Device Target as they are for now.

Note: Device Target is a useful assignment if you are using two or more controllers. For example, one controller could be assigned to Deck A's functions while the other is assigned to Deck B's, and so on.

Assigning Traktor Controls to MIDI

After you have created your MIDI controller within Traktor's Controller Manager, use these instructions as a generalized guideline for assigning Traktor controls to your MIDI hardware.

Note: Bear in mind that Traktor's Interaction modes are entirely dependent on the type of hardware control and the specific Traktor command you are assigning. For example, if you are binding a software command to a key on your computer keyboard (a button), Interaction mode will display a drop-down menu containing options such as Hold, Direct, Inc/Dec, and Reset. The naming is fairly logical, and therefore each type behaves much as you might expect.

- Hold actions only engage while the relevant key is held. This would make sense for a Traktor command, such as an EQ kill.

- Toggle actions act as switches, turning commands on and off, such as starting and stopping the Play/Pause function.

- Trigger actions are for one-off events that have no reference duration—for example, setting a cue point or starting an autoloop.

- Direct actions control a specific action from a specific hardware button— for example, using a button to select a precise FX type—or from a specific hardware fader to control Traktor's volume fader or pitch.

- Inc/Dec incrementally steps through next/previous functions, respectively.

- Reset jumps a parameter back to its default value.

- Output is a unique type of output parameter that is used to control the on/ off LED states on certain compatible MIDI controllers.

1. Under Assignment Table click Add In (see Figure 8.3).

Figure 8.3 The Add In button.

2. Choose Transport > Play/Pause. As you can see in Figure 8.4, Traktor Control Play/Pause should appear within the Assignment Table.

3. Under Device Mapping click the Learn button shown in Figure 8.5. The button will highlight, signifying that Traktor is "listening" for incoming MIDI input.

4. Press any button on your MIDI controller. A MIDI message of some form should appear directly to the right of the Learn button. Disable the Learn command.

5. Under Mapping Details, click on the Interaction Mode drop-down menu and choose Toggle, as shown in Figure 8.6. Toggle regulates the "switch" behavior of the Play/Pause button, such that the first button press engages Play and the second engages Pause.

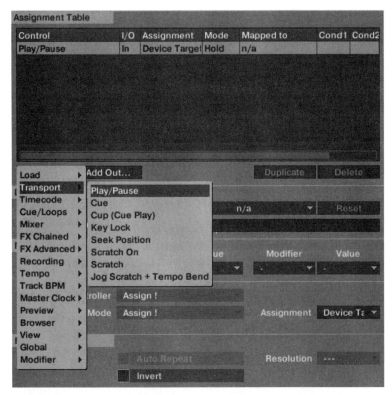

Figure 8.4 Use this drop-down menu to find all of Traktor's available MIDI commands.

Figure 8.5 Once Learn is enabled, tap/click/twist/hit any MIDI controller parameter to bind the assignment.

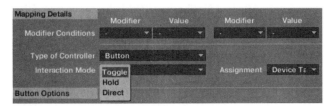

Figure 8.6 Use this drop-down menu to configure how you want to interact with the Traktor MIDI command.

6.   Under Assignment choose Deck A, as I have done in Figure 8.7. Assignment does one of two things: Either it filters incoming commands directly to a specific Deck (or Focus Deck) or it delegates overall control to the assigned Device Target under Device Setup.

At this point, simply load a track into Deck A and press the newly assigned MIDI control button to start playback; press it again to pause. Simple, right?

Figure 8.7 Select which Traktor Deck you want the MIDI assignment to affect.

Tip: Keep in mind that you don't have to stick every single parameter onto your MIDI controllers. Your computer keyboard is just as useful for button-specific commands. In fact, Native Instruments constructed a default Key Mapping layout—the behaviors of which are clearly laid out within a one-page PDF document. You can find the document within the Traktor root folder under Settings > Keyboard Mappings > (choose either Perform or Preparation).

Don't worry if the Controller Manager feels slightly overwhelming and cumbersome. If I have one complaint about Traktor, it is that the Controller Manager's window is too small to clearly display all of the necessary information. Nonetheless, once you gain a bit of familiarity, your workflow with MIDI controller mapping will grow to be quick and effective.

Unfortunately, defining Traktor's 200 or so available parameter assignments and interaction subsets goes beyond the scope of this book. I highly suggest that you refer to the last section of the Traktor manual for detailed information on all available parameters and how their behaviors can benefit your performance.

However, there is one particularly potent section of Traktor's Controller Manager that I feel needs highlighting: modifiers.

Modifiers

Throughout the process of personalizing Traktor's MIDI configuration, you may have noticed how easy it is to run out of unassigned MIDI controller knobs, buttons, faders, and so on. Even mapping Traktor's controls across the most comprehensive MIDI devices requires a fair amount of planning, preparation, and everyone's favorite: patience! As you sequentially map out Volume faders, FX panels, EQs, loops, cues, and so on, at some point you will probably run out of unassigned hardware controls. So, what then?

Meet Traktor's modifiers...

For basic comparative terms, think of a modifier as the Shift, Ctrl (OS X: Command), or Alt (OS X: Option) keys on your computer's keyboard. Also known as keyboard *shortcuts*, Traktor's modifiers are somewhat like the standard Save, Copy, Edit, and Print hotkeys used by most word processing applications.

In essence, a modifier activates an alternate task when used in combination with any key/button/fader/knob. When you run out of unassigned hardware controls, defining a modifier will, for example, allow you to use one knob to control Traktor's EQ, filter, and FX parameters.

Traktor provides DJs with eight modifiers per mapping—each of which is unique to the mapping in question. In other words, they do not cross over to other mappings, and they can be used afresh within each new mapping you create—for example, if you use two or more MIDI controllers. Each of the eight modifiers has eight assignable values (0 to 7). The bar labeled Modifier State within the Controller Manager is specifically designed to help you troubleshoot which modifier is assigned to where and at what value. For example, if you press a button on your MIDI controller that is currently assigned as a modifier, one of the modifiers (1 to 8) will flash the value assigned to it (0 to 7).

Confused?

Out of context, Traktor's modifiers and their relationship to MIDI hardware can be somewhat complex. The point of this section is to get you experimenting with modifiers. Don't forget, you always have the option to start over. For this example, let's start from a clean slate with the Faderfox DX2 controller displayed in Figure 8.8.

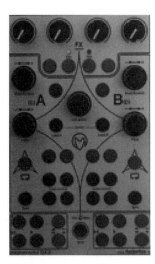

Figure 8.8 Faderfox's DX2 MIDI controller.

Note: As I was wrapping up the writing stage for *Part 1* of this two-book project, Faderfox released the third generation of their wonderful compact MIDI controllers. I have not had a chance to play with the new series yet, but based on my past experience with the second generation, I can recommend the devices without out even touching them. If you have used any Faderfox controllers in the past, the most drastic difference is that they now operate via USB 2.0—no more MIDI-only from Faderfox! Check them out at www.faderfox.de.

At the top of the DX2 there is a bank of four knobs and four buttons. Perhaps unsurprisingly, this section is labeled FX Control. Considering that each of Traktor's FX panels combines four effect parameters with four effect buttons, it seems logical to tie the two together. The immediate problem is that the DX2 FX Control section only provides enough control for one Traktor FX panel.

Upon the DX2, the four central, gray unassigned/unlabeled buttons shown in Figure 8.9 are a logical location to assign four independent modifiers.

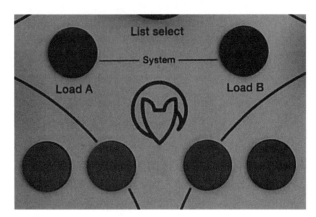

Figure 8.9 Our four modifier buttons.

Unless you are also using a DX2, disregard the values within the Mapped To sections that follow, as they will differ from your MIDI controller. I have simply included them as a reference point to show two things: the first to show how a standard MIDI assignment would appear, and the second to display macros, or multiple Traktor commands mapped to the same MIDI fader/knob/button. I encourage you to adjust and apply the following steps to your own control surface.

Here is but one way you could use modifiers to transform the DX2's top-left FX Control knob from one Advanced FX Wet/Dry Knob to four.

1. Open Preferences > Controller Manager.

2. Under Assignment Table, choose Add In > Modifier > Modifier #1.

3. Repeat Step 2 and add Modifier #2, #3, and #4.

4. Highlight Modifier #1 and click Learn.

5. Press DX2 button 1 to bind (learn) the assignment.

6.   Repeat Steps 4 and 5 for Modifier #2, #3, and #4.

7.   Under Assignment Table, choose Add In > FX Advanced > Wet/Dry Advanced.

8.   Highlight Dry/Wet Advanced and click Learn.

9.   Twist DX2 FX Control knob 1 to bind (learn) the assignment.

10.   While Dry/Wet Advanced is highlighted, click Duplicate three times.

Next, verify the behavior of the parameter by adjusting the mapping details so that they mirror the following:

Traktor Command	Type of Controller	Interaction Mode	Assignment	Button Options	Mapped To	Cond1	Cond2
Modifier #1	Button	Hold	Global	Set to Value: 1	Ch16.NoteD6		
Modifier #2	Button	Hold	Global	Set to Value: 1	Ch16.NoteD#6		
Modifier #3	Button	Hold	Global	Set to Value: 1	Ch16NoteA6		
Modifier #4	Button	Hold	Global	Set to Value: 1	Ch16NoteA#6		
Dry/Wet Advanced	Fader/Knob	Direct	FX Unit 1	Soft Takeover: On	Ch.16CC.006	M1=1	
Dry/Wet Advanced	Fader/Knob	Direct	FX Unit 2	Soft Takeover: On	Ch.16CC.006	M2=1	
Dry/Wet Advanced	Fader/Knob	Direct	FX Unit 3	Soft Takeover: On	Ch.16CC.006	M3=1	
Dry/Wet Advanced	Fader/Knob	Direct	FX Unit 4	Soft Takeover: On	Ch.16CC.006	M4=1	

Now, let me explain this mishmash. The four unlabeled DX2 buttons sequentially send a value of 1 from Modifier #1, 2, 3, and 4. Each button in turn represents the activation of respective FX panels 1, 2, 3, and 4. The leftmost knob on the top of the DX2's FX Control is now assigned to control the wet/dry balance for all four FX panels. (As you can see within the preceding table, as well as in Figure 8.10, Mapped To shows the same value for all four Dry/Wet Advanced parameters.)

Because we are trying to control four independent FX panels from one small MIDI control surface, it is important to understand that hardware knob positioning will not transfer from one Traktor FX panel to another—the software state remains as it was previously left. For example, if we hold Modifier #1 and twist DX2 knob 1 fully clockwise, FX panel 1's dry/wet balance will be 100-percent wet. However, the other FX panels may be at oppositional depths—for example, 0 percent or dry. If we press Modifier #2 in this situation and twist DX2 knob 1, Traktor's wet/dry mix in FX panel

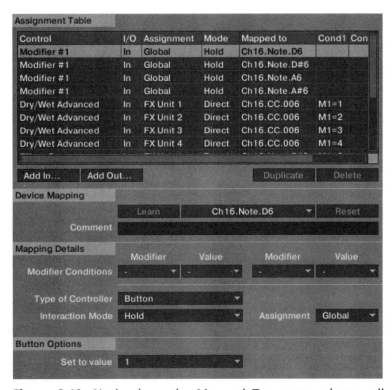

Figure 8.10 Notice how the Mapped To commands are all duplicates of one another but assigned to different FX units.

2 will "jump" to the current DX2 knob position—in other words, roughly 100 percent, which is not what we want.

Thus, make sure that Soft Takeover is set to On in these scenarios. The FX Panel parameter will remain at its current position until the DX2 knob meets/matches the software position.

Within the current configuration, if no modifier button is held, the DX2's leftmost FX Control knob does nothing. On the other hand, if I hold the leftmost button on the DX2, Modifier #1 is sending out a value of 1. (Within the Controller Manager, the Modifier State #1 indicator displays the number 1.)

Note: Notice that each repeated dry/wet control in the preceding table has a modifier value (1 to 4) attached to it. As mentioned, unless a Modifier button is held, the DX2 knob doesn't do anything. Expanding upon our example, you could assign each DX2 FX Control knob to Traktor's FX Select parameter (Add In > FX Advanced > Effect Select) for each independent FX panel. Leave no control behind!

So, what does this mean?

Another way to think of modifiers is as if/then statements.

If Modifier #1 button 1 is held on the DX2, *then* FX panel 1 is active. *If* Modifier #1 button 2 is held on the DX2, *then* FX panel 2 is active. And so on... Because we assigned the leftmost DX2 knob to the Wet/Dry control for *all* FX panels:

- (Modifier #1 = 1) + (Twist DX2 Knob 1) = Wet/Dry FX Panel 1 control.

- (Modifier #2 = 1) + (Twist DX2 Knob 1) = Wet/Dry FX Panel 2 control.

> **Note:** You could also configure this setup with Modifier #1 value numbers (1 to 4) rather than entirely separate modifier numbers (1 to 4). Experiment with your hardware to see which works best.

There are two primary Interaction modes within which modifiers will be used the most: Hold and Direct. For the most part, Hold mode is self-explanatory. Holding down the Modifier button maintains the modifier value until released—much like the Shift or Ctrl key on a computer keyboard.

On the other hand, Direct mode engages a permanent modifier value state—somewhat like a computer keyboard's Caps Lock key. If you took the previous example and switched the values of each modifier to Direct, there would be no need to hold down the Modifier button—pressing the button could be used to set a particular mapping "page" as permanently active until switched, or disengaged. A bit of confusion arises with Direct mode in that it does not act like a toggle switch—in other words, clicking the modifier turns that value on, but clicking it again does not turn it back off.

To make a modifier behave like a toggle switch, duplicate the following settings:

Traktor Command	Type of Controller	Interaction Mode	Button Options	Cond1
Modifier #1	Button	Direct	Set to Value: 0	M1=1
Modifier #1	Button	Direct	Set to Value: 1	M1=0

If that's not enough modifier action, let's go a little bit further.

Leaving all of our previous settings as they are, let's say that I want to expand upon the single Wet/Dry FX Panel control. I still want independent control over the individual FX panels, but I also want to use the same DX2 FX Control knobs as used for the wet/dry mix to select the types of effects across all four panels.

This would be a perfect example of a situation within which to use two modifier conditions. The concept is the same, but the implementation takes one more step—that is, pressing an additional "Shift" function. Once again using the computer keyboard example, the action of two modifiers is a lot like emptying your trash on Mac OS X—Command+Shift+Delete.

Another way to think of utilizing two modifiers is as if/and/then statements. "And" in this equation represents the second modifier. *If* Modifier #1 *and* Modifier #2 are held, *then* knob 1 on the DX2 is set as the effects selector for FX panel 1.

As mentioned, we will build upon the previous assignments explained within the modifier examples above. To assign the second modifier and relevant controls:

1.   Open Preferences > Controller Manager.

2.   Under Assignment Table, choose Add In > FX Advanced > FX Select.

3.   Highlight FX Select and click Learn.

4.   Twist DX2 FX Control knob 1 to bind (learn) them.

5.   Duplicate FX Select and repeat Steps 3 and 4 for DX2 FX Control knobs 2, 3, and 4.

When you have all four FX Select parameters learned to DX2 knobs 1 through 4, adjust the FX Select settings to mirror this table:

Traktor Command	Type of Controller	Interaction Mode	Assignment	Button Options	Mapped To	Cond1	Cond2
FX Select	Fader/Knob	Direct	FX Unit 1	Soft Takeover: On	Ch16.CC.006	M1=1	M2=1
FX Select	Fader/Knob	Direct	FX Unit 2	Soft Takeover: On	Ch16.CC.004	M1=1	M2=1
FX Select	Fader/Knob	Direct	FX Unit 3	Soft Takeover: On	Ch16.CC.025	M1=1	M2=1
FX Select	Fader/Knob	Direct	FX Unit 4	Soft Takeover: On	Ch16.CC.023	M1=1	M2=1

To translate this into English, DX2 FX Control knobs 1 through 4 are now used as the effects selector for FX panels 1 through 4, respectively. However, the knobs still won't do anything until modifiers have been engaged. Cond1 and Cond2 each represent the if/and of the conditional formula; by this I mean each modifier must be active in order to select effects with the DX2's FX Control knobs.

Explained another way, Modifier #1, 2, 3, and 4 are still assigned to the same gray DX2 buttons 1, 2, 3, and 4. So the setup now is that when no modifiers are held, the

DX2 FX Control knobs don't do anything. If one of the DX2's buttons 1, 2, 3, or 4 is held, FX Control knob 1 controls the wet/dry balance for FX panels 1, 2, 3, and 4, respectively. Now, while simultaneously holding DX2 buttons 1 *and* 2, DX2 FX Control knobs 1, 2, 3, and 4 change the effect type for FX panels 1, 2, 3, and 4, respectively.

Now, let's say that we want to get really crazy with our effects—yay! Just for fun, let's assign one last dual-condition modifier to simultaneously control the wet/dry mix for all four FX panels. The relevant assignments could be:

1.   Open Preferences > Controller Manager.

2.   Under Assignment Table, highlight the bottom-most Dry/Wet Advanced within the list, as I have done in Figure 8.11.

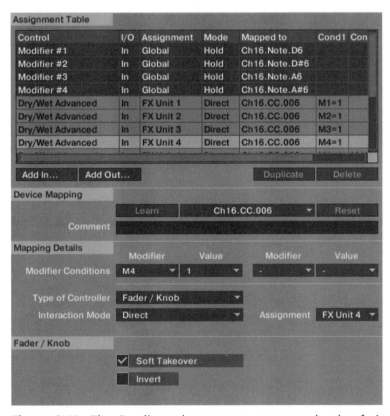

Figure 8.11 The Duplicate button can save you loads of time inside the Controller Manager.

3.   Click Duplicate four times.

Notice within the following table that by duplicating the Wet/Dry Advanced parameter, we have retained the MIDI Learn (Mapped To) assignment. Again, we still want to use DX2 knob 1 to control the overall wet/dry balance—we're just taking it one step further. Make the appropriate adjustments to the modifier conditions of the new Traktor commands:

Traktor Command	Type of Controller	Interaction Mode	Assignment	Button Options	Mapped To	Cond1	Cond2
Dry/Wet Advanced	Fader/Knob	Direct	FX Unit 1	Soft Takeover: On	Ch.16CC.006	M1=1	M4=1
Dry/Wet Advanced	Fader/Knob	Direct	FX Unit 2	Soft Takeover: On	Ch.16CC.006	M1=1	M4=1
Dry/Wet Advanced	Fader/Knob	Direct	FX Unit 3	Soft Takeover: On	Ch.16CC.006	M1=1	M4=1
Dry/Wet Advanced	Fader/Knob	Direct	FX Unit 4	Soft Takeover: On	Ch.16CC.006	M1=1	M4=1

Using double modifier conditions, we can now control the Wet/Dry Advanced parameter for *all four* FX panels from DX2 knob 1. Remember that Modifier #1 and 4 are bound (learned) to DX2 buttons 1 and 4, respectively. Now if we hold DX2 buttons 1 and 4 and then twist DX2 knob 1, the wet/dry balance on FX panels 1 through 4 are all simultaneously adjusted. Wow!

Tip: Create periodic backups during the construction of your MIDI controller mappings. If something goes wrong, this will allow you to revert to a previously functional version of the current mapping. To export a .TSI file specific to the current mapping, navigate to Preferences > Controller Manager > Device Setup > Edit tab and choose Export.

When you are working with modifiers, one of the most important concepts to keep in mind is versatility. On paper, modifiers are often somewhat confusing to new Traktor users. My intent in pairing the previous examples was not only to explain how modifiers work, but also to demonstrate how a few creative assignments can virtually triple the size of small MIDI controllers, such as the Faderfox DX2.

You could apply similar frameworks to Traktor's EQs, loop controls, hot cues, or even Browser functions.

Tutorial Control Examples

As you can see, once you throw modifiers into the mix, Traktor's control potential skyrockets. A handful of modifier assignments can turn one tiny MIDI controller into four, thus letting you prioritize one set of controls without abandoning others.

DJs willing to invest a little bit of time and effort can create incredibly powerful performance tools with a few extra commands. To clarify everything that we've covered so far, I have constructed the following examples to demonstrate how to pick up Traktor's features and transfer them over to your control surface.

The following tables are intended to communicate the pertinent Traktor controls and how each assignment should be configured within the Controller Manager. Throughout the process, I encourage you to reassign, add, or subtract controls as you see fit. For example, most of the Assignment parameters within my examples say Deck A (or Device Target). The Assignment property simply dictates which of Traktor's Decks the current control will affect. The only reason I used Deck A is to remain consistent for those following along. The option to select Device Target simply means that the currently selected control will affect the same source as governed by the overall controller mapping chosen within Device Setup. Basically, feel free to assign each control anywhere you want.

Although it is somewhat of a double-edged sword, there is no perfect way to create these assignments. So, don't forget: You aren't going to break anything. If you make a mistake, just roll back a few steps.

One-Touch Expandable Track Browser

One drawback to performing with four expanded Decks is that Traktor's features virtually eclipse the track Browser. Unsurprisingly, there is a workaround, made even easier if you have a controller with click-down rotary encoders (such as the Faderfox DX2). The following represents the relevant MIDI assignments for your controller's single rotary encoder. If your knob does not have click-down functionality, simply transfer the following button assignments over to any unassigned MIDI controller button.

Controller	Traktor Command	Type of Controller	Interaction Mode	Assignment	Button Options
Knob Twist Assignment	Only Browser Toggle	Button	Hold	Global	
	List Select Up/Down	Encoder	Relative		(adjust as needed)
Knob Button Assignment	Load Selected	Button	Trigger	Deck A (or Device Target)	
	Only Browser Toggle	Button	Direct	Global	Set to Value: 0

Twist the newly assigned encoder to jump into Browser Only view and skim through your tracks. Once you click down to load, the Browser will bounce back to your previous layout configuration.

One-Button Deck Sync

If you use Traktor's Sync functions, consider augmenting your workflow with a macro assignment to link the Sync state of all four Decks.

1. Open Preferences > Controller Manager and select the relevant mapping under Device Setup.

2. Click Add In > Tempo > Sync.

3. Duplicate the Sync control three times. There should be one for each Deck.

4. Click Learn and sequentially assign the same keyboard key or MIDI control button for each duplicate.

5. Ensure that the Assignment Table reflects the following list:

Traktor Command	Type of Controller	Interaction Mode	Assignment	Button Options
Sync	Button	Direct	Deck A	1
Sync	Button	Direct	Deck B	1
Sync	Button	Direct	Deck C	1
Sync	Button	Direct	Deck D	1

Synchro Start

At this stage, you should have some understanding of the symbiotic relationship between Traktor's Beatgrids and its internal Sync functions. This interconnection ought to be fairly easy to see after you have loaded, synced, and mixed a few tracks together. However, this process gets pretty powerful once Traktor has been configured for an entirely synced playback state, known as Synchro Start.

Essentially, Synchro Start initiates an endless playback state, whereby loading any track automatically plays and syncs the song to whatever source is defined as the master tempo. There are a few conditions that must be met prior to using Synchro Start:

■ Traktor's Deck modes must be set to Internal. As mentioned previously, the Sync function does not work while spinning with the timecode control vinyl/CD.

■ Verify that the tracks all have a properly defined Beatgrid. If the tracks are not syncing properly, go back and run through the Beatgrid tutorial in the previous chapter.

■ Uncheck the box: Preferences > Loading > Stop Playback at End of Track.

■ Uncheck the box: Preferences > Loading > Loading Only into Stopped Deck.

■ Check the box: Preferences > Loading > Initially Cue to Load Marker.

Once you have adjusted the settings accordingly, open a layout that exposes all four Traktor Decks. This particular style of mixing is fantastic when you're dropping tracks quickly. For example, when you're playing short sections, loops, or a capellas, Synchro Start will let you rip through your playlists while simultaneously automating some of the mundane processes, such as the Play button. It's like riding a bike without brakes... well, not really, but hopefully you can see where I'm going.

1. Set the Clock Master to Internal within the Master Clock panel.

2. Load tracks into all four Decks.

3. Engage the Sync button on each Deck. You should see the Deck tempos jump to follow the Master Clock tempo.

4. Press Play on all four Decks. All tracks should be playing back in sync.

5. Use the Traktor Browser to load tracks into the various Decks and notice that they immediately jump into synced playback.

Autoloop Loading

If you like the idea of the Synchro Start function, the next natural step belongs to Autoloop Loading. Not only will your tracks immediately load presynced, but they will also cue to a designated playback position with looping engaged. This style of performance is particularly powerful when executed across playlists of preconfigured tracks. Ensure that Traktor is properly set for Synchro Start playback as listed previously and then modify the following:

1. Store a load cue point at the desired start position within a handful of tracks.

2. Store a loop point of the desired length directly on top of the load cue point—in other words, click the load cue point hot cue, click the desired autoloop size, and then click the next unassigned hot-cue slot (or the Store button) to store it.

3. Open Preferences > Controller Manager and select the relevant mapping under Device Setup.

4. Select Add In > Load > Load Loop Play.

5. Click Learn and press a key on your keyboard or a button on your MIDI controller.

6. Test out the assignment on a few different tracks.

Note: If you have or use extremely short loops (think: locked grooves), you may want to adjust the Auto-Detect Size slider in Figure 8.12 from within

Preferences > Transport > Loops. Traktor will automatically assign a loop to any track shorter than the displayed length.

Figure 8.12 As a safety measure for playing short loops, check the looping Auto-Detect Size.

Setting Looping Controls

With NI's understanding of the creativity looping affords a modern DJ performance, it was vital that the company paid special attention to Traktor's loop engine. It must be seamless and transparent—instinctual, not procedural. Fortunately, Traktor gives DJs numerous looping options to work with.

For example, if you tend to stick to loop sizes of around four to eight beats, you may only need to assign two buttons to your MIDI controller—one for each loop size. Clicking the button sets an automatic four- or eight-beat loop; clicking it again disables it. MIDI Learn these specific controls to your mapping.

1. Open Preferences > Controller Manager and select the relevant mapping under Device Setup.

2. Click Add In > Cue/Loops > Loop Size + Start.

3. Click Learn and press a button on your MIDI controller.

4. Repeat Steps 2 and 3.

5. Ensure that the Assignment Table reflects the following list:

Traktor Command	Type of Controller	Interaction Mode	Assignment	Button Options
Loop Size + Set	Button	Direct	Deck A (or Device Target)	Set to Value: 4
Loop Size + Set	Button	Direct	Deck A (or Device Target)	Set to Value: 8
And so on...				

Understandably, you may also want to sweep through the range of loop sizes via MIDI controller buttons. If so, create and MIDI Learn these specific assignments to your controller:

Traktor Command	Type of Controller	Interaction Mode	Assignment	Button Options
Loop Size	Button	Inc (next)	Deck A (or Device Target)	
Loop Size	Button	Dec (prev)	Deck A (or Device Target)	
Loop Set	Button	Trigger	Deck A (or Device Target)	

Now, if autolooping is not achieving what you are after, disable the Snap function from the Master panel and test out manual looping—effectively engaging precise control over loop-in and loop-out points. This is the perfect configuration if loop playback sync is not important, or if you want to set any other loop demarcations by hand—for example, triplets, and so on. Essentially, Loop In/Set Cue and Loop Out control the placement of your loop markers once the Snap function has been disabled within the Master panel.

MIDI Learn these commands to your control device:

Traktor Command	Type of Controller	Interaction Mode	Assignment	Button Options	Mapped To	Cond1	Cond2
Modifier #1	Button	Hold	Global	Set to Value: 1	Ch16.Note.D6		
Modifier #2	Button	Hold	Global	Set to Value: 2	Ch16.Note.D#6		
Loop In/Set Cue	Button	Trigger	Deck A (or Device Target)	NA	Ch16.Note.A-1	M1=1	M2=0
Loop Out	Button	Trigger	Deck A (or Device Target)	NA	Ch16.Note.D6	M1=0	M2=1
Cue/Loop Move Mode	Button	Direct	Deck A (or Device Target)	Loop	Ch16.CC.014	NA	NA
Cue/Loop Move	Encoder	Relative	Deck A (or Device Target)	NA	Ch16.CC.014	M1=1	M2=1
Cue/Loop Move Mode	Button	Direct	Deck A (or Device Target)	Loop Out	Ch16.CC.014	M1=0	M2=1
Cue/Loop Move	Encoder	Relative	Deck A (or Device Target)	NA	Ch16.CC.014	M1=0	M2=1
Loop Size	Encoder	Relative	Deck A (or Device Target)	NA	Ch16.CC.014	M1=0	M2=0
Loop Set	Button	Trigger	Deck A (or Device Target)	NA	Ch16.Note.A-1	M1=0	M2=0
Cue/Loop Move Size	Encoder	Relative	Deck A (or Device Target)	NA	Ch16.CC.014	M1=1	M2-0
Store Cue/Loop	Button	Trigger	Deck A (or Device Target)	NA	Ch16.Note.A-1	M1=1	M2=1

The benefit of setting up your MIDI controller as listed here is that through the simple combination of a click-down rotary encoder and two buttons, you can drop either auto or manual loops and easily resize them. If you accidentally drop a loop in the wrong location, you can define how far you want to move it and instantly jump the loop to a new location. If your loop-out point isn't quite precise enough, define a move amount and shift your loop-out point over by whatever degree you deem necessary. Once you are looping what you want, store it to the next unassigned hot-cue slot.

Here is an overview of the control actions as they stand in the preceding assignment table:

Encoder	Button 1	Button 2	Result
Twist	NA	NA	Define autoloop size
Push	NA	NA	Set autoloop
Push	Hold	NA	Set manual loop-in point
Push	NA	Hold	Set manual loop-out point
Twist	NA	Hold	Move loop-out point
Twist	Hold	NA	Set loop move size
Twist	Hold	Hold	Loop jump
Push	Hold	Hold	Store currently active loop to the next unassigned hot cue

Do not forget that this process is 100-percent modifiable to suit your needs. If you don't like the behaviors, by all means substitute the buttons/knobs to fit around your MIDI controller. Better yet, experiment with an entirely different blend of configurations.

The Hot-Cue Sampler

A lot of the language in this chapter, and with Traktor in general, speaks of a "synced" performance within which absolutely nothing falls off the Beatgrid. Remember that this is purely an option, not a requirement. If you uncheck Quantize from the Master panel and the Sync buttons from the Decks, Traktor's cue-related behavior jumps into a free-run state—in other words, if you don't click a hot cue in time with the master tempo, playback sync will fall apart spectacularly.

This is obviously not the best configuration if you are aiming for smooth transitions in your mixing; however, without automatic quantization enabled, you can trigger hot cues at will, much like a groovebox phrase sampler or a drum machine. Further, if you also uncheck Snap mode, cue-point behavior will not magnetically snap to the closest Beatgrid.

Why does this matter? Because now you can set a cue point anywhere inside a track—in other words, hot cues do not have to sit on beat. Store a hot cue on a kick, snare, hat, and ride. Map each hot cue to individual MIDI controller buttons (think: NI's Maschine controller). What do we have? An improvised drum sampler!

Don't limit yourself to mapping the drums from tracks you already have. Create your own loops, find one-shot sound FX on the Internet, even record your own found sound—DJ software doesn't get much more individualized than this.

1. Uncheck Quant and Snap from the Master panel.

2. Set the Mouse Control to Vinyl from Preferences > Transport > Mouse Control.

3. Load a track with some interesting percussion.

4. Click and drag to any drum sound within the Waveform display—for example, a kick drum.

5. Click an unassigned hot-cue slot or click Store and remap your hot cues.

6. Open Preferences > Controller Manager and select the relevant mapping under Device Setup.

7. Click Add In > Cue/Loops > Select/Set + Store Hotcue.

8. Click Learn and press a button on your MIDI controller.

9. Repeat Steps 4 through 8 up to six more times. (Hot cue #1 is usually the first grid marker.)

10. Ensure that the Assignment Table reflects the following table:

Traktor Command	Type of Controller	Interaction Mode	Assignment	Button Options
Select/Set + Store Hotcue	Button	Hold	Deck A (or Device Target)	Set to Value: 1
Select/Set + Store Hotcue	Button	Hold	Deck A (or Device Target)	Set to Value: 2
Select/Set + Store Hotcue	Button	Hold	Deck A (or Device Target)	Set to Value: 3
And so on...				

Once you have four or so hot cues mapped out to your MIDI controller, start a track within another Deck and start banging around on the new hot cues. Enable Deck Sync and Quantize once again and notice the behavior change once Traktor forces tempo-locked playback.

Tip: Experiment with some effects on top of your improvised sampler Deck. If your hot cues are drum hits, saturate delay or reverb tails with a bit of distortion to add presence to your drumming.

HID Devices

A relatively recent feature addition to Traktor, HID (Human Interface Device) technology represents a step forward from traditional MIDI. What HID has over MIDI is a more accurate control response; for example, it is specifically useful with extra-sensitive pitch adjustments. Additionally, HID hardware displays replicate track information sent directly from Traktor's Decks.

While configuring hardware devices within the Controller Manager, you may have noticed a few manufacturer names within the Device drop-down menu. Denon's DN-HC4500 and several of Pioneers CDJs, including the CDJ-400, CDJ-900, MEP-7000, and the new CDJ-2000s, shown in Figure 8.13, are all preconfigured for Traktor through the HID technology.

Figure 8.13 Pioneer's CDJ-2000.

One particularly useful feature of HID devices becomes immediately apparent when creating MIDI mappings. The moment you MIDI Learn a command, rather than a MIDI CC or note-on/off message, Mapped To assignments display named parameters, rather than numbers. In other words, the Play/Pause button of a CDJ will show up as... Play/Pause!

If you use any of these devices, remember that once you are happy with a MIDI mapping, simply click Duplicate within the Edit drop-down menu. Define the In-Ports for both controllers (Out-Ports are locked), set the Device Target to the respective Deck A, B, C, or D, and you should be good to go.

Traktor Kontrol X1

In light of how long Native Instruments has developed the Traktor product line, it seems somewhat surprising that it took so many years for the company to independently manufacture its own DJ controller. However, considering DJ culture climate in 2010, all appearances show that it was worth the wait.

A string of design similarities is apparent when comparing a few of the X1's direct competitors, such as Faderfox's DX3 and Allen & Heath's Xone:1D. Small form factor; readily accessible knobs, faders, and buttons; rugged build quality; and bilateral symmetry speak to the mirrored configurations of traditional and digital DJ stage setups. However, the advantage users gain with the X1 lies within the fact that NI developed a controller intended primarily for its own DJ software.

Software integration is enhanced through what NI refers to as its bidirectional Native Hardware Library (NHL) control protocol. This proprietary data stream gives DJs nearly four times the resolution of MIDI's 128 steps, which is great when considering the importance of smooth filter sweeps, accurate FX control, and so on.

Plugging in the X1 provides instant plug-and-play functionality out of the box. If you have Traktor launched and you pop in the X1 via the provided USB 2.0 cable, you are prompted with the instructions as shown in Figure 8.14. Click OK and touch any of the X1 controls—magic! If you use all four Decks, hot-plugging a second X1 instantly provides control over Decks C and D.

Figure 8.14 The X1's connection prompt.

The X1 Layout

The X1 hardware itself is built upon a similar chassis to NI's Maschine controller—robust and designed for the inevitable rough treatment gear receives in transit. I was fortunate enough to be in NI's Berlin office on a few occasions during the early stages of the X1's development, so I got to witness various degrees of the X1's progression from its concept stage to its final release. A commendable effort was focused on the finer details, from the knobs of the X1's Effects section, to the push encoders of the Browse and Loop Sections—even the mechanics of the click-down buttons scattered around the rest of the X1 were all carefully chosen.

Most of the default Traktor assignments are sound: The click-down encoders in Figure 8.15 make browsing Traktor's collection fast and effective. Figure 8.16 displays Traktor's intuitive Transport section, controlling syncing, cues, Beatjumps, scratch controls, and so on. FX inserts are assigned via the clearly labeled FX buttons; however, for me the most important part of the entire controller is the Loop section shown in Figure 8.17. DJs are given direct access to loop in/out and autoloops, nested immediately adjacent to the Hotcue page command—the primary controls I consistently reach for track after track.

Figure 8.15 Each knob represents independent browsing/Deck-loading functionality.

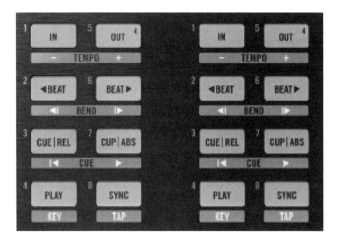

Figure 8.16 Use the X1's Transport section to control Traktor's playback behaviors.

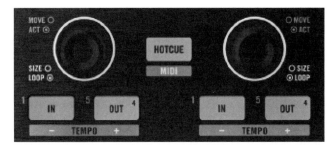

Figure 8.17 Use the Loop knobs for experimental repetition...tion...tion...tion (sorry).

Under the Hood

You may have noticed the dedicated X1 tab within Traktor's Preferences. Shown in Figure 8.18, assignable X1-exclusive controller behaviors are configurable directly inside Traktor. Calibration settings, button actions, and premapped Deck prioritization are a few of the available customizations. Should you accidentally mess everything up, rather than walking back through dozens of assignments, simply click Restore, and the X1 will default to the factory preset.

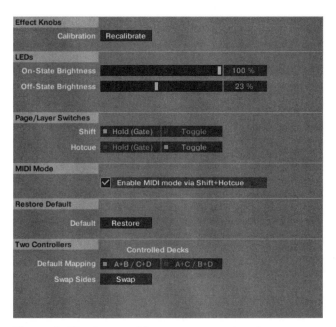

Figure 8.18 Access this menu to customize some essential X1 hardware behaviors.

Of particular note is the X1's MIDI mode. Like all of NI's other controllers, the X1 also shares NI's Controller Editor software. If you own any of the NI hardware controllers—for example, the Kore 2, Rig Kontrol 3, Maschine, or X1—you are probably familiar with the GUI shown in Figure 8.19. If not, simultaneously clicking Maschine's Shift and Hotcue buttons flips the controller into MIDI mode (see

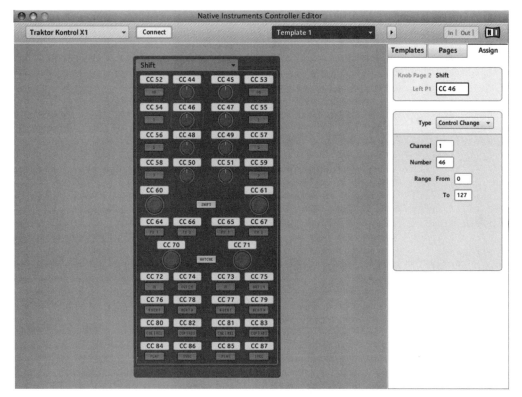

Figure 8.19   Configuring my X1's MIDI actions within NI's Controller Editor software.

Figure 8.20   The Hotcue button.

Figure 8.20), the controller state from which you can send/receive traditional MIDI control parameters. Launch the Controller Editor from your Applications/Program Files folder. From here, you are able to exhaustively customize any X1 (or other NI controller) MIDI parameters. The preconfigured layout of the X1 is a good starting point; however, as I mentioned previously, most DJs need a personalized control surface.

As an example, if you hold down the X1's Shift button, you open an alternate "page" for the controller, enabling a secondary set of functions akin to the modifier actions described a few sections ago. When you're using the X1's default template, the Effects knobs in Figure 8.21 logically control the FX panel's parameters. Yet, while you're holding Shift within the confines of the factory template, the Effects knobs remain unassigned. Taking into account the X1's hardware layout, notice that the Effects knobs are positioned like the EQ section of any standard DJ mixer.

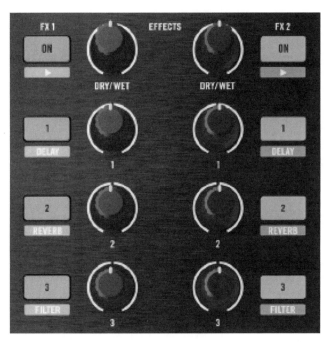

Figure 8.21 The X1's FX controls.

Assigning X1's Controls

Let's assign Traktor's EQ to the X1 Effects knobs.

1. Open: Preferences > Controller Manager and select Traktor Kontrol X1 under the Device Setup.

2. Click Add In > Mixer > EQ > EQ Low.

3. Click Learn within Device Mapping.

4. On the X1, hold Shift and twist the bottom-left Effects knob to bind (learn) the assignment.

5. Repeat Steps 2 through 4 for the rest of Traktor's EQ section.

Notice two things. First, while in Traktor's MIDI Learn mode, the X1's Shift button behaves somewhat like a predefined modifier—there is no need to assign modifier conditions for simple X1 Shift actions. (They can, of course, still be used.) Second, pay particular attention to the Mapped To section in Figure 8.22. Each assignment displays a name instead of a MIDI CC/note message—to some extent sharing HID device behavior. Obviously, this presents tremendous benefits when troubleshooting your .TSI mapping file as well as customizing the X1 as a whole. Further, when assigning LED outputs, which are explained in the next section, rather than having to flip through a huge string of MIDI CC/note messages, you can select precisely where you want to send Traktor's LED outputs by name.

Assignment Table

Control	I/O	Assignment	Mode	Mapped to	Cond1	Con
Playback Mode Int/Rel~	Out	Deck A	Output	Shift.Left.CUE		Dec
Playback Mode Int/Rel~	Out	Deck B	Output	Norm.Right.CUE		Dec
Playback Mode Int/Rel~	Out	Deck B	Output	Shift.Right.CUE		Dec
Playback Mode Int/Rel~	Out	Deck A	Output	Norm.Left.CUP		Dec
Playback Mode Int/Rel~	Out	Deck A	Output	Shift.Left.CUP		Dec
Playback Mode Int/Rel~	Out	Deck B	Output	Norm.Right.CUP		Dec
Playback Mode Int/Rel~	Out	Deck B	Output	Shift.Right.CUP		Dec
EQ Low	In	Device Target	Direct	Shift.Left.P3		

Figure 8.22   All the X1's parameters' Mapped To commands are clearly labeled within the Controller Manager.

Some other suggested configurations surround the Snap and Quant buttons within the FX section shown in Figure 8.23. In most cases, these two previously mentioned functions are generally left on or off, so there is little reason to waste two buttons on functions that you won't touch regularly. Try mapping out the button combination Shift + Right FX2 (Quant) to transform the overall Deck A/B control into overall Deck C/D control—effectively turning one X1 into two. Next, map out the button combination of Shift + Left FX2 (Snap) into control over FX panels 3/4. The simple fact that Traktor displays button presses makes this process significantly faster than mapping out standard MIDI messages.

Figure 8.23   Use the FX section to assign FX and assign Master panel behaviors.

LED Output

Previous generations of MIDI controllers offered very little in the way of visual feedback information—perhaps understandably, given that they were primarily designed to send out MIDI rather than to receive it. However, if you look at any number of examples from this current generation of MIDI hardware, it is pretty rare to find a device that isn't dominated by flashing buttons and knobs.

While we have seen that Traktor responds to incoming MIDI commands with varying degrees of complexity, the software is also capable of sending outgoing MIDI information to hardware controllers offering LED feedback. Fortunately, as far as assigning outbound MIDI commands goes, the process is nearly identical to what we have already covered while MIDI Learning Traktor's internal controls.

LED feedback is incredibly useful for several reasons, but the most important in my eyes is that you can look away from your computer and focus instead on your performance instruments.

Assigning LED Outputs

Let's say that I want to launch Deck Play/Pause from my Maschine controller's Transport section and have the hardware Play button blink in tempo with the Deck's bpm. Note that the following LED output steps can be mirrored for almost any backlit MIDI hardware control.

Create the following control assignments:

1. Open Preferences > Controller Manager.

2. Choose your controller from the Device drop-down menu. Configure the In-Port and Out-Port such that Traktor is sending to and receiving from the device.

3. Click Add In > Transport > Play/Pause.

4. Select Learn and press the relevant MIDI button on your MIDI controller.

5. Click Add Out > Transport > Play/Pause.

6. Click Add Out > Output > Beat Phase Monitor.

Notice that I did not include Learn steps for the two Out commands. That's because there aren't any. When sending LED outputs messages, you have to determine what MIDI channel your hardware controller receives on in addition to whether it listens for MIDI CC (control change) or MIDI note-on/off messages. Check your hardware's user documentation, as that is most likely where you will find that information.

To illustrate, here is what my Assignment Table looks like within the Controller Manager:

Traktor Command	I/O	Type of Controller	Interaction Mode	Assignment	Button Options	Mapped To
Play/Pause	In	Button	Toggle	Deck A (or Device Target)	NA	Ch01. CC.104
Play/Pause	Out	LED	Output	Deck A (or Device Target)	NA	Ch01. CC.104
Beat Phase Monitor	Out	LED	Output	Deck A (or Device Target)	NA	Ch01. CC.104

Notice that all three commands reference the same MIDI CC assignments. As mentioned previously in this chapter, the Mapped To configuration will most likely differ. However, the point is for you to see that all three assignments will ultimately refer to the same hardware control. As you can see in Figure 8.24, the drop-down list lets you manually set the relevant MIDI output message.

Figure 8.24 Determine your hardware MIDI settings before assigning LED outputs.

Press the newly assigned Play button on your MIDI controller and notice the behavior as it blinks in time with the Beatgrid. Additionally, click Traktor's Play/Pause button with your mouse and note your hardware's response.

Note: Many modern MIDI controllers let users configure the inner workings of their hardware through specially designed Controller Editors. In many cases, you can completely reconfigure the state of every button on the device. If control features are not behaving properly, or you simply want them to behave differently, open the respective Controller Editor and verify the actions of the relevant MIDI controls.

I am not going to exhaustively detail the LED output commands, but you should be aware that all of the MIDI input controls are duplicated at the MIDI output stage. Though, as you have seen with the Beat Phase monitor, there are powerful LED output assignments exclusive to the MIDI Output drop-down menu. For example, some MIDI controllers have LED VU meters. You could very easily send Traktor's master output to your hardware device in order to monitor the master volume.

Further, controllers such as AKAI's APC40 or Novation's Launchpad have additional multicolor LEDs. As an example, you could assign Traktor's different cue-point types to different colors on the controller. Additionally, color-code loop assignments, Deck playback states, Deck mode, and so on. Needless to say, LED output is a feature that you shouldn't overlook.

Syncing Traktor via MIDI Clock

I have to admit that I never truly realized Traktor's potential until I synced it with some of my MIDI-capable gear. For sure, Traktor arms performers with multiple paths of creative exploration; however, incorporating a variety of tools into a performance allows artists to more faithfully express themselves.

Rather than jump into different setup options right this second, let's take a look at where to begin when considering linking Traktor up with other MIDI-capable gear.

Note: Please note that this section is intended as a primer to the advanced setups discussed in *Part 2* of *The Laptop DJ Handbook*.

Effectively, Traktor will fit within a MIDI-synced setup in two ways.

Traktor as Master

When you use this configuration, Traktor will serve as the Master Clock source; in other words, the MIDI Clock sync signal will be sent from Traktor to a separate slave destination—for example, another MIDI-capable application upon the same computer, another computer running Traktor, a drum machine, an effects unit, and so on.

1. Navigate to Preferences > MIDI Clock.

2. Check the Send MIDI Clock check box, shown in Figure 8.25.

Figure 8.25 Adjust these settings to fine-tune Traktor's MIDI Clock output.

3. Click on the Controller Manager tab, click Add under the Device heading, and choose Generic MIDI from the drop-down menu.

4. Leave the In-Port set to None for now.

5.   Click on the Out-Port drop-down menu and choose:

- OS X: Traktor Virtual Output.

- Windows: You will need a dedicated internal MIDI application, such as MIDI Yoke (www.midiox.com).

- If you are syncing external hardware or another computer, you will set the Out-Port to the MIDI out port of your MIDI interface—for example, Audio 8 DJ MIDI Ouput Port 0.

6.   Close the Traktor Preferences.

7.   Click on the Metronome icon within the Global section to switch to the Master Clock panel.

8.   Click Int under the Clock Master heading.

9.   Click the Play/Pause button under the MIDI Clock Master heading.

10. Click the Sync button under the MIDI Clock Master heading after configuring the slave hardware/software. This Sync button pulses a MIDI Stop > MIDI Start message to resync all devices.

11. Load and play a track within Deck A. Click Deck A's Sync button so that playback reflects the Master Clock.

12. If the playback between the devices is not synchronized, slowly adjust Traktor's MIDI Clock Sending Offset slider found under Preferences > MIDI Clock and shown in Figure 8.26.

Figure 8.26 Use this panel to control Traktor's MIDI Clock playback performance.

Note: When you're performing with synced setups, one MIDI complication is that it has a tendency to drift over extended periods of time. Occasionally, it helps to give these drifting devices a "slap" on the back of the head in the form of a MIDI Sync message. Although the function is readily located within Traktor's Master Clock panel, it helps to map the function out to a MIDI controller button.

MIDI Learn the assignment Preferences > Controller Manager > Assignment Table > Add In > Master Clock > Master Tempo Clock Sync MIDI.

Traktor as Slave

The functional opposite of Traktor as Master, Traktor as Slave sets all tempo control functions on "receive"—in other words, Traktor's Sync functions are all determined by an external master source, such as another computer running Traktor, a drum machine, and so on.

1. Navigate to Preferences > MIDI Clock.

2. Uncheck the check box labeled Send MIDI Clock.

3. Click on the Controller Manager tab, click Add under the Device heading, and choose Generic MIDI from the drop-down menu.

4. Click on the In-Port drop-down menu and choose:

   - OS X: Traktor Virtual Input.

   - Windows: You will need a dedicated internal MIDI application, such as MIDI Yoke (www.midiox.com).

   - If you are syncing external hardware or between two computers, you will set the In-Port to the MIDI in port of your MIDI interface—for example, Audio 8 DJ MIDI Input Port 0. To avoid potential confusion, set the selected device's Out-Port to None.

5. Close the Traktor Preferences.

6. Click on the Metronome icon within the Global section to switch to the Master Clock panel.

7. Click Ext under the Clock Master heading displayed in Figure 8.26.

8. Load and play a track within Deck A. Click Deck A's Sync button so that playback reflects the tempo of the master MIDI Clock source (the other hardware/software sending the MIDI Clock signal).

9. You should see the Master Clock tempo fluctuating with the incoming MIDI Clock signal.

10. If playback between the devices is not synchronized, slowly adjust the offset function from the master (external) MIDI hardware/software.

Moving Forward

I hope that having read this chapter, you are now able to understand the significance Traktor represents within DJ culture. Through Traktor, NI imagined an application that would let performers rethink their performance boundaries in ways unimaginable as few as 10 years ago. Not content with playing one record after another, NI has managed to entirely encapsulate DJ culture and shape Traktor into the powerful tool that it is today.

In the next chapter, we'll use a similar approach to examine a second progressive model of digital DJ software, Serato Scratch Live.

9 Serato Scratch Live

Societies around the world are commonly understood through their cultural norms; customs, belief structures, mannerisms, and so on all come together to shape an external view (or a popular understanding) of who a group of people are. It's a classification system that applies well to multilayered groups of like-minded people—collectives, if you will—such as the youth movement constantly redefining DJ culture.

Part of what keeps DJ culture so fresh is the continuous challenge to these norms by a steady stream of new ideas, new talent, and, of course, new tools. Sure, it's not what it was, but cultural throwbacks are constantly bubbling up through the cracks and being adopted by the next generation of DJs.

At the root of these societies are the subcultures: the support structures that keep the bigger picture dynamic enough to remain relevant. Turntablism, for example, almost singlehandedly established the DJ-as-artist archetype by morphing a playback device into a performance instrument. Today, through companies such as Native Instruments, Serato, and Ableton, DJ culture is once again evolving into the next generation.

With 2004's release of Serato Scratch Live (commonly known as SSL or just Serato), the Serato/Rane partnership gave the DJ market a product that is quite possibly DJ culture's truest summary.

Getting Started

As software DJ products go, getting Serato up and running couldn't get any easier. The software itself is relatively undemanding from a computer's perspective—you do not have to spend hundreds of thousands of dollars on the computer market's latest hotrod.

Serato runs equally well on both Macs and Windows-based PCs, but be aware that system requirements present a lowest common denominator scenario—Serato should launch and run, but using all of the advanced features might bring a low-spec computer to its knees. Before you go out and buy a laptop, remember that if your machine meets but does not exceed the requirements, you may run into problems once you push Serato to its limits. Double-check Serato's latest system requirements at serato.com/scratchlive#minispecs.

If you did your research, you saw that SSL offers several different hardware/software combinations. Unless otherwise noted, all of the following references to SSL refer to a fully licensed copy of Serato Scratch Live 2.1 as bundled with the SL3 (see Figure 9.1), because this represents the most appropriate feature set in line with the themes of this book. If you are unsure about which version to go for, dig through the Products section on Serato's website at www.serato.com.

Figure 9.1 SSL 2.1 bundled with the SL3 interface.

Installation, Registration, and Updating

As I mentioned before, software installation processes vary not only from developer to developer, but also between Mac and PC platforms as well as current operating system versions—for example, Mac OS X 10.5.x versus 10.6.x. Refer to the software documentation or the company's online knowledge database for specific information on software and driver installation, troubleshooting, and, if necessary, technical support. For visual learners, I have also found that trawling YouTube for hardware (and software) setup tutorials often yields some fantastic results.

With SSL, Serato users buy into a particularly attractive ideal: There is no registration process, and all updates are completely free. Yes, free. Updates are regular, include dozens of fixes/improvements, and involve the massively devoted user base in regular public beta tests. With the relatively recent update to SSL version 2.1, Serato included a level of product enhancements typically associated with paid upgrades. Most software companies charge for these major service updates, especially when graduating a full point level, such as 1.0 to 2.0. Not Serato. I cannot pretend to know how the company pulls it off, but this is unarguably enticing from a consumer's perspective.

Be that as it may, this exception does come with one major caveat. Serato runs in what the company refers to as *Offline mode* when no hardware is connected—that is, with much limited functionality. The SL3 effectively acts as SSL's hardware dongle, in that full software functions are linked to a mandatory hardware connection.

Depending on what you're after, this difference really may not be that big of a deal; SSL's Offline mode still retains the entire feature set essential to pre-gig collection maintenance, which we will discuss in the section titled "Your Music Collection and the Serato Browser."

Manually Configuring Your Audio Setup

If any one single process is absolutely crucial to DVS technology, it is the hardware setup. Do whatever it takes to remember the sequence of steps. Practice in your home or studio, create a mental checklist, tattoo it onto your hand...trust me, it will pay off in the end.

Note: To be sure, the Serato/Rane partnership has yielded a powerful DJ tool; however, you should understand that the hardware/software combination does have certain limitations. For example, Native Instruments' Audio 4 or Audio 8 hardware is required to use Traktor's timecode vinyl; however, the Audio 4/8 double as "true" audio interface solutions—that is, they can be used as soundcards for DAW applications or for general computer use. Further, Traktor's software audio engine is compatible with virtually any third-party audio card. If you perform with Traktor "internally" (no control vinyl/CDs), your audio output options are still completely open-ended.

In this regard at least, the SL3 and Serato operate in a relatively closed environment. The hardware doesn't function as a soundcard outside of Serato (whereas the Audio 4 or 8 can be used as a standalone audio interface in conjunction with other studio applications, such as Ableton or Logic), and SSL does not offer a software-only internal mixing mode. (Serato's ITCH application does offer software-only mixing, however, so check the serato.com website for more information.) There has been talk about releasing, for example, ASIO drivers for the SL3 for some time; however, as of the writing of this book the driver is currently unavailable.

Finally, the most potentially deadly situation Serato users find themselves in concerns the moment when artists switch over. Unlike Native Instruments' "passive" DJ products, which pass signal through the multicore cables from the turntables (using real vinyl) or CDJs (using standard CDs) with or without a computer connected, the SL1 and SL3 require either an external power supply or a direct connection to a computer via USB. If this connection gets severed during a performance, the audience is treated to a loud thump followed by silence. If you're prepared, this doesn't really pose an issue, so just be aware of this minor difference.

Note: If you are unfamiliar with the term, *software-only mixing* refers to the ability to open your laptop—on an airplane, for example—and mix without connecting any external hardware.

Setting Up the SL3 Hardware

Figure 9.2 clearly displays the basic hardware routing process of SSL and the SL3. After you have set up Serato a few times, the process simply becomes a matter of muscle memory—an absolute must if you tend to "enjoy yourself" at a gig!

When you've made all of the physical connections, double-check a few things:

- Ensure that the Dip switches are correctly set for the control medium you are using—such as Up for Phono (turntables), Down for Line (CDJs).

- Connect your SL3 directly to your laptop. Do not use a USB hub, as you may experience dropouts when it's coupled with other USB devices.

- Ensure that your SL3 is plugged into the mains with a power supply. If you don't and the SL3 is accidentally unplugged (for example, during changeover), all music will completely cut out with a very loud pop.

- If you're using turntables, verify that the grounding forks are in good shape and are properly connected to your SL3 or the DJ mixer's grounding post.

- Set the DJ mixer channel inputs to Line. (See the section titled "Preparation and Performance" for information on playing with both "real" vinyl and SSL's control vinyl.)

- If you're using CDJs, make absolutely sure that any keylock or master tempo features are disabled.

Setting Up the SSL Software

Once the SSL hardware is properly set up, it is important to instruct your computer how to "speak" with the connected audio interface. I mentioned this already, but the efficiency of communication between your computer and its audio hardware is known as *latency*. Within DVS software, latency is understood as the time it takes between moving the control vinyl and actually hearing the result of that movement (for example, scratching) out of the speakers. As you can see in Figure 9.3, the degree of Serato's latency is controlled from Setup > Hardware > USB Buffer Size (Latency).

Figure 9.2 Hooking up the SL3 to a DJ mixer.

Figure 9.3 Use this slider to adjust SSL's latency settings.

Tighter control is achieved with a lower buffer size; unfortunately, though, there is no magical, absolute value. Because the degree of this setting is ultimately controlled by the speed of your computer, try lowering the setting until you experience dropouts, pops, and/or glitching. Just above that point is your optimum value.

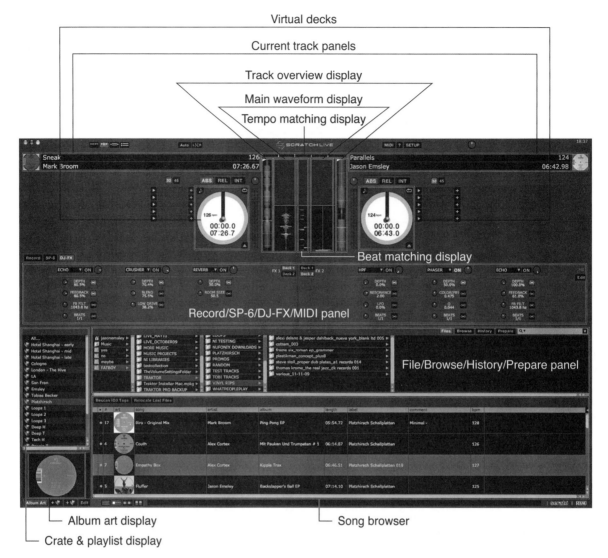

Figure 9.4 Serato's GUI.

Note: Notice the Line/Phono Status under the Hardware Setup. The list corresponds to the SL3's input dipswitch settings. When you are using Phono (turntables), a menu titled Phono Sensitivity appears. For optimum performance, match this value to the measurement provided by the manufacturer of your needles.

Additional Performance Settings. If Serato is giving you trouble and raising the USB buffer size doesn't help, open the Setup page and click on the Display tab. Maximum Screen Updates controls how many times per second Serato refreshes its GUI. Turning this value down gives your processor a little bit more headroom to perform more important functions.

On the other hand, Audio Cache determines how many seconds of your song to allocate into RAM once it's loaded into a Deck. A larger cache may load tracks a bit slower, but it also provides a wider viewing angle within the Waveform view.

Navigating the User Interface

SSL's strongest facet is its uncomplicated approach to DJing. In line with Serato's obvious nod to vinyl purism, very few steps exist between opening the box and mixing your first tracks. Figure 9.4 shows Serato's unmistakably direct software GUI design choices.

If you've had the opportunity to play around with a few different DVS bundles, you've probably noticed that they all share a degree of similarity. What sets an application such as Traktor or Serato apart from the rest is how all of these elements combine into a cohesive workflow. As developers, Serato's obvious grasp on how a DJ's mind works is immediately apparent with one glance at SSL's intuitive interface.

Tip: While you are learning your way around SSL, click on the ? icon (see Figure 9.5) located at the top of the Serato interface. Helpfully, when you click on the icon, a list of Serato's preset keyboard shortcuts appears. When the tooltips option is enabled, hovering over any icon within the GUI (including within the Setup page) brings up a synopsis of the feature as well as keyboard shortcuts and/or behaviors related to that function/section.

Figure 9.5 Click this icon to display a list of Serato's preset keyboard shortcuts.

Display Modes

Speaking of how a DJ's mind works…because performance styles are unique to the individual, Serato optimized the SSL interface into four views. Visualizing precisely how audio files play in relation to one another is a crucial factor within the realm of digital DJing; as such, SSL's four Display modes represent one of the application's most defining characteristics. In particular, each Display mode provides a unique view over how a song's transient data corresponds to that of an opposing Virtual Deck.

Click on any of these Display Mode icons (see Figure 9.6) to change SSL's layout perspective.

Figure 9.6 Click one of these four buttons to change Serato's layout appearance.

Library Mode. If you click on the Library Mode button, Serato's Virtual Decks are effectively squashed down into minimal info windows, while the Library Track List is expanded to allow comprehensive Crate/Main Library viewing (see Figure 9.7). Tracks continue to play, and SSL's behaviors are still accessible, of course, but this view is plainly intended for browsing.

Figure 9.7 SSL's Library mode.

Tip: Hit the spacebar to jump back and forth between your current performance mode and the Library mode.

Classic Vertical Mode. The first of SSL's three performance modes, this view takes both the main waveform display and the track overviews and vertically aligns them between the Virtual Decks (see Figure 9.8).

Figure 9.8 SSL's Classic Vertical mode.

Classic Horizontal Mode. The second of SSL's three performance modes, this view takes both the main waveform display and the track overviews and stacks them on top of one another between the Virtual Decks (see Figure 9.9).

Figure 9.9 SSL's Classic Horizontal mode.

Stack Mode. The third of SSL's three performance modes, this view takes both the main waveform display and the track overviews and stacks the entire Virtual Deck section into horizontally scrolling rows (see Figure 9.10). For reference, Serato compares this expanded waveform view to the horizontal structure of DAW arrangement windows. If not enough Virtual Deck data is available, click the Show/Hide Deck Controls button.

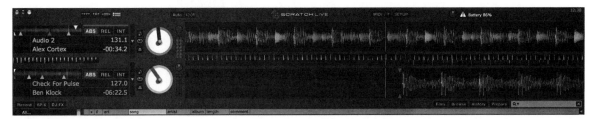

Figure 9.10   SSL's Stack mode.

> **Note:** You will only be able to see SSL's third (or fourth with the right hardware) Deck within Stack mode.

Library View

Considering the importance of music to a DJ set, it's hardly surprising that the success of a digital DJ app partially hinges on the capabilities of its track browser. After all, what's the point of DJing with a digitized music library if you don't have immediate access to your tracks?

Fortunately, Serato is keen on direct visual cues, as evidenced by SSL's four different Library views. Click one of the icons found at the bottom of the GUI, shown in Figure 9.11, to flip through the available Library layouts.

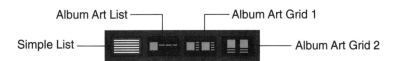

Figure 9.11   Click one of these icons to flip through the available Library layouts.

- **Simple List.** A text list arranged by the criteria of your collection metadata—for example, artist, title, and so on (see Figure 9.12).

- **Album Art List.** Basically the same as the Simple List, but with album art as well (see Figure 9.13).

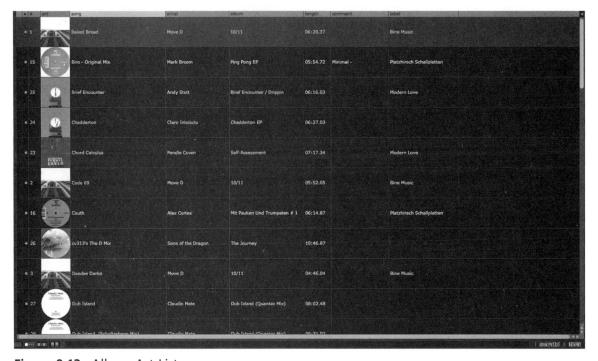

#	song	artist	album	length	comment	label
1	Baked Bread	Move D	10/11	06:20.37		Bine Music
15	Biro - Original Mix	Mark Broom	Ping Pong EP	05:54.72	Minimal -	Platzhirsch Schallplatten
25	Brief Encounter	Andy Stott	Brief Encounter / Drippin	06:16.03		Modern Love
24	Chadderton	Claro Intelecto	Chadderton EP	06:27.03		
23	Chord Calculus	Pendle Coven	Self-Assessment	07:17.34		Modern Love
2	Code 69	Move D	10/11	05:52.05		Bine Music
16	Couth	Alex Cortex	Mit Pauken Und Trumpeten # 1	06:14.87		Platzhirsch Schallplatten
26	cv313's The D Mix	Sons of the Dragon	The Journey	10:46.87		
3	Deedee Darko	Move D	10/11	04:46.04		Bine Music
27	Dub Island	Claudio Mate	Dub Island (Quantec Mix)	08:02.48		
28	Dub Island (EchoReshape Mix)	Claudio Mate	Dub Island (Quantec Mix)	06:31.92		
4	Emotionally Yours	Move D	10/11	05:28.80		Bine Music
17	Empathy Box	Alex Cortex	Kipple Trax	06:46.51		Platzhirsch Schallplatten 019
5	Evil	Move D	10/11	06:02.11		Bine Music
29	Exigen	Pendle Coven	Self-Assessment	10:47.34		Modern Love
30	Experiment 3 (MLZ Remix)	DJ Ghosthunter	One Cycle EP	06:15.04		
18	Fluffer	Jason Emsley	Backslapper's Ball EP	07:14.10		Platzhirsch Schallplatten
6	FM Heaven	Move D	10/11	04:53.33		Bine Music
31	Folder	Geoff White	Force Inc.		Questions & Comments	
32	In the Beginning	Move D & Benjamin Brunn	In The Beginning / Don't Forget	07:24.29		
33	Intrusion's Lost Dub	Sons of the Dragon	The Journey	06:27.89		
34	Isolate	Quantec	Isolate EP	08:42.03		
7	Jo Interlude	Move D	10/11	04:06.91		Bine Music
8	Just Do It	Move D	10/11	11:12.55		Bine Music
35	König der Welt (Sven's dWorld Mix)	Freund der Familie	Konig Der Welt EP	09:51.36		
9	Mayfirst	Move D	10/11	08:06.71		Bine Music
44	Minus	Pacou	Sound Device	05:18.20		Cache
19	Mood Organ	Alex Cortex	Kipple Trax	05:38.01		Platzhirsch Schallplatten 019
45	Mystery Of Nazerus (version 2)	Marco Bernardi	Mystery Of Nazerus Remxed	04:45.05		Clone Records
20	Parallels	Jason Emsley	The Journey	06:42.98		Platzhirsch Schallplatten
36	Phase90 Reconstruction	Sons of the Dragon	The Journey	11:01.47		
10	Raise This Flap	Move D	10/11	05:09.63		Bine Music
37	Reel Life (CV313 Dimensional Space Mix)	Luke Hess	Ignite The Dark Remixes	08:16.65		
38	Sailing Stars	CV313	Sailing Stars	09:58.13		
39	Sark (Taron Trekka Remix)	Freund der Familie	Sark	07:13.63		
40	Slight Transition	Brendon Moeller	Safari ep	06:50.59		
21	Sneak	Mark Broom	Mit Pauken Und Trumpeten # 2	07:26.67		Platzhirsch Schallplatten
41	SQX Mix	Sons of the Dragon	The Journey	10:49.01		
11	Stringent	Move D	10/11	05:19.95		Bine Music
42	Supra	Quantec	Isolate EP	06:25.04		
46	Trust	Terrence Dixon	Trust / Miles Per Hour	03:59.88		Open Concept
12	Twin Towers	Move D	10/11	02:08.52		Bine Music
22	Untitled	Superkord		05:57.09		Platzhirsch Limited
49	Vermillion	Bvdub	Wish I Was Here	11:48.05		MoM
43	Wish I Was Here	Bvdub	Wish I Was Here	11:52.05		MoM
48	Xine Rising	Sven Weisemann	Xine Zero	09:14.87		

Figure 9.12 Simple List.

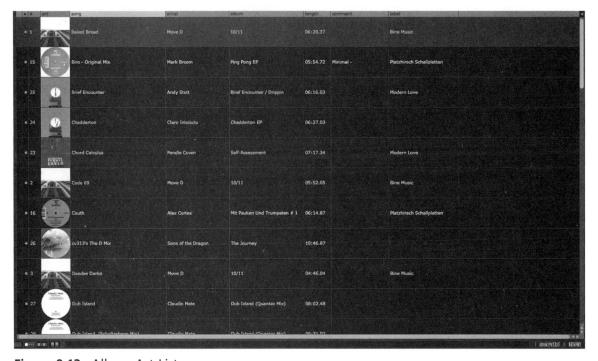

Figure 9.13 Album Art List.

- **Album Art Grid 1.** iTunes-styled list with track metadata nested to the right of the cover art (see Figure 9.14).

- **Album Art Grid 2.** Again, an iTunes-styled list with track metadata nested underneath the cover art (see Figure 9.15).

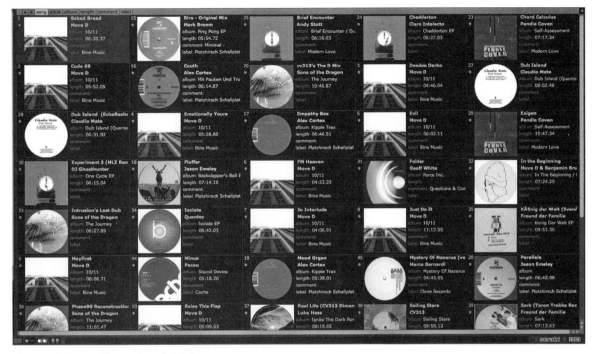

Figure 9.14 Album Art Grid 1.

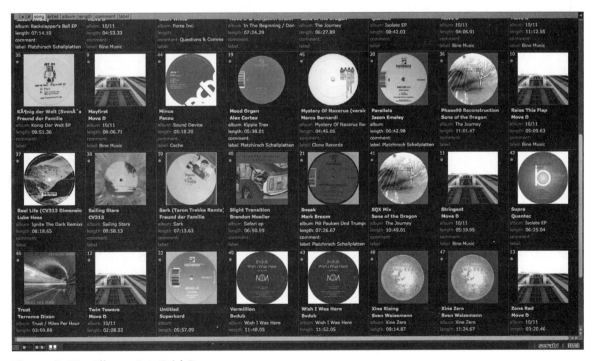

Figure 9.15 Album Art Grid 2.

Note: Adjust the font and cover art view sizes under Setup > Library > Font Size/Album Art Size.

Your Music Collection and the Serato Browser

Once you have Serato installed, launch the application after disconnecting the SL3 (or other supported hardware device). Serato's GUI should appear somewhat like mine in Figure 9.16. This is SSL's Offline mode that I mentioned earlier. Offline mode gives you access to a few critical features; most importantly, you can quickly perform track analyzation.

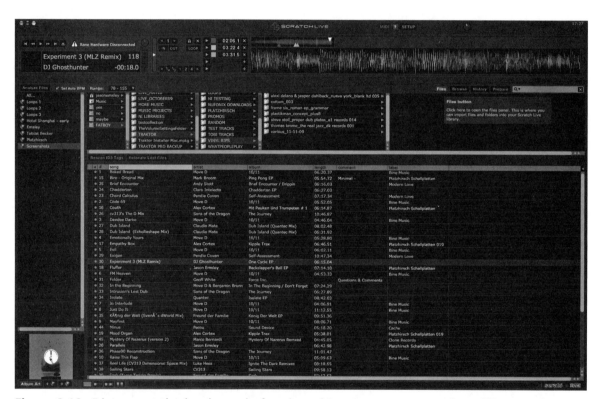

Figure 9.16 Disconnect the hardware before launching Serato to open the Offline mode.

Loading and Importing Your Music

Because no two performers use the same process to store their music, Serato's Library was intentionally designed to make importing music files as versatile as possible. Of the various methods, the most effective begins by clicking the Files button on the right side of the interface (see Figure 9.17). When the folder tree shows up, navigate to the folder

Figure 9.17 To import music into Serato's Library, click the File button and point Serato to your music folders.

or files that you want to import. Click and drag the folder (or files) and drop it (or them) on the icon labeled All within the Crates and Playlists window, found on the left side of the screen. You can apply this process to individual audio files, subfolders, or an entire directory of music.

As I said, there are also a handful of other import methods available:

- Open the OS X Finder/Windows Explorer and drag files or a folder directly into the Crates and Playlists window. Dropping the files/folder onto the All icon will import all of the songs into the overall Library, dropping the files/folder onto a Crate will import all of those songs into that Crate, and dropping the files/folder onto a blank space will create a new Crate with all of the relevant songs.

- Open the OS X Finder/Windows Explorer and directly drag and drop files onto one of Serato's Virtual Decks. The track is immediately ready to play and now resides within the Library.

- Navigate to Setup > Library > Read iTunes Library. Selecting this option will show and import the files within your iTunes Library. Bear in mind that this does not include any DRM-protected .m4p files—on the other hand, .m4a iTunes Plus files are supported.

- Load a CD into your laptop's CD/DVD drive, and it will appear within the Crates and Playlists window. The CD's contents will appear within the Track List and are readily available to drag and drop directly onto a Virtual Deck. Note: This method won't lend well to scratching; it is always a best practice to import your music and perform any required maintenance beforehand.

Note: Remember, if you are dragging files/folders from random locations on your hard drive, Serato won't automatically know if you delete, move, or rename those files. Once again, think of an organizational structure for your music and stick with it. You can find file-management information within the section titled "Organizing Your Music Library."

Analyzing Your Library

If you read through the Traktor chapter, then you already have an idea of what the Analysis process does to your music collection. Just like analyzing music files within Traktor, Serato's Analysis function scans your Library for corrupted files, creates the waveform track overview, measures track bpm, and compensates for a track's loudness levels with the Auto-Gain feature.

To analyze your files, make sure that your SL3 (or other supported hardware) is disconnected. Click the Analyze Files button shown in Figure 9.18. If you have thousands of

Figure 9.18 As I have done here, click Analyze Files to begin scanning the music within your Serato Library.

songs, you might want to go do something else for a while—if you own tens of thousands of tracks, that "something else" should be going to bed for the night. Even though Scratch simultaneously analyzes several files, large music collections take quite a long time. Alternatively, you can always drag and drop an individual Crate or selection of songs on top of the Analyze Files button, enacting the analyzation process manually.

Note: Once you have analyzed your Library, keep your eye out for the Corrupt File icon shown in Figure 9.19. Make absolutely sure that you delete these files from Serato's Library, as they are occasionally the reason why audio applications crash. Helpfully, Serato provides a breakdown of SSL's error messages within the user documentation.

Figure 9.19 The Corrupt File icon.

The fix? Often re-encoding audio files into a compatible format resolves issues with corrupted files. If it doesn't work, then make sure that you delete the file from your machine, because it could cause unforeseen problems beyond just SSL.

Set Auto BPM. As noted, analyzation estimates a track's tempo and writes a bpm tag into the .ID3 data. If you know that your collection falls within a particular bpm range, check the Set Audio BPM box and choose a tempo range from the drop-down menu shown in Figure 9.20. Doing so prevents Serato from accidentally doubling or halving the actual track bpm.

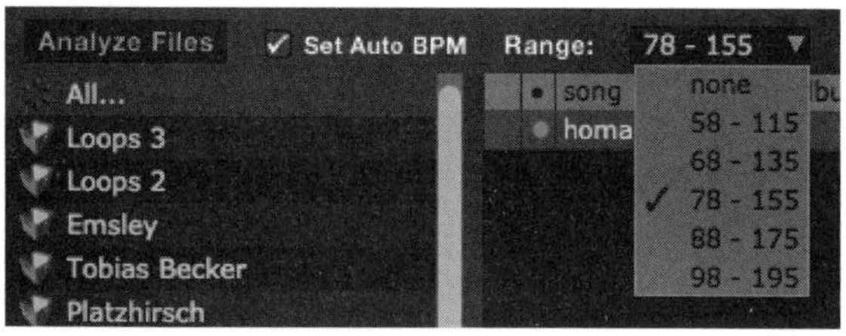

Figure 9.20 Use this drop-down menu to define a tempo window prior to analyzing the Serato Library or individual Crates.

Organizing Your Music Library

At the core of Serato's organizational structure lies the Crate concept—an obvious throwback to storing and transporting vinyl. Within the Serato Library, Crates generally refer to a collection of music files, whereas playlists (minus the iTunes Library) assume their radio heritage by referring to a schedule of what was or will be played.

Semantics aside, Serato's organizational structure is arguably the most efficient and effective on the DJ software market. Considering how complex a 500-GB music drive can get, organizational subtleties are that much more indispensable.

Crates

Serato provides you with two different Crate types: regular Crates and Smart Crates. Standard Crates are essentially folders that are used to organize your tracks in any way that you see fit. Smart Crates, on the other hand, intelligently organize your tracks through include/exclude criteria. Double-click on the text of either Crate type to rename it. Select any Crate and click Ctrl+Delete to delete it from your Library.

To create a normal Crate, click on the small brown Make New Crate icon (see Figure 9.21) located in the bottom-left corner of the GUI. With regard to standard Crates, any single song can be held within multiple Crates; you can reorder Crates by dragging them up and down the list, or you can drag and drop one Crate on top of another to form sub-Crates.

Figure 9.21 The Make New Crate icon.

For example, create a folder for hip-hop and then drag and drop specific subgenres on top of the parent hip-hop Crate. When you click and hold on a Crate, a dotted line will appear on the left side of the list. Drop the Crate on the left to reshuffle; drop the Crate on the right to create a sub-Crate. Depending on how deep you want to go, Crates with sub-Crates can even be dropped onto one another to create organizational hierarchies.

To create a Smart Crate, click on the small blue Create Smart Crate icon (see Figure 9.22) located in the bottom-left corner of the GUI. Use the subsequent pop-up window (see Figure 9.23) to define the Smart Crate's automated sort rules. This type of system cuts an immense amount of time out of organizing a music collection. Instead of having to perform the mundane task of keyword-searching specific groupings of songs or albums, dragging them to predefined Standard Crates, and repeating the process for hours on end, you could create a Smart Crate and define specific criteria, such as hip-hop and artist

Figure 9.22 The Create Smart Crate icon.

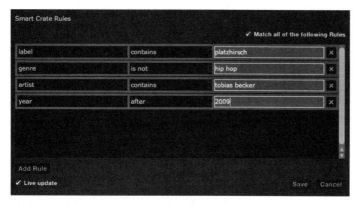

Figure 9.23   Use this window to define what tracks you want to include in/exclude from your Smart Crates.

a, b, c, and d. And to remain fresh, you could include the fact that you added the tracks to your collection within the last three months or so. Further, if you enable the Live Update function, this process is even further simplified because from now on any new tracks that fit the criteria will automatically filter into that specific Smart Crate. Easy!

1. Click Add Rule to create the first filter.

2. Use the first drop-down menu to select the filter criteria.

3. Use the second drop-down to select the include/exclude criteria.

4. Use the third field to specify the search term(s).

5. Click the X field to delete the rule.

6. Check Match All of the Following Rules to ensure that the results match up with every rule. Uncheck it to ensure that the results match up with at least one rule.

7. Check Live Update if you want Serato to automatically refresh the Crate if and when tracks are added or metadata is edited. If this option is unchecked, you will have to manually refresh the Smart Crate's contents by clicking the Refresh Crate icon shown in Figure 9.24.

Figure 9.24   Use the Refresh Crate button to update the contents of your manually managed Smart Crates.

8. Click Save to create the new Smart Crate or click Cancel to exit.

9. Double-click within the relevant text box to (re)name your Smart Crate.

10. If you need to make changes to your Smart Crate filters, select the Smart Crate and click the Edit button to the right of the Create Smart Crate button.

Tip: If you want to avoid making accidental changes to your Serato Library, navigate to Setup > Library and check Protect Library.

The Song Browser

The Song Browser is a criteria-based organizational overview of the tracks contained within your entire Serato Library or within individual Crates/playlists. Clicking on the header of any criterion will reshuffle the Song Browser into that order (or its reverse)—for example, click on Artist, and your tracks will alphabetize by Artist Name tags; click it again to reverse the order.

Tip: If you are having a hard time viewing the Song Browser's text, press Ctrl++ or Ctrl+−. This will grow or shrink the font size, respectively.

Further, right-click (OS X: Control-click) on any header, and a drop-down criteria checklist will appear. Select/deselect the metadata that you want displayed within the Song Browser, rearrange the columns by clicking and dragging the column header titles (such as Artist, Label, and so on), and then resize any columns by dragging left or right on the relevant handlebars that separate each column header.

Browsing, Preparing, and Searching. Searching for music during a performance can get pretty hectic. One obvious downside of having access to so much music is that once you go on the hunt for something specific, there are so many other tracks getting in the way. Serato really thought this one through, as is evidenced within a section that we have seen once already, shown in Figure 9.25.

Figure 9.25 Turn to these functions when quickly searching through your music collection is a must.

Let's say, for example, that during a gig I am looking for a track cataloged on the label that I release some of my music with, Platzhirsch. I have already created a Smart Crate that filters for tracks tagged with the label name, but for this scenario I want to be a bit more specific.

As you can see in Figure 9.26, I have enabled the Browse function by clicking on the button located on the right side of SSL's GUI. With Browse active and any random Crate selected, I am given an intuitive filter system of the fixed criteria: Genre, BPM, Artist, and Album. When I select an artist name, the Crate is then narrowed down to files tagged with that data.

Figure 9.26   Use the Browser function to perform fast searches across fixed criteria.

The Prepare panel, on the other hand, is Serato's virtual equivalent of "earmarking," or angling vinyl in a record box. While tearing through your Crates at a gig, simply press Ctrl+P to drop a track into this purpose-made "temporary" Crate. Don't worry too much about filling the Prepare panel; earmarked tracks are immediately erased when they're loaded into a Virtual Deck.

Tip: If you want to keep the Prepare panel's contents for future use, highlight the tracks and drag and drop them onto an empty space within the Crate list or directly on top of the Make New Crate icon.

Finally, if you know more or less what you're looking for but you can't find it, turn to the Search function. Press Ctrl+F to jump into the Search box. When you begin typing, the Song Browser intelligently filters around your text entry—a great feature, as you don't often have to type the full name. When you're ready, press the Tab key to jump into the Song Browser and skim through the search results. If you prefer not to search through specific criteria, click on the magnifying glass and uncheck the topics that you do not want searched (see Figure 9.27).

Figure 9.27   Use this list to remove specific criteria from your searches.

History

When you have invested some time into SSL, you'll have a pretty healthy collection of data from past sessions. This data is all stored within the History panel. From here, you can access detailed session information, such as what tracks you played, when you played them, how long they were played, and so on.

Tip: When you have a great set, navigate to the relevant session within the History panel. Drag and drop that session on the Make New Crate button—now you have a Crate holding all of the tracks that you played, in the order that you played them.

History Crate. You can export playlist data for distribution in various formats. SSL also offers a function that allows you to export and post Serato playlists to your serato.com profile. Moreover, using the Live Playlists option lets you post this information in real time! Enable or disable these plug-in options under Setup > Plugins.

Take note that several other History options are accessible; for more detailed information on the History panel's functions, refer to your Serato documentation.

Caution: Be aware that turning off all network-related services during a performance is an industry-wide practice with good reason. Even if you are not connected to a WiFi network, your wireless card will still actively scan for one; as a result, you may experience USB dropouts and/or general poor audio performance. If you must have an Internet connection, test in your home or studio before trusting the setup at a gig.

File Management

Undoubtedly the most fascinating part of digital DJing, file management is a necessary evil that is required knowledge of all performers. On the surface, file management primarily concerns two functions: working with .ID3 tags and the how and where of track locations on your hard drive. Editing .ID3 data (the metadata tags saved to your music files) is the simple behavior of, for example, changing the artist name or adding a comment to one of your tracks. This data is stored onto the file itself, so if you bring the track to another computer, the same data instantly appears exactly as you stored it.

Press Ctrl+E to jump into the Tag Edit mode. If you hold down Ctrl and press the left or right arrow keys on your keyboard, the text-entry box will jump to the previous or next field, respectively. As an alternative, you can simply double-click within a field to make quick changes to specific track info.

Album Art. One particularly useful addition to DJ software is the inclusion of album art. Not only is it a good way to tie visual aids to your music, but it also helps inject a bit of character into the inherently dry nature of digital file structures.

If your .ID3 tags do not already contain any album art images, simply drag any .JPEG or .PNG image file from the OS X Finder/Windows Explorer and drop it directly onto the relevant audio file while one of the Album Art views is visible. Alternatively, select a track within the Song Browser and drag and drop the image file directly onto the Album Art window located in the bottom-left corner of the GUI (see Figure 9.28). If you want to hide the Album Art window, simply click the Album Art button to toggle it on/off. To change the viewable image size, navigate to Setup > Library and adjust the album art size accordingly.

Figure 9.28 SSL's Album Art window.

Gone Missing. When the "S" hits the fan and you see the icon shown in Figure 9.29, for one reason or another your file(s) cannot be found. Luckily, Serato put measures in place to resolve these issues quickly and easily. If you ever find yourself in this situation, the buttons in Figure 9.30 are your safety net.

Figure 9.29 This icon indicates that your files cannot be found.

Figure 9.30 Use these two buttons to perform Serato's automatic collection maintenance functions.

Rescan ID3 Tags automatically scans your tracks for their original tag data. Inconsistencies show up as missing tracks and can then be resolved with the adjacent button, Relocate Lost Files. Click the Relocate Lost Files button to scan your entire hard drive to relink any and all files that the Library believes are missing.

To save time, you can apply both of these functions to lower tiers of the file structure—for example, dragging and dropping your Music folder also includes all tracks from within any folders underneath. You can drag and drop Crates and tracks onto either, though perhaps more effectively, you can grab folders or individual drives from the File Browser and drop them on one of the buttons—the result is that the scan process completes much more rapidly.

> **Tip:** A good way to re-create a function like Traktor's consistency check inside Serato is to first run the Rescan ID3 Tags function. Reshuffle the Song Browser so that all missing files are bunched together. Highlight all of the missing files and drag and drop them on top of the Relocate Lost Files button. If the files exist on any of your drives, Serato will eventually find them.

Copying, Moving, and Deleting Crates. If you are playing back to back with fellow artists, in some cases it doesn't make sense for all of them to bring their own laptops and hard drives. Copying a few Crates/sub-Crates to a jump drive is simply more efficient. To copy your Crates:

1. Open the File panel.

2. Navigate to your external jump drive within the File panel.

3. Drag and drop a Crate/sub-Crate onto the external drive.

4. Choose Copy from the window that pops up (see Figure 9.31).

Figure 9.31 Choose Copy.

5. When the progress bar finishes, doubles of your tracks will pop up within the Song Browser. Additionally, direct copies of the Crate's contents will appear on the external jump drive.

> **Note:** The previous actions apply not only to Crates, but also to drive-based files and folders moved within the File panel.

In an altogether different situation, follow these steps, but instead choose the Move command from the list shown back in Figure 9.31. Moving the files would be more appropriate when you're rearranging or restructuring your Library, as the function also changes file-path references.

When you get around to doing a bit of Library cleansing, deleting Crates and tracks is as simple as pressing Ctrl+Delete. However, be aware that deleting tracks from Crates/sub-Crates does not delete them from the *All heading. To completely remove a track from your Library, you must delete it from the main collection—in other words, from under the *All Crate.

In the end, if you want any file permanently expunged from your hard drive, simply select it under *All and hit Ctrl+Shift+Delete. Before emptying your computer's trash can, double-check that you really want the contents permanently deleted.

Preparation and Performance

From the sound systems to the equipment in the DJ booth, every venue is completely different from the next. Even DJ booths implanted with the typical "industry standards" have variations that have the potential to create havoc with your DVS product—from grounding, wiring, or setup complications to crowd and loudspeaker noise. Each situation has to be treated individually.

Fortunately, Serato uses a powerful calibration system that lets you manually adjust your setup on a case-by-case basis. If you have never touched a DVS application before, the process might seem a little bit complicated at first, but trust me, once you've done it a couple of times it becomes second nature.

On a cheerier note, Serato boasts several performance modes, features, and behaviors that cater to various performance styles. It's an application that doesn't care whether you are a hobbyist or a professional musician; just remember that knowing your instruments simply provides you with the ability to clearly communicate your inspiration. More often than not, this knowledge comes through a little bit of good ol' preparation.

When Should I Calibrate?

The intent of Serato's calibration process is not unlike that of any other DVS technology. Essentially, the record passes along an analog control signal, which in Serato's case is a combination of a 1-kHz sine wave and what it refers to as the *Noise Map*. Without getting too deep into things, the tone is used for both track playback speed and direction, and the Noise Map is used as a song position pointer.

Considering all of the unforeseen variables between the control record/CD and the SSL software, every scenario has to be independently configured. For example, bad tonearms and/or bad needles give Serato a headache—nearly as badly as dodgy wiring.

Another major factor is the amount of background noise where you are performing. Needles/styli are extremely sensitive tools; if ever you rip vinyl, try the silly game of yelling really loudly at your needle. Play back the audio file and listen closely. You should be able to hear yourself—and yes, I've actually tried it (sad, right?). Now imagine continuously amplified noise, and you have your event space.

With all of that background noise, Serato needs to know what information to keep and what to ignore; this point is referred to as the *threshold*. To calibrate Serato:

1. Click on the Setup tab so that you can see the scopes (see Figure 9.32).

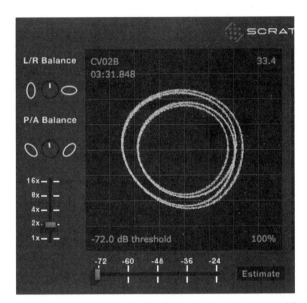

Figure 9.32 Adjust all of the appropriate Calibration settings from this Scope panel.

2. If you're using a turntable, set the needle on the record but leave the deck stopped. If using a CDJ, insert the CD but leave the CDJ paused.

3. Click and hold the Estimate button found at the bottom-right of the Scope panel (refer to Figure 9.32) until the threshold more or less stops moving.

4. Start playback on the turntable/CDJ. The scopes should jump to life.

5. Use the zoom (1×, 2×, and so on) if the view seems distant.

6. Adjust the L/R Balance and P/A Balance controls so that the innermost ring is as close to a perfect circle as possible.

Notice that the four corners of the Scope panel each contain different values. Top left displays current playback position on the timecode record; top right displays the RPM— that is, vinyl's 33 RPM or 45 RPM; bottom left is the estimated threshold level; while the bottom right represents the most important value—the fidelity of the control signal. For the best performance, you'll want this number at or above 85 percent—if it falls below, try recalibrating your system.

Tip: One of DVS technology's biggest snags stems from grounding issues. With the needle on the vinyl and the turntable stopped, you want the RPM value in the top right of the Scope panel holding steady at 0.0. If the value seesaws up and down, try adjusting the threshold. If you hit −24 and the problem persists, first double-check the turntable's grounding forks (ensure they're fastened to your Serato hardware or to the DJ mixer). If they seem okay, try moving power sources, such as power strips, away from your setup. If they can't be moved, shift your setup somewhere else in the booth.

Scratch Live Modes

From the beginning, SSL was formulated to augment the vinyl DJ's experience without abandoning DJ culture aesthetics. Part of the difficulty was that Serato not only had to encapsulate performance mechanics well over 30 years in the making, but it also had to counterbalance the old with the new, all in order to remain relevant within a massively fickle consumer market.

The result is Serato's own recipe of external vinyl/CD control, with an approach quite similar to that of its direct competitor, Traktor Scratch Pro.

Absolute Mode

While you are performing in Absolute mode (see Figure 9.33), needle positioning on the control vinyl/CD directly corresponds to the playback position of the loaded track—in other words, "needle dropping" with the timecode vinyl emulates needle dropping with real vinyl. Use Absolute mode if you want Serato to behave as true to vinyl as possible.

Figure 9.33 SSL's Absolute mode.

Note: You may have noticed that the Loop functions are missing from Absolute mode. The reason for this is simple: Once a loop is engaged, the "absolute" positioning of the control record is no longer relevant—in other words, the audio file's playback position becomes "relative" to the control vinyl/CD's playback speed/direction only. Switch to Relative mode to combine Loop functions with external vinyl/CD control.

Relative Mode

While you are performing in Relative mode (see Figure 9.34), the control vinyl/CDs only control the forward/backward (scratching) movements—in other words, needle positioning has no relation to track playback positioning. Use Relative mode if you are after skipless playback—if the needle accidentally jumps (for example, while scratching or when some punter bumps the decks), the track picks up precisely where it left off.

Figure 9.34 SSL's Relative mode.

Additionally, you should immediately notice that Relative mode offers several additional performance features over Absolute mode. Not only can you further develop your performance with SSL's Cue and Loop functions, you can also access the Load Prev/Next and Fast Forward/Rewind features.

Note: If you run out of record while using Absolute or Relative mode, the Virtual Deck automatically switches to Internal (also known as Emergency) mode. Once you drop the needle back into the control vinyl's lead-in zone, the relevant Deck will switch back to Absolute mode.

Along with that theme, if you run into trouble with your control vinyl/CDs (such as dust or skipping), hold Ctrl and click the Internal (INT) button with your mouse. Not only does this switch the Deck mode to Internal, but it also resets the Pitch fader to 0% so that you can immediately jump back into Relative mode (pitch is the same, position is not) when the problem is resolved.

Internal Mode

While you are performing in Internal mode (see Figure 9.35), the control vinyl/CDs are not used, and all playback functions are controlled within the computer. As vinyl/CDs are not controlling the Virtual Decks, use the mouse (or a MIDI controller rotary "platter") to scrub through the main waveform display or for large jumps within the track overview display.

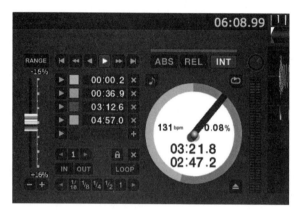

Figure 9.35 SSL's Internal mode.

Tip: Press Ctrl+I/Ctrl+K to drop a temporary cue point within the left/right Virtual Decks, respectively. These cue points exhibit the same behavior as a CDJ's Cue button—in other words, hold down the I key, and the left Deck will play until you release the key, when it jumps back to the cue point. Further, tap the I key to audition the playback position.

As expected, the Pitch fader controls the Virtual Deck's playback tempo, but note that by clicking on the Range button, you can change the % Pitch adjustment from 8% to 10, 16, 50, and 100%. Click and drag up or down on the pitch to decrease or increase playback tempo, respectively. Hold the Shift key to adjust pitch in finer increments.

All playback, cue point, and looping functions have preassigned keyboard shortcut assignments. Check the SSL documentation to see what those are.

Caution: Be careful when you switch from Internal to Absolute or Relative mode. If the Internal Deck is playing to the audience and you switch to Absolute or Relative mode, the Pitch fader will jump from the "internal" tempo to the turntable/CDJ tempo—not the most pleasant surprise for a dance floor!

Aux Deck Plug-In

Since SSL was released, Serato and Rane have made some great decisions when enhancing their DJ software/hardware design. One of the best thus far was SSL 2.0's addition of a third Deck via the SL3's Aux Deck plug-in.

Third Deck Setup

Navigate to Setup > Plugins > SL 3 Aux Deck and check Enable SL 3 Aux Deck Plugin (see Figure 9.36).

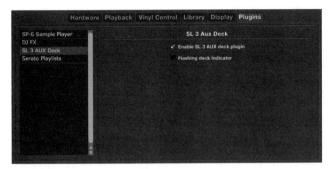

Figure 9.36   Ensure that you enable the Aux Deck plug-in if you want to use SSL's third Virtual Deck.

From the hardware side, simply route your connections in the same manner as the left and right Decks. The only obvious difference is in the labeling—that is, you route in and out through the Aux 1/2 input/output on the hardware, as you can see back in Figure 9.2.

Note: One minor drawback of employing the third Virtual Deck is that you are only able to view the waveform displays via the Stack View mode; however, the third Deck still functions no matter which display you choose. It may take a little bit of getting used to, but in my opinion, the option of using a third Deck versus not using a third Deck far outweighs being a stickler over GUI layouts.

Cue Points and Loops

Cue points and loops are one of DVS technology's unquestionable attractions. DJ software's digital feature sets almost always bring forth some form of attack from the analog crowd; cues and loops, on the other hand, rarely elicit any negative responses because of what they bring to a DJ set.

Of all the tools in Serato's arsenal, it feels as if SSL's Cue and Loop functions could use a bit of refining. Don't get me wrong; they work well. However, within a performance setting, Serato simply doesn't execute cues and loops quite as elegantly as Traktor does.

Cue Points and Hot Cues

SSL lets you embed up to five cue points/hot cues within a track's .ID3 data—more than enough for most purposes. How you seek out cue-point positions is a simple matter of how you are using Serato. For example, with the offline player (hardware disconnected), playback behaviors are controlled by the keyboard and mouse; whereas with the control vinyl/CDs, cue points are best found by needle dropping and/or spinning backward/forward within the track.

Note: Remember that by definition, cue points and loops can only operate within Relative (REL) and/or Internal (INT) modes.

Figure 9.37 displays the Cue Point section. When you find a good location, setting a cue point is a simple matter of clicking the + icon within an empty cue slot. Jump to cue points with the Play icon, delete a cue point by clicking the X icon, reshuffle cue-point ordering via drag and drop, and even change cue-point coloring by clicking directly on the colored box. On the other hand, if you prefer that your cues remain chronologically ordered, navigate to Setup > Playback and check Sort Cues Chronologically. (Note: Refer to the user documentation for a full list of keyboard playback controls.)

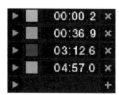

Figure 9.37 Use this panel to control and manage your cue points.

Cue-point playback behavior while in Internal mode is straightforward: Launch a cue point while a track is playing, and the track jumps back and continues playback from the cue point; hold the cue point, and the track engages a stutter loop. On the other side, launch a cue point while a track is stopped, and the track jumps to the cue position. Hold the cue point, and the track plays until released, at which point the track jumps back to the cue point and stops.

Tip: The difference between a cue point and a hot cue is simple: Cue points are generally managed and preset, whereas hot cues are still standard cue points, but they are designed for performance. To enable hot cues, go to Setup > Playback > Enable Hot Cues.

Hot-cue playback is MIDI-assignable, but it is also mapped out to and controlled by the keyboard's number keys: The left Deck is 1 through 5, and the right Deck is 6 through 0.

To set hot cues during a performance, simply click a number key corresponding to an empty cue slot. To overwrite an existing cue point, press Ctrl in combination with the respective cue-point number key.

Looping...Looping...Looping...

The Loop controls, shown in Figure 9.38, provide instant access to SSL's real-time looping behaviors. You can store up to nine loops per track, each of which is embedded into .ID3 data for future use and cross-Library compatibility. The simple, yet powerful parameter controls encourage performance-focused looping as a seamless, inspired process. For example, sparse drum intros are perfect for looping and lend well to layering with other tracks. If you produce your own music, use the airplane/train/car to quickly throw together some interesting drum loops, sound FX, beds, pads, and so on and use them to add some individuality to your DJ set. If you're into mash-ups, looping is one of the most powerful features you will find within DVS products. Get the crowd's attention by creatively remixing the hooks or other recognizable elements of popular songs on the fly. Def Leppard and Kanye never sounded so good!

Figure 9.38 SSL's performance-focused looping controls.

Basically, autolooping factors in a track's bpm data so that looped playback remains audibly seamless and perfectly in time. The action of setting an autoloop is as simple as clicking one of the five visible number buttons at the bottom of the Loop section. Each number represents a number of beats—for example, four beats make up one bar in 4/4 time, so clicking the number 4 sets a one-bar loop.

Let's say that you have engaged a four-beat (one-bar) loop. Click 4 again to disengage the loop. Alternatively, you can also click the Loop button to engage/disengage looping. While an autoloop is engaged, clicking another autoloop length will automatically adjust the loop length and continue playback. If the visible loop lengths are too long or too short, simply click the left or right arrow to expose further length options.

Once a loop is engaged, a fluorescent-green tinge spreads over the length of the selected loop (see Figure 9.39).

Figure 9.39 Although it doesn't look green in this black-and-white book, you can see the tinge that spreads over the selected loop.

Tip: The visible autoloop lengths are MIDI assignable, but they're also instantly accessible with the hotkey combinations: The left Deck uses Alt+1 through 5, and the right Deck uses Alt+6 through 0.

If autolooping doesn't offer enough precision, use the manual loop-in/loop-out commands for increased looping accuracy. There are a few different methods of working with manual loops.

From a stopped Deck:

1. Click the In button.

2. Use the mouse (or control vinyl/CD) to scrub to a desired endpoint. Alternatively, the left and right arrow keys on the keyboard make micro adjustments—hold Shift to make larger ones.

3. Click the Out button.

4. Start playing.

From a playing Deck:

1. Click the In button.

2. When the playhead reaches a desired endpoint, click the Out button. You should see the In/Out buttons start flashing.

3. If you need to adjust your manual loop points, click In to adjust the loop-in point or Out to adjust the loop-out point. If you selected In, Out will continue flashing...and vice versa. Although the track appears to have stopped, playback will continue.

4. Use the mouse (or control vinyl/CD) to scrub to the desired In or Out point. Alternatively, the left and right arrow keys on the keyboard make micro adjustments—hold Shift to make larger ones.

5. If you're editing the loop-in point, click In again to exit...or vice versa.

6. Continue playing.

If you are unable to (or you do not want to) use the control vinyl/CDs to manipulate the loop points, ensure that the function is enabled from Setup > Vinyl Control > Adjust Loops with Vinyl.

(Auto)Loop Roll. Of all SSL's looping functions, Loop Roll represents the most powerful of the lot. When applied creatively, Loop Roll can be combined with autoloop hotkeys (or MIDI assignments) for some pretty interesting results.

1. Set an autoloop with the hotkey combinations: The left Deck uses Alt+1 through 5; the right Deck uses Alt+6 through 0.

2. Holding the Ctrl key, drop out of the autoloop by hitting the same combination. In other words, if you set an autoloop by pressing Alt+1, drop out of the loop by pressing Ctrl+Alt+1. Notice that the track instantly jumps forward to where it would be if looping was not engaged.

As an alternative to this example, you could also continue bouncing between different autoloop lengths while holding down the Alt key. As long as you disengage the autoloop while holding the Ctrl+Alt macro, the Deck jumps the track forward to the exact playback position had looping not been used.

Now, if during all of this you discover loops that you want to keep, click on the tiny disk icon (see Figure 9.40), and the loop will be saved to the next available loop slot. To prevent accidental changes, click the Lock icon that appears, and if you no longer want the loop, simply click the X icon immediately to the right.

Figure 9.40 Save the loop to the next available loop slot.

Recording

DJ mix tapes have been around for years, and with the prominence of online social networks they are more prevalent than ever. In combination with the SL3, Serato's Record function provides an easy means of archiving a performance or throwing together a demo mix. Alternatively, you can also use Serato's Record function to archive your vinyl collection for use within your Serato sessions.

Using the hardware routing example back in Figure 9.2 as a guide, ensure that you are sending a copy of the DJ mixer's master output to the SL3's Aux In—for example, this could be a dedicated record out, a monitor/booth, or a second master output.

To record within Serato:

1. Set the quality of your recordings from Setup > Hardware > Recording Bit Depth. CD-quality audio is 16-bit, and that is more than sufficient for demo mixes; 24-bit, on the other hand, records at a higher quality, ideal for archiving your vinyl collection.

2. Select the Record button from the left side of the SSL GUI.

3. Within the Record panel, choose Aux from the Input Source drop-down menu.

4. Test your volume levels and adjust the Gain knob so that the maximum peaks register just below the red clipping point of the VU meter.

5. Click the red Record button to begin recording. The button will flash while recording audio.

6. Click the Record button again to stop recording.

7. Type a name within the Filename text box and click the small Save icon to archive your file.

8. When saved, all recordings appear within the Crate titled RECORDED. Don't worry if you don't see it; the Crate is automatically created with your first recording.

DJ-FX Plug-Ins

What DJ tools are more fun than effects? That's right…none! There really is no perfect time to use Serato's DJ-FX. In general, effects allow you to shape your own sounds by morphing a prerecorded track in real time. They can add ethereal space to a dry vocal or just as easily grime it up with some bit-crushing distortion. Slap a little delay on a static drum loop for some extra groove or thicken up melodic tracks with a phaser effect. The key here is to experiment with Serato's different effects types by using different kinds of sounds. For example, delays, echoes, and reverb (incidentally, each is actually a type of delay) sound entirely different on percussion than they do on vocals. Test them out on tracks you know first; then build outward from there.

Given the fact that Serato's software effects plug-in, Pitch 'n Time, remains a professional staple within the audio industry, discovering the level of professionalism in SSL's DJ-FX is hardly surprising.

Intro to the DJ-FX Plug-Ins

The first thing that you want to do is enable the DJ-FX plug-in from Setup > Plugins > DJ-FX > Enable DJ-FX Plugin. Next, click on the DJ-FX tab (see Figure 9.41).

Figure 9.41 Click the DJ-FX tab.

With the DJ-FX panel open, it should be pretty easy to grasp what's going on. The somewhat modular signal flow of SSL's DJ-FX offers two effects units that are freely assignable to any or all of the Virtual Decks, each of which is independently capable of holding up to three chained effects. Note that the audio signal flow passes from the left unit through to the right, so you should definitely try some experiments with the ordering of your effects. Unfortunately, Decks can only utilize one effects unit at a time; however, with three chainable effect types this shouldn't pose too much of a problem.

SSL's DJ-FX offers two different performance modes:

- **Ultra Knob mode.** Use this mode (see Figure 9.42) and its single knob to globally control a customized blend of parameters from all three effects units. As you can see in Figure 9.43, using this effect is simply a matter of turning on the effect, assigning a Virtual Deck number, and twisting a single knob. In this easy way, you have access to infinitely more parameters than you have hands available.

Figure 9.42 Select Ultra Knob mode.

Figure 9.43 SSL's Ultra Knob mode.

- **Super Knob mode.** Use this mode (see Figure 9.44) and its three knobs when you want more precise control over the three provided DJ-FX. As shown in Figure 9.45, using this effect requires at least one of three effects to be selected. Once one is chosen, assign the DJ-FX panel to your Deck(s), turn on the effects, and tweak away.

Figure 9.44 Select Super Knob mode.

Figure 9.45 SSL's Super Knob mode.

Customizing the DJ-FX

When you're ready to start customizing, click on the Show Parameters button (see Figure 9.46) to reveal a deeper level of individual effects parameters and the Macro Edit Mode button (see Figure 9.47) to enter Macro Mapping mode (see Figure 9.48). Once this mode is uncovered, the basic principle for customizing the DJ-FX in either Ultra or Super Knob mode is this:

Figure 9.46 Click the Show Parameters button.

Figure 9.47 Click the Macro Edit Mode button.

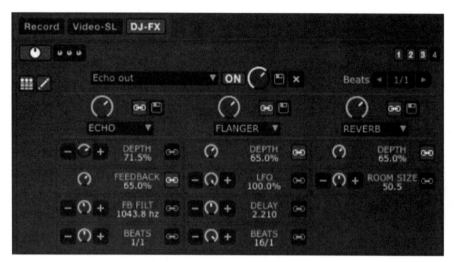

Figure 9.48 The DJ-FX Macro Mapping mode.

1. Use the Link button (see Figure 9.49) to bind/unbind the relevant parameter to the Ultra or Super knob. To customize a parameter's behavior, ensure that the relevant knob is unlinked.

   Figure 9.49 The Link button.

2. Twist the Ultra or Super knob to a start position for the custom mapping—for example, 9 o'clock.

3. Twist the relevant parameter's knob to the lowest desired position and click the Macro Min button (see Figure 9.50). This sets the minimum travel point for the value.

   Figure 9.50 The Macro Min button.

4. Twist the Ultra or Super knob to an end position for the custom mapping—for example, 3 o'clock.

5. Twist the relevant parameter's knob to the highest desired position and click the Macro Max button (see Figure 9.51). This sets the maximum travel point for the value.

Figure 9.51 The Macro Max button.

6. Bind the mapping assignment by clicking the Link button again—an active link is backlit orange.

7. Click the Save button (see Figure 9.52) if you want to keep your DJ-FX mapping. The Save button located beside the Super knob saves individual custom effects; the Save button located beside the Ultra knob saves a global combo.

Figure 9.52 The Save button.

In the end, it is quite difficult to explain what effects actually sound like. I could throw a bunch of adjectives and adverbs at you, but that's better left to the marketing guys. Your best bet is to just start messing around with all of the different settings and find out what works for you. Again, experimentation is the key.

SP-6 Sample Player

Aside from turntables, if any one instrument could be used to define DJ culture, it would have to be the sampler. In the studio, samplers provide artists with the tools to appropriate, shape, and then musically reproduce snapshots of virtually limitless source material. On the stage, however, samplers have steadily adapted over time to serve the immediate needs of a live performance. It's there whenever you need to fire off the infamous one-shot alarm siren, vocal phrases you have edited out of a track, drum fills, pads, as well as virtually any other audio source you can imagine. Drag and drop any playing track from a Deck onto an SP-6 slot for an instantly doubled backdrop readily primed for creative layered scratching. Echo out a track, use the SP-6 to drum out some one-shots, and slam back into your music for some improv action that energetic crowds tend to go nuts over.

Serato's relatively recent addition of the SP-6 Sample Player presents DJs with new possibilities that blend well with the long-prescribed techniques of turntables in DJ culture. Among other things, turntablism has always been about creatively piecing together phrases of different records—samples—to form entirely new versions of existing songs "live." The SP-6 is simply a new evolutionary limb grown off of turntablism's musical delivery.

Intro to the SP-6

First, enable the SP-6 from Setup > Plugins > SP-6 Sample Player > Enable SP-6 Sample Player Plugin and then click on the SP-6 tab (see Figure 9.53).

Figure 9.53 Click the SP-6 tab.

With the SP-6 panel open, click on the drop-down Display menu found in the top-right corner of the Player (see Figure 9.54).

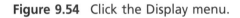

Figure 9.54 Click the Display menu.

Ensure that each option is checked so that the SP-6 shows up fully loaded (see Figure 9.55). The following list describes the SP-6 Player's functions and behaviors:

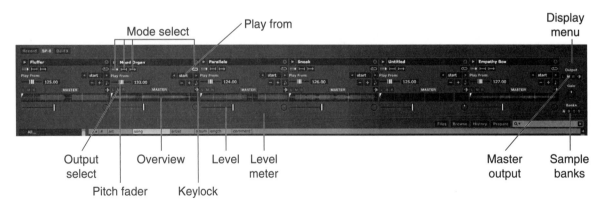

Figure 9.55 SSL's SP-6 Sample Player.

- **Mode.** Select how the SP-6 plays the loaded sample—in other words, the sample is triggered, switched on/off, held, or repeated.

- **Output Select.** Configure which output the SP-6 sends its signal through—for example, Left (L), Mix (M), Aux (A), Right (R), or Master. Outputs are independently assignable for each slot or globally for the entire SP-6 master output.

- **Pitch.** Use the Pitch fader or Bend, Nudge, and Keylock controls to manipulate how the loaded sample sounds against the music playing through the Virtual Decks.

- **Play From.** Defines how the SP-6 plays back the loaded sample—Start launches the sample from the beginning, Cue defines which cue point to start playback from, and Loop selects the loop-in section to launch from. Note that cue and loop launch behaviors are dependent on the mode selection—in other words, using Loop will play the sample from the loop-in point through to the end of the sample unless Repeat mode is chosen.

- **Overview.** Displays the loaded sample's waveform data, including all stored cue and loop points.

- **Level.** Use the Volume fader and Gain knob to control and optimize output volumes, respectively. Note that the SP-6 also utilizes its own overall gain output, located on the right side of the panel.

- **Level meter.** Use the Level meters to meter individual slot output volumes in order to avoid clipping.

- **Sample banks.** Use these buttons to flip between the four sample banks. With six slots per bank, the SP-6 offers 24 sound source options and configurations that are automatically saved and recalled within each new session.

Using the SP-6

From a performance perspective, the SP-6 Sampler was intentionally designed for quick actions—a feature absolutely essential to spontaneity. For example, using the hotkey combination of Ctrl+Alt+Z through N instantly loads samples, loops, or entire tracks into Slots 1 through 6. Alternatively, highlight up to six samples within the Song Browser and drag them up to Slot 1; drop the files to automatically map them across all six slots.

When you have loaded a few samples, launch them by clicking the Play button, by hitting the hotkey combination of Ctrl+Z through N, or by mapping the SP-6 buttons onto an external MIDI controller.

Tip: Because manually beatmatching the SP-6 slots to the Virtual Decks is somewhat awkward, apply the Virtual Deck technique of Instant Doubles to automatically match a track's playback position and Gain and Pitch values. While the track playback automatically does its thing in the SP-6 Player, you can manually do your thing with an instantly doubled copy layered on top!

SP-6 Play Modes

Before you jump into a performance with the SP-6, it's a good idea to get comfortable with the mechanics behind each of the Play modes.

■ **Trigger mode.** Pressing the Play button plays the audio file through to the end (see Figure 9.56). To stop, hold the Alt key and click the currently playing slot's Play button or press the appropriate Alt+Z through N hotkey combo. Press the Play button repeatedly to retrigger the loaded sample from the beginning.

Figure 9.56 Trigger mode.

■ **Hold mode.** Holding the Play button plays the audio file as long as the button is pressed (see Figure 9.57). Release Play, and playback stops.

Figure 9.57 Hold mode.

■ **On/Off mode.** The Play button acts as a toggle—clicking Play launches the sample, and clicking it again stops playback. The sample does not restart as with Trigger mode. See Figure 9.58.

Figure 9.58 On/Off mode.

■ **Repeat mode.** When this mode is active, launched samples will repeatedly play from start to finish until playback is stopped (see Figure 9.59). Load loops within the Play From function to engage automatic looping.

Figure 9.59 Repeat mode.

Additional Vinyl Behaviors

Because SSL is almost entirely constructed around the technology of Serato's control vinyl, it is pretty easy to understand that the records do much more than just move the Virtual Decks. Open Setup > Vinyl Control, and you will find a list of additional features specific to the Serato records.

For example, I mentioned earlier that loop-in/out points are adjustable with the control vinyl, but several other useful behaviors also exist. The relative-specific option Drop to

Cue Points is particularly useful; in this mode, the first five intro segments of the control vinyl instantly jump the Virtual Deck to any and all corresponding cue points established within your tracks.

Choose Enable Next Song on Flip, and you can jam through a sequentially organized Crate without touching your computer—keep flipping the record to load the next song in line. If that is not enough, if you choose to Enable Vinyl Scroll, the innermost track of control vinyl side A and control CD track 2 allow you to manually scroll through the currently selected Crate. With the vinyl, move the needle to the innermost track, scroll through your playlist (if you cannot find the track you want, pick up and drop the needle within the lead-out section prior to the vinyl scroll section to change crates), rinse, and repeat. When you have your track, drop the needle back at the intro, and the track will instantly load it and play. Adjust the additional setup options to configure how fast vinyl scroll jumps through your Library and/or choose to reverse the scrolling behavior.

Finally, use the Vinyl Start Offset dials to adjust where playback begins within the lead-in section of your control vinyl. Record wear is a natural part of DJing with vinyl, and fortunately Serato has compensated for that fact.

Additional Deck Behaviors

If you are new to digital DJing and DVS technology, one of the first options that you should enable is found at Setup > Playback > Lock Playing Deck. Checking this box will protect you against accidentally dropping/replacing a track upon a Deck that is currently playing to the dance floor.

Other useful options that we haven't discussed already can be found from the Playback page, such as Track End Warnings and Hi-Fi Resampler. The latter setting in particular is useful because it uses a more efficient time-stretching algorithm that maintains high-quality audio playback when scratching or repitching your tracks.

Intro to Controller Assignments

And, of course, all of this brings us to the most important aspect of digital DJ software: control. It doesn't really matter if you are using a keyboard and mouse or a tabletop of MIDI control hardware; as long as you are able to use your tools to perform, then you are doing your job.

If you have past experience with MIDI-capable software, there are parts of Serato's controller assignment that will instantly feel familiar, and there are others that might feel somewhat limiting. Of particular note is Serato's lack of external MIDI clock and LED output functionality. The former allows performers to sync drum machines and/or other performance software, such as Traktor or Ableton; the latter allows customizable, bidirectional LED states on certain MIDI control surfaces. A common application of LED status deals with parameter on/off buttons, such as with Deck playback or effect unit states (don't confuse this with Serato Approved hardware, which does support this behavior).

Keyboard Shortcuts

SSL's control behaviors are probably best exemplified through keyboard shortcuts, or hotkeys. Because Serato upgrades are released fairly often and quite commonly with new feature additions, it would be best to refer to Serato's user documentation for a list of supported hotkeys.

Personally, I prefer to have the option to customize control behaviors within my software; it's simply the way that my brain works. Thus, when I first used Serato years ago, my nose was a little bit bent out of shape when I discovered Serato's static key assignments. Admittedly, SSL's keyboard control template is highly logical; however, there is no leeway if and when the end user wants to customize certain actions.

The other side of this argument brings to mind another audio industry standard: Pro Tools. Using a fixed keyset, engineers can jump in/out of any Pro Tools–based studio and expect the exact same results every time they touch the keyboard. This also makes perfect sense in Serato's case when, for example, DJs tag with other artists. Sure, they may still need to bring their own tracks on a USB stick; but while playing, everyone is on the same page, no matter whose computer is getting used.

Tip: For Mac users, a company called iSkin designed a customized keyboard overlay that fits Apple's MacBook line of laptops. The overlay displays SSL's keyboard shortcuts in a logical, color-coded arrangement. One additional benefit of the overlay is that it protects your keyboard from the inevitable spillage, dust, and key wear. Visit www.rane.com and navigate to the Ranestore for more information.

Assigning MIDI Controls

If you are new to working with audio software and/or hardware, get into the habit of seeking out and installing the latest software, audio driver, and/or firmware updates prior to testing everything out. So before proceeding, check to see that you have the latest updates from the manufacturer of your MIDI control surface(s).

Within the last Traktor chapter, I mentioned that one of my biggest gripes about the application is how controller assignments are handled within the Controller Manager. Although Traktor supplies the most versatile MIDI implementation of any DJ software, the window is simply too small and is a bit clunky to work with.

However, within SSL (and Ableton, as you will see next), MIDI assignment is simple and elegantly carried out. To assign a MIDI command:

1. Ensure that your MIDI devices are all connected properly via USB 2.0 or an external MIDI interface.

2. Click the MIDI button from the top-right corner of SSL's GUI. You will see the MIDI panel pop out underneath the Virtual Decks. Within most audio applications, this mode is commonly known as MIDI Learn—clicking a software command with the mouse tells the application to "listen" for incoming MIDI messages. Any incoming MIDI data—from a hardware knob, for example—is then bound to the software command.

3. To view SSL's "hidden" parameters—for example, commands for the Left Deck, Library, or the Right Deck—click the Show MIDI Panel button (see Figure 9.60).

Show MIDI Panel

Figure 9.60 The Show MIDI Panel button.

4. As an example, let's say that we want to assign a MIDI control knob to scroll the Song Browser. Hover your mouse over the knob icon. As you can see in Figure 9.61, open commands display a gray pop-up window stating Unassigned to MIDI Input.

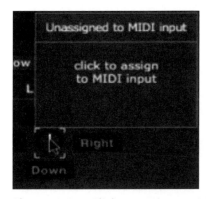

Figure 9.61 Click to assign to MIDI input.

5. Click on the software command and notice that the pop-up window immediately turns orange, signifying that SSL is "listening" for incoming MIDI data.

6. Twist whichever hardware knob you want to scroll SSL's Song Browser. Notice that the pop-up window shifts to green and now displays the assigned MIDI message.

7. Click the MIDI button from the top-right corner to turn off MIDI Assign mode.

Repeat these steps until you have a MIDI layout that suits your performance style. When you are finished, navigate to Setup > MIDI and notice that your controller mapping shows up under MIDI Presets. This preset management window is particularly useful if you have multiple controllers and/or you use Serato on more than one computer. As I have said before, creating the perfect controller mapping takes a bit of patience and even more experimentation. Remember to try things out—you're not going to break anything!

Serato Approved

Creative partnerships within the digital DJ market are quickly becoming commonplace. Serato's forthcoming venture with Ableton is a huge deal. A partnership with Novation has just (as of the writing of this book) released the Dicer (see Figure 9.62), a tiny pair of devices dedicated to cue points and loops. And of course we can't ignore the fact that Serato exclusively licenses out the SSL software for use with Rane's hardware. Another type of collaboration that results in some handy DJ hardware/software combos is Serato's "Approved" line of third-party USB controllers.

Figure 9.62 Novation's Dicer: an ultra-portable cue and loop control surface.

Companies such as Denon, Pioneer, Numark, and recently Novation have all developed hardware that instantly integrates with the SSL software. What this means for DJs is seamless access to a feature list premapped across hardware that offers platter (Deck) control, buttons, and faders—all of which cater to a specific style of digital DJing. I mentioned earlier that SSL lacks a MIDI LED out functionality; Serato Approved hardware bypasses that issue.

SSL's HID (*Human Interface Device*) support adds an impressive level of information feedback to hardware devices such as the CDJ-2000 (mentioned in the previous Traktor chapter). For example, with the Scratch Live 2.1 update, CDJ-2000s enable the remote browsing of SSL's Song Browser. So what? Well, not only can you use the CDJ-2000's hardware display to access SSL's Library, but the CDJ monitor also displays album art and even the waveform overview and cue/loop points once a track is loaded. Further, although Serato still requires a Rane audio interface for outputs (SL3 and so on), no control CDs are required because of a direct connection to the CDJ itself. To top it all off, HID supplies the software/hardware combo with increased low-latency responsiveness.

Serato ITCH

In line with these partnerships comes Serato's hardware/software combo, ITCH. Serato's intent with the ITCH software is to provide a platform for the hordes of digital DJs who are actively seeking out new methods of performance. Relationships with respected hardware developers such as Allen & Heath, Numark, Denon, and Vestax have resulted in some interesting hardware/software solutions.

In particular, the Allen & Heath Xone:DX mixer provides hardware control over ITCH'S internally focused mixing environment. With a specifically designed DJ mixer of Allen & Heath caliber, ITCH is coupled with a hardware device that provides a powerful USB 2.0 soundcard and unmatched control over the DJ-FX, cues, looping, and especially ITCH's four Decks with tempo matching and beat sync.

Needless to say, because of the boom in laptop-based DJing, it will be interesting to see where Serato takes the ITCH concept over the next few years.

10 Intro to Ableton Live

As mentioned in the previous chapter, the millennium-bordering years represented a significant turning point not only for DJ culture, but also for the music industry as a whole. Copyright and ownership became the ubiquitous themes that permeated industry discourse. By the time litigious bickering reached a fever pitch, a newly digitized music culture had silently moved on.

Surrounding the year 2000, computer market forces created the perfect environment for a new era of digital artistry. Laptops were powerful, relatively inexpensive, and capable of processing hard drives rammed full of digital audio files alongside software-based instruments and effects. Modern recording technology took what was once a stage full of gear and compressed it to fit inside a backpack.

We examined how with Traktor, NI was able to capture and streamline years of performance standards into an advanced performance interface, thereby revolutionizing DJ culture and maturing it into the digital age. Within this chapter you will see how Ableton applied a similar design philosophy to the studio paradigm and then threw the result onstage. This result was Ableton Live.

So, What Is Live?

Try to think of your laptop as a contemporary musical instrument. Much like a guitar, computers today accompany musicians everywhere between the studio and the stage. However, unlike a guitar, a laptop is also a drum machine, a synthesizer, a sampler, an effects rack, and a multitrack audio recorder. With Live, the same machine can be used for recording vocalists, teaching music theory, controlling theater sound design, remixing, engaging in multitrack music production, scoring to picture, composing art installations, running a record label, networking with international music communities…or specifically in relation to this book, performing.

While Traktor progressed DJ culture's methodologies, Live, on the other hand, optimized studio workflows into a product that is equally comfortable for a pasty studio tan or a lead singer's big hair. Go to Google Images and type something like "recording studio." Results will range from tiny in-home project studios to beautiful, wood-lined, multimillion-dollar control/live rooms. For fun, search for "Vince Clark studio." How's that for a control room? Now, how do you get all of that gear on stage?

Simple: Ableton Live...

To its credit, Live's inherent modular nature makes it very difficult to pigeonhole. You may be familiar with the "Big Five" digital audio workstations (DAWs): Pro Tools, Logic, Cubase/Nuendo, Digital Performer, and SONAR. You may also be familiar with some of the loop-based production suites: ACID, Reason, FL Studio, and so on. As with all software, each of these examples has relative pros and cons. What Live manages more effectively than any of the aforementioned is that it provides a vehicle for an artist's "Live" experience on the stage, in the studio, and in the figurative "gray area" in between. Yet, for these same reasons, Live is also somewhat more difficult to describe.

Is Live a DJing application? In the traditional sense, no. That is a realm more aptly fitting software such as Traktor or Serato. However, as I stated in Chapter 1, I don't believe that tools or venues should necessarily define DJs. Instead, only a broad answer describing the action of DJing is necessary. The fact that so many artists are using Live not only for music production, but also as the heart of their stage performance speaks volumes about the adaptability and potential Live offers performers.

With that said, how does one DJ with Live?

The tricky part of answering this question is that Live is so much more than a DJ product. If you want to mix two tracks together, it's easy. If you want to mix your music files alongside your own productions in combination with plug-in VST or Audio Units instruments and effects, you can do that, too. On one hand, Live provides the means to deconstruct tracks into pieces and reshuffle them as desired. On the other hand, Live also provides the means to construct tracks from the ground up, piece by piece. Imagine a DJ mixer in which each channel represented individual instruments—for example, drums on Audio 1, basslines on Audio 2, vocals on Audio 3, and so on. Don't like particular sections of a track? Within seconds you can edit them out. Every music collection contains tracks that would exhibit a higher degree of dance-floor sensibility with a bit more (or less) X, Y, Z. Unlike other DJ applications, Live provides several creative alternatives to shape that "something" into existence.

We will take a closer look at this later, but at some level, Live's Warp function and resultant Warp Markers can be compared to Traktor's Beatgrid and grid markers. For example, once a track is warped, playback is entirely synced to Live's Master Clock tempo, and thus, beatmatching is automated.

On the other hand, if you are into turntablism, you want to manually beatmatch your music, or you simply love the aesthetic of turntables and/or CDJs, Live is probably not what you are looking for.

Note: Since I started writing this book, Ableton and Serato have joined in a creative partnership to release the Bridge. Using what is termed *Ableton Transport Control (ATC),* Bridge provides you with tempo control over your Ableton Live sets via Serato's timecode vinyl and software. It is still early days for the software, but ATC stands to be an incredibly powerful means of manipulating Live's clips, track levels, sends, and so on within the Serato GUI.

As I mentioned in the previous chapter, synced playback frees artists from beatmatching's unavoidable time constraints. In turn, this time can be creatively refocused toward other performance techniques. Again, this approach is neither better nor worse. It's simply different.

Installation, Registration, and Updating

As I mentioned in Chapter 5, the process of software installation varies from developer to developer as well as between the Mac and PC platforms. Please refer to the software documentation or the company's online knowledge database for specific information on software and driver installation, product authorization, troubleshooting, and, if necessary, technical support.

Once Live is installed, activated, and updated, ensure that your computer is also running the most recent, relevant hardware drivers for any audio interfaces or MIDI control surfaces you plan on using. You can check that you are running the latest Live version by clicking Help from the application menu bar and selecting Check for Updates.

Live's Preferences

When you're new to any music software application, it's a good practice to do a little digging inside the Preferences. As a performer's location changes, so do the requirements of audio routing and MIDI hardware, as well as the look, the feel, and the overall behavior of an application. These simple reasons are but a few that spell out why an artist must learn to adjust the nuts and bolts that hold together his software.

For the purposes of *Part 1* of this book, the audio and MIDI preferences are the most relevant. Other settings and configurations will be noted as needed, of course, but take note that *Part 2* will necessarily delve into more of the advanced Live configuration settings.

Configuring Your Audio Setup

Part of what makes Live such a strong performance platform is the flexibility of its internal signal routing. Unlike the fixed signal path of traditional DJ mixers, Live's Mixer section enables performers to customize precisely how audio flows throughout the application on its way to an audience. Further, with a multichannel audio interface, artists can freely send multiple audio streams to any desired external destination—for example, a headphone cue mix or external effect sends—or they can connect independent track outputs to a mixer for DJ-styled control.

Audio Device

All of Live's external signal routing begins within the Audio Preferences tab shown in Figure 10.1. Your options for Driver Type will primarily depend on what type of computer you are using. For example, OS X users should only see Core Audio, whereas PC users will likely find MME/DirectX and/or ASIO. As mentioned in Chapter 3, Steinberg's ASIO driver will yield better performance and lower latency. If there is not an ASIO driver available, download the free ASIO4ALL driver at www.asio4all.com.

Immediately following Driver Type are Live's Audio Input/Output settings. As you can see in Figure 10.1, I have selected my RME Fireface 400. (Windows users will only see one option, whereas OS X users are given independent input/output options.) If you are not recording or receiving any external audio, simply leave Audio Input Device as No Device. Click the Audio Output Device menu and choose the appropriate soundcard. If your audio interface does not show up within the drop-down list, double-check that it is connected properly and then download/install the latest hardware driver from the manufacturer's website.

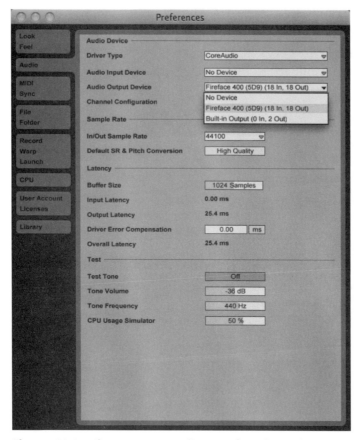

Figure 10.1 Choose your audio interface from the Audio Output Device drop-down menu.

Once you have selected the appropriate driver and soundcard configuration, you need to tell Live where audio is coming from and where you want it to go. If you have chosen No Device for your Audio Input Device setting, Input Config remains grayed out.

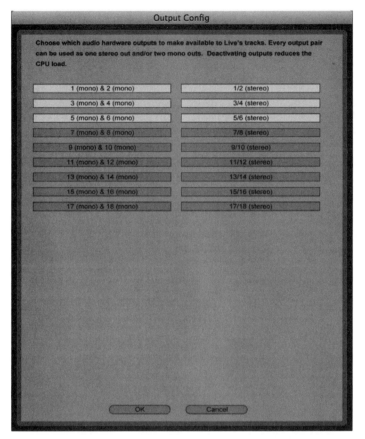

Figure 10.2 Use this window to enable any outputs that you plan on using.

Alternatively, if you need to record or process external audio in any way (synths, microphones, and so on), click on the Input Config box and enable/disable the relevant mono/stereo inputs. Next, click on Output Config (see Figure 10.2) and enable/disable the outputs relevant to your setup. One piece of advice: Disable any unused input/output options to save processing power.

To help put this in perspective, if you want to blend your tracks with a hardware DJ mixer, you have to enable a stereo output pair for each software audio track in question—in other words, Track 1 to 1/2 (stereo), Track 2 to 3/4 (stereo), and so on. Each software output should coincide with an available hardware output on your audio interface. In this external mixing situation, all cueing/pre-listening is done from the DJ mixer itself. The downside of this setup is that audio routing to Live's internal effects, or return tracks, is slightly more convoluted.

On the other hand, if you use a MIDI control surface to do your mixing, other setup options are possible. For example, rather than dedicating individual track outputs to your audio interface, the only stereo outputs required are one pair for the master out and one pair for the cue out. This type of internal mixing offers the most flexibility with regard to Live's internal signal routing—for example, for effects and so on.

Sample Rate and Latency

Now that Live recognizes your setup's audio input/output settings, you have to tell the software how best to handle these audio signals. Simply stated, Live's Sample Rate determines the quality at which Live records and plays your audio files. There are too many factors involved to cover in this brief chapter, but suffice it to say that 44,100 Hz should be enough for most purposes, as this is the same Red Book standard used for CD-quality audio.

Default SR & Pitch Conversion effectively instructs Live to process audio files with a higher-quality algorithm. What this translates to is a higher degree of accuracy when pitch shifting and a more precise result with Live's real-time sample-rate conversion. There are few reasons to turn this setting off; however, note that it can be disabled from individual clips via the little Hi-Q button.

I've already mentioned latency a few times; however, it remains a major industry buzzword, particularly concerning recording technology. In case you haven't been following along sequentially, *latency* can be simply defined as the time it takes to convert analog audio to digital data and back. Every system will have a degree of inherent latency that is unavoidable; however, to what extent is primarily determined through the combination of audio drivers and CPU power. Lower latency will re-create a more accurate experience at the expense of CPU drain. Specifically, there is always a measure of milliseconds between twisting a knob (or pressing a key, button, and so on) or singing into a mic (playing a synth and so on) and hearing the result through your speakers. Within Live, the length of this delay is controlled through the Buffer Size setting.

Think of a buffer this way: Say you go to a breakfast that serves endless cups of coffee. The cup is your buffer, the coffee is the digital audio signal, conversation is the analog audio signal, and the poor server is a depiction of your slightly aging CPU. Given that it's 7:30 a.m. in our example, nobody can bother talking until a full coffee is in hand. Halfway through the first cup, the server returns and tops you off. Conversation ensues unbroken. Once again, you finish half of your coffee, and, miraculously, the cup is full again. This is a properly configured buffer. Not only are you amped, but also breakfast conversation has flowed along wholly uninterrupted. As the restaurant gets busier, your table has to work harder to maintain a conversation. On top of that, the coffee is going down like water. All of a sudden, you pick up your mug to find the dregs sloshing around the bottom. Conversation halts, and you have to flag down the server for more of the good stuff!

This break in conversation is analogous to what happens when an audio buffer goes "dry." With a larger cup of coffee, the server wouldn't have to work as hard to keep your cup full once it gets busy. Conversely, coffee gets cold in an oversized cup, you won't drink it, and thus your 7:30 a.m. responsiveness will dissipate. With a tiny cup, forget it. Anyway, there is a happy medium in there somewhere, but it requires a bit of experimentation.

If the basics of audio buffers are still confusing, substitute coffee with beer and the waiter with a bartender and it might make more sense.

Like the coffee (or beer) in the previous example, the rate at which the buffer is expended varies on a case-by-case basis. Every computer is different, and every artist configures his Live set individually; thus, each Live set will make different demands of the CPU. My optimum Latency Setting will differ from yours, and we will each have to arrive at that point with a bit of trial and error. Within OS X, adjust the Buffer Size by dragging the horizontal slide display with your mouse or by clicking directly on the value and typing in a new number. Within Windows, click the Hardware Setup button and make the necessary adjustments directly from your soundcard's dedicated control panel.

Start from a higher value and gradually work downward. If your computer is relatively new, a good buffer size to start from would be 512. If you hear unpleasant audio artifacts (clicking, popping, and so on), you have gone too far. Raise the value until the artifacts go away, and you should be good to go. Be aware that adding further plug-ins and audio files might make this value irrelevant once your CPU strains to keep Live's input/output in order.

Tip: Concerning the perfect balance of input/output latency, check the Live Lessons found under Help > Help View from Live's application menu bar. Once the Live Lessons panel opens on the right-hand side, you can view the full list of Ableton Lessons. Under the heading Hardware Setup, walk through both Setting Up Audio I/O and Driver Error Compensation. Bear in mind that this process is absolutely critical to Live's overall latency and therefore performance. Get comfortable with adjusting these settings, because they are vital to using Live with any type of external hardware, whether in the studio or onstage.

Configuring Your MIDI/Sync Setup

Now that you are able to make some noises with Live, the next step is to exert some hands-on control over how those noises sound while escaping. With Live's Preferences open, click on the MIDI/Sync tab. Shown in Figure 10.3, the MIDI/Sync Preferences define global behaviors of all currently connected MIDI devices.

The top half of this dialog is used to assign any/all natively supported MIDI devices. Any device displayed under the Control Surface drop-down menu utilizes preset control templates referred to by Ableton as *instant mappings*. Simply choose your device from the menu and use the subsequent Input and Output drop-downs to select the relevant port connections. Given that the most modern MIDI controllers utilize USB 2.0, the Input/Output ports should list most devices by name. MIDI-only (think: Fader-fox second generation) control surfaces won't show up under the Input/Output; rather, select the name of the MIDI interface to which they are connected. Some controllers require Live's Dump command to connect with the appropriate template presets. If the button is grayed out, your device does not require it.

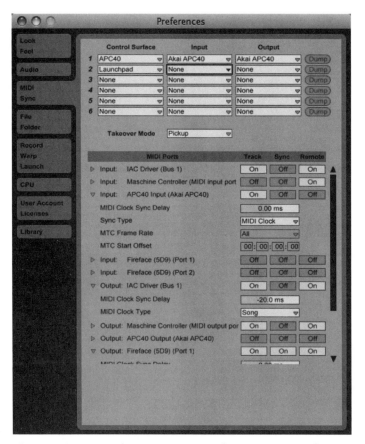

Figure 10.3 Use the MIDI/Sync Preferences to configure Live's MIDI behaviors.

If your control surface has features that send absolute values—for example, a knob that has finite clockwise/counterclockwise positions—use Takeover mode to assign the behavior of that parameter. For example, if a knob on your hardware is turned counterclockwise, and the Live control it manipulates is turned clockwise, once you touch the hardware knob, the software state will "jump" to the hardware value—which is usually a bad thing when controlling, for example, an effect's wet/dry mix. The change with None selected is abrupt, whereas Pickup is fixed until the hardware value meets the software value. Value Scaling smoothly transitions between the two positions until they meet in the middle.

The lower half of this dialog is used to manually configure specific behaviors of your MIDI devices. As you connect/disconnect any hardware to/from your computer, you should see it appear/disappear from this list. Enabling the Track Input function ensures that Live's MIDI tracks receive incoming MIDI information, such as notes played on a MIDI keyboard controller. On the other hand, Track Output sends MIDI data from one of Live's MIDI tracks to external sources, such as a synthesizer.

Sync Input and Output are independently used to slave Live to incoming MIDI clock or to establish Live as the MIDI clock master source, respectively, as well as to calibrate Live's sync offset. Notice the EXT button that pops into the top-left corner of Live's GUI if you click on/off Sync Input. Don't worry too much about this just yet; we will cover how to sync Live at the end of Chapter 12, "DJing with Ableton Live."

Finally, the Remote setting enables the selected hardware to control virtually any of Live's parameters. Remote Input instructs Live to "listen" for incoming MIDI control data and lets users assign this data to Volume faders, aux sends, plug-in parameters, clip and scene control, playback behavior, and so on. On the other hand, Remote Output enables Live to send feedback to controllers that are able to receive bidirectional status information. For example, AKAI's APC40 (see Figure 10.4) and APC20 (see Figure 10.5) and Novation's Launchpad (see Figure 10.6) use pads that light up green, amber, or red depending on the state of Live's clip playback. Obviously, this is quite useful in dark venues.

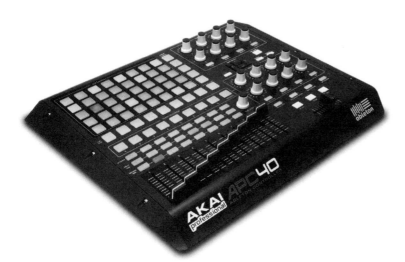

Figure 10.4   AKAI's APC40.

Creating and Saving Your Live Set

A *Live set* is Ableton's name for a snapshot of one specific session within a larger Live project. Live projects contain and organize all Live set-related information: clips, device presets, audio files, and so on. One project can contain several sets. For example, suppose you have a handful of gigs across a few different cities. If you know that your setup won't change between gigs, you can create a set for each city you perform in and, for example, export each gig recording for promotional purposes, and so on.

As another example, suppose you are working on an EP. Each set could represent individual songs and/or versions of the songs. Thus, you could use the project file to house every conceivable piece of project data. You can collect the original track and all remixes into one large file for seamless integration across all of the participating artists. Not only does this structure help keep everyone organized, but it also aids with archiving and file backup.

Live's File Manager is far too vast to cover in this chapter; however, there are a couple of key features that are absolutely essential to become familiar with. Under Live's File

Figure 10.5   AKAI's APC20.

Figure 10.6   Novation's Launchpad.

menu, choose Collect All and Save. As you can see in Figure 10.7, you will need to determine what data you want copied into the project file. If your Ableton DJ set consists of a music collection in WAV format, copying all of this information will take ages and could also chew an enormous chunk out of your hard drive. On the other hand, if

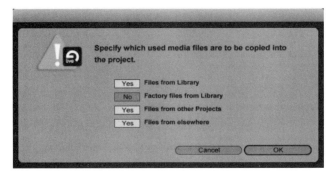

Figure 10.7 Determine what files you want kept within your Live project folder.

you are using sample-based plug-ins, it is often wise to copy this information over, especially if the project file will be going between multiple computers or artists. Regardless, if you are DJing with other people or simply archiving your current DJ set, Collect All and Save is absolutely essential to ensuring that your Live set opens at gigs error free —this is not always a situation where surprises are welcome.

One other essential File Management feature is relevant when audio files go missing from your Live set or project. If this happens, go to Live's File menu and choose Manage Files. As you can see in Figure 10.8, this process can be applied to the current Live set or across the entire project file. For this example, let's choose Manage Project under the Project header. In Figure 10.9, you can see that Live has caught a missing file. Clicking Locate takes me to the window shown in Figure 10.10, through which I can manually locate the missing audio file or allow Live to automatically scan specific portions of my hard drive.

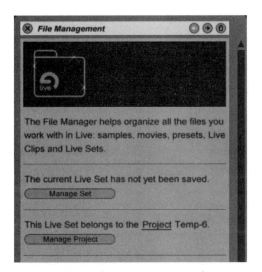

Figure 10.8 File Management lets you maintain files across individual sets or larger projects.

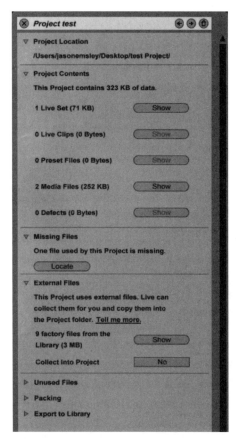

Figure 10.9   Whoops, found a missing file. Click Locate to resolve missing file errors.

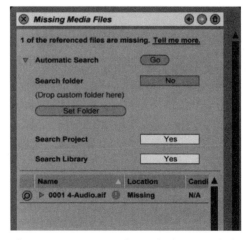

Figure 10.10   Use this window to define missing-file search criteria.

Live's Interface

Through Live, which is at odds with many of the industry's most popular DAW applications, Ableton has managed to design a GUI that feels right at home on a (relatively) small laptop monitor—a widely visible precondition of digital DJing. One way that Ableton accomplished this was by optimizing Live's GUI into two pages—the Session view and the Arrangement view—each of which is further subdivided into scaling, fold-able windows.

Note: Simply launch Live and press the computer keyboard's Tab key to jump between the two views.

Although undeniably powerful, many DAW applications can hardly be described as fun or engaging. Live's GUI, on the other hand, actually is a hell of a lot of fun to use!

Arrangement View

Figure 10.11 shows Live's Arrangement view. If you have any experience with DAW applications, this page should feel somewhat familiar. If you don't, the primary thing you need to know is that this page is where a song's composition takes place—it is where all of the ideas that form a production are brought together to form one cohesive piece. Though playback is nonlinear by design (unlike the tape machines of old), Live's playhead still follows the horizontally scrolling, timeline-based playback workflow shared by DAWs such as Logic, Pro Tools, Cubase, and so on.

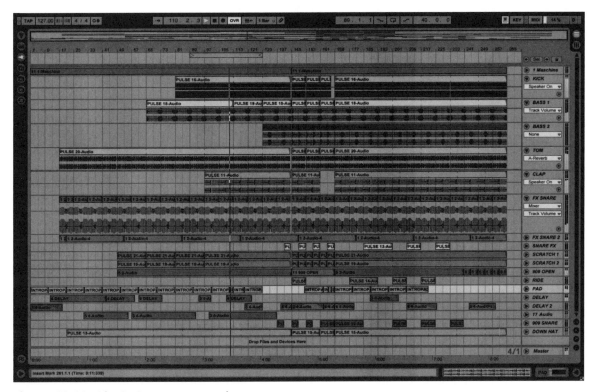

Figure 10.11 Live's Arrangement view.

Putting aside the production realm for now, let's look at two key areas for performers to bear in mind regarding Live's Arrangement view encompass (1) recording and polishing performances, and (2) editing audio files (songs, a capellas, and so on). With regard to recording, once you click on the transport control bar's Record button (see Figure 10.12 and 10.13), every MIDI-related action you make is recorded into the Arrangement page—an incredibly useful feature for archiving one-off performances or catching the elusive "lucky mistake" that only ever seems to happen in the moment.

Figure 10.12   Use the Live transport control bar to instruct Live's playback behaviors.

Figure 10.13   The Record button.

As you become familiar with Live's efficient audio-editing features, you make yourself dependent on the Arrangement view for virtually all of your audio reworking. As I am a big fan of analogies, think of the Arrangement view as equal parts workbench, draftsman's table, easel/canvas, sewing kit, and Lego set. The tools within this page let you break, melt, mend, combine, cut, paste, copy, and duplicate both audio and MIDI data to creative effect.

Regrettably, given the brevity of this chapter, I am only going to cover Live's Session view, for it exhibits the necessary feature sets for the performance style upon which this first book is based. The second book in this series will take a more focused look at Live's Arrangement view—specifically, the vital features it presents to adventurous DJs.

Note: Don't forget that there are many useful Live-specific handbooks out there. Of particular note are *Ableton Live 8 Power!* (Course Technology PTR, 2009) by Jon Margulies and *Ableton Live 8 and Suite 8: Create, Produce, Perform* (Focal Press, 2009) by Keith Robinson. Check them out!

Session View

Figure 10.14 shows Live's Session view. At first glance, the interface appears somewhat simplistic and dry. Trust me when I say that this is a good thing. Live's Session view is structured such that necessary features are compartmentalized and can be shown/hidden for clear, instantaneous access. Live performers do not need years of technical experience as producers, audio engineers, or DJs to understand Live's logical signal flow.

Within the performance realm, the vast majority of artists utilize Live's Session view because it represents a methodical approach to controlling sounds "live"—not too far removed from the straightforward audio routing inherent to a DJ mixer. One

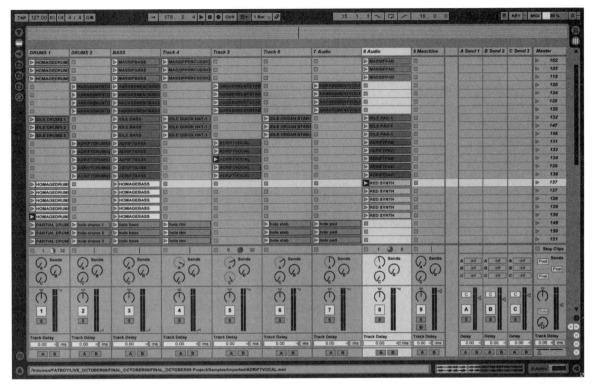

Figure 10.14 Live's Session view.

advantage is that this particular DJ mixer isn't hardwired, meaning that you can add and remove components as you like. Don't have enough channels? Add a few more. Need some more effects? Drop them in an aux track. Don't like nightclub DJ mixers? Find a MIDI controller that you love and use the intuitive MIDI Mapping mode to construct your own!

Notice that Figure 10.15 shows four types of channel strips: audio, MIDI, return, and master. Each type provides independent audio sources with a discrete signal-routing path to virtually any location inside Live's internal audio/MIDI signal flow, or sound can be bussed through a dedicated external audio interface to any number of exterior destinations—for example, a cue mix, hardware effects units, a DJ mixer, and so on. You can apply effects individually to each independent audio or MIDI channel, centralize them upon aux sends, or apply them across the entire master output.

Live's Session view is divided into a few discrete sections, most of which can be shown, hidden, and resized via an assortment of controls arranged around the rim of the Live GUI. For example, click the black triangles in the upper-left and lower-left/right corners to show/hide the respective Browser, Info, and Detail views (see Figure 10.16). Further, click and drag the thick black lines bordering each section to resize that particular panel.

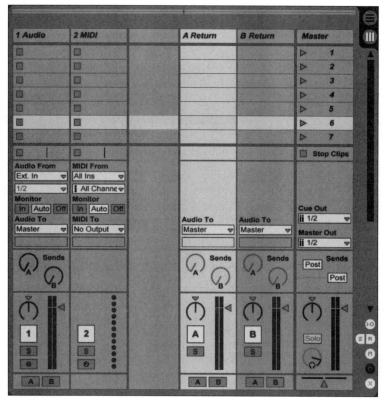

Figure 10.15 Live's various track types.

Figure 10.16 Click to show and hide Live's various view panels.

Tip: If you are new to Live, click the small, black triangle in the bottom-left corner of the GUI. (You can also press Shift+? on your keyboard.) When the Info view is visible, a concise parameter description is provided describing the feature currently located under the mouse pointer.

Live's Session view, shown in Figure 10.17, can be broken down into a number of functional sections:

- Transport control bar
- Session Mixer
- Clip/Track view
- Live Browser
- Info view

1. Transport control bar

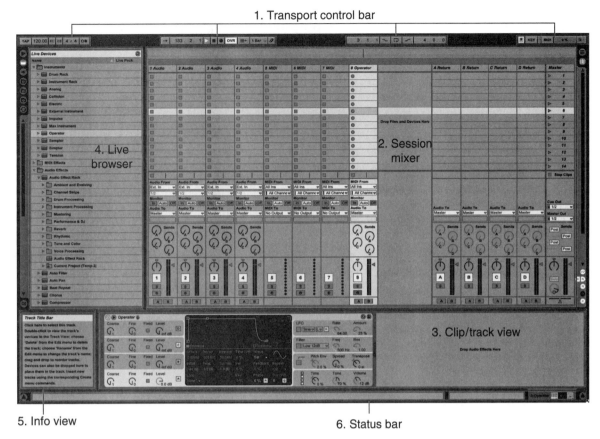

4. Live browser

2. Session mixer

3. Clip/track view

5. Info view

6. Status bar

Figure 10.17   Live's Session view.

- Status bar

- Overview

Together, these sections form the fluid structure that sets Live apart from other DAWs. Unlike the mix/edit approach of many other sequencers, what could be considered Live's "Mix" view was also intentionally designed as a performance interface. The grid-based clip slots (see Figure 10.18) smack-dab in the middle of the Session view

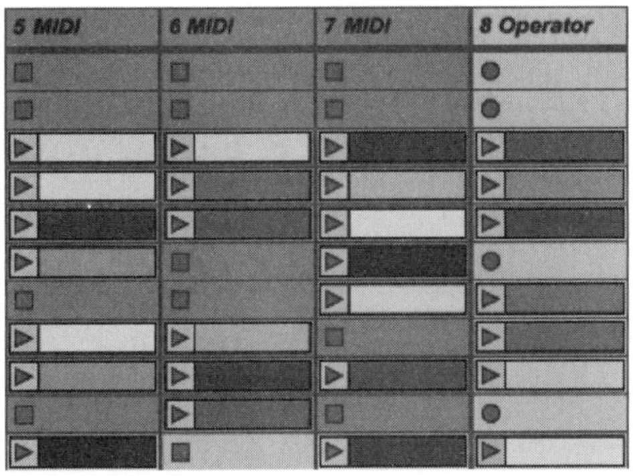

Figure 10.18   Use the clip-slot grid to hold, play, record, and arrange all of your Live clips.

were constructed as the antithesis of the timeline-based Arrangement view. Rather than following a scrolling sequence of events, audio and MIDI files in the form of Live clips (explained in Chapter 12) are triggered, or "played," using a methodology unconcerned with linearity.

The overall principle is fairly simple: The clip grid is composed of clip slots, each of which holds independent clips housing individual sounds, be they loops, samples, entire songs, or MIDI files. Entirely dependent on you as the performer, clips can be individually fired off in an improvised "remix" fashion, or they can be arranged into horizontal rows and launched in combination as a scene (think: independent rows dedicated to a song's intro, verse, chorus, and so on). Whereas individual clips house their own playback features, note that scenes (rows) of clips also have their own dedicated play and stop controls directly under the Master track header (see Figure 10.19).

Figure 10.19 Use scene launchers to play an entire row of clips.

To serve as an example, some performers strip tracks down into constituent "instruments," such as drums, bass, vocal, synth, and so on, while others use Live's audio tracks as virtual turntables to mix entire songs "DJ style."

Finally, nearly every visible feature, from track Volume faders, pan pots, effects sends, and Mute/Solo buttons, to those less visible, such as view states, track selection, and clip controls, are all readily assignable to computer keyboard keys and/or MIDI control surfaces. In short, Live does the adapting; the performer doesn't.

Session Mixer

Earlier on, I mentioned one particularly powerful Session Mixer feature—its modularity. In form, the Session Mixer somewhat resembles the structure of mixing desks most often found entrusted to studio engineers; however, in function it caters to artists ranging from DJs and producers to sound designers and composers—once again, with the live-performance angle at the forefront.

Each channel strip section can be broken down into functional sections. You can show/hide each individual section to reduce the amount of screen clutter—a useful feature for artists preferring a cleaner performance interface.

Glance to the series of six icons located on the far-right side of Live's interface (see Figure 10.20). This collection of buttons allows you to show/hide the various features of the Session Mixer. For example, even though a visible in/out section is essential when routing your audio and MIDI signals, you probably won't touch it during a performance. Try toggling some of the buttons and take note of the changes in screen real estate.

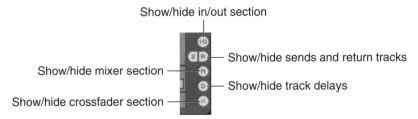

Figure 10.20 Click through the various Show/Hide buttons and notice how each button's on/off state affects the Session Mixer.

Depending on how accurate you like to be with your mixing, Live 8 allows you to extend the travel distance of your Volume faders, thus affording deeper mixing precision. There are two simple ways to adjust the size and appearance of your tracks.

1. Use your mouse to "grab" the horizontal line bordering the top of any VU meter/fader (see Figure 10.21). Drag up or down to expand or contract the overall size of Live's track volume.

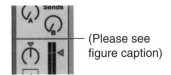

Figure 10.21 Grab and drag up/down to resize the track Volume faders.

2. Move your mouse to any track title bar (for example, 1 Audio). Click and drag the right-hand border of the text box (see Figure 10.22) to expand or contract the overall width of the Live track.

Figure 10.23 shows an example of a widened and fully extended fader. Each check mark delineates the logarithmic dB (decibel) curvature inherent to the internal hardware components of many professional studio/DJ mixers—and of no coincidence, the biomechanics of human hearing!

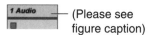 —— (Please see figure caption)

Figure 10.22 Grab and drag left or right to resize the track width.

Figure 10.23 Expanded Volume faders. How exciting!

Note: We will cover controller-assignment specifics in Chapter 12; however, until then, remember that you can map virtually everything you see within the Session Mixer to commands on your MIDI controller or computer keyboard.

Live's Tracks

Live's audio/MIDI signal flow is managed, sourced, and fed through one of four types of tracks. To some extent, all of Live's tracks share similarities; for example, the track Volume fader on an audio track behaves exactly the same as it does on a return track. Nevertheless, it is important to know where these differences lie. Thus, the following is a brief breakdown of the various track features provided within the Session Mixer.

Audio Track. When you're DJing with Live, audio tracks are the performance "bread and butter." For example, you could use one audio track to play songs from your music library; another to pipe a singer's voice through effects on Live's aux tracks; yet another for one-shots, FX, and/or pads; and a few more for snippets of your own productions. Further, audio tracks are able to host any assortment of effect plug-ins under the VST and Audio Unit formats or chosen from Live's wide array of bundled audio effects.

Figure 10.24 shows an example of an audio track. Dragging the triangular track Volume handle (fader) determines a track's signal output level, whereas dragging the track pan pot shifts the output balance left and right across the stereo field. The numbered Track Activator button turns a track's status on (yellow) and off (gray), essentially acting as a mute button.

In Solo mode, engaging the Solo/Cue button (S) singles out the chosen channel by muting all of the other tracks. In Cue mode, engaging the Solo/Cue button (headphone

Figure 10.24 Live's audio track.

icon) reroutes that particular channel's output through a specified physical output on your audio interface—in other words, this is one way you could cue or monitor your tracks before blending them into the main mix. Which output this is depends on the interface output that you choose from under the Cue Out drop-down menu (found on the master track).

Note: To switch between Solo and Cue modes, click the Solo/Cue button directly to the left of the master track Volume fader. Be aware that in order to switch from Solo mode, you must have independent outputs assigned from under Cue Out and Master Out.

Directly below Solo/Cue is the Arm Session Recording button. Until a track is armed for recording (red), the Record button remains grayed out. Engage this button when you are ready to record something.

The aux send (Sends A, B, and so on) pots resting on top of the track volume/pan are used primarily for effects. In short, the controls within this section take a duplicate signal from the current track and pipe it over to the corresponding return track (A Return, B Return, and so on), located on the right-hand side of the Session view.

Above the sends you will find an audio track's In/Out section. We'll cover this in a few pages under the section titled "Audio Routing," but for now remember that menus and controls within this area instruct Live on how to handle the sending and receiving of your audio streams.

Atop the In/Out section lies the Session Mixer's primary clip functions. You can place clips loaded into an audio track in any order within the vertically cascading clip slots, and you can stop them by clicking the Clip Stop button at the bottom of the clip slot grid. Notice the space alongside the right of the Clip Stop. Known as the *Track Status display*, this compact area provides quite a bit of information regarding what is happening in that particular track—for example, clip loops present a looping "pie chart" (see Figure 10.25) that cycles with the length of the loop, one-shots have a min:sec countdown, you get bar:beat feedback while recording, and so on.

Figure 10.25 A clip loop "pie chart."

Finally, click on a track title (name) at the top of a channel strip and press Ctrl+R (OS X: Command+R), and the track title bar will open up for renaming—quite a useful organizational feature.

MIDI Track. As I mentioned earlier, Live's tracks share several parallels. This is especially the case with audio and MIDI channel strips. For example, if you take a look at the MIDI track in Figure 10.26, the Track Activator, Solo/Cue, and Arm Session Recording (despite the tiny quarter-note icon) buttons are essentially the same. Further, within the context of the clip slot grid, MIDI and audio clips are handled exactly the same. The most obvious differences are the track Volume fader and the lack of aux sends.

By default, MIDI tracks are created for "traditional," or standard, MIDI purposes—in other words, they are meant to route MIDI signals somewhere else. As an example, MIDI clip data could be sent to play external hardware outside of Live, such as a synthesizer, or it could be sent to another MIDI track inside Live that contains a plug-in instrument device. Output volume would most likely be controlled directly from the hardware instrument while using this type of MIDI track; thus, there are no track Volume faders on a standard MIDI channel strip. The situation is the same with the lack of aux sends. MIDI data is just that—data; therefore, there is no need for sends on this particular type of MIDI track.

This changes once you drop a plug-in instrument on top of any MIDI track. Since the MIDI clip's data is now directly sent to the currently loaded plug-in, track volume and

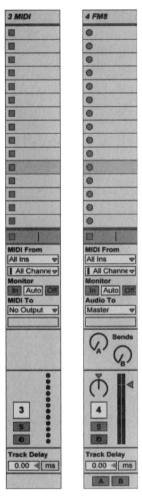

Figure 10.26 Standard MIDI track (left) and a MIDI track with plug-in instrument (right).

aux sends now make sense because the instrument is producing sound. Thus, the track appears nearly identical to an audio track—or an *instrument track*, if you will—which can be seen in Figure 10.24.

You'll find the final major difference within the In/Out section. Earlier, I mentioned that this area is where you instruct Live on how to handle the sending and receiving of audio streams. The concept on a MIDI track is basically the same; however, instead of audio streams you are managing the routing of MIDI data.

Return Track. In short, a return track (see Figure 10.27) is a throughput-only audio track designed as a meeting point for several audio signals—hence the reason it has no clip slots. Think of a return as a funnel that guides multiple signals to a controlled output. Live lets you create up to 12 of these funnels, each of which can handle individual instances or complex chains of plug-in effect units. We'll cover some of the various uses of return tracks under the section titled "Effects" in Chapter 12.

Master Track. On the surface, the master track performs one obvious function: output. In most performance setups, this is audio's last stop before hitting external sources and/

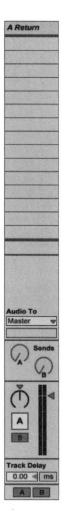

Figure 10.27 Live's return track.

or the speakers. Note that this particular channel strip shares the track Volume/Pan discussed previously, but also the toggle for the global Solo/Cue mode. While in Cue mode, use the Preview/Cue Volume pot to adjust the output signal.

Often, performers choose to apply subtle dynamic treatments, such as multiband compression and/or limiting as well as a touch of EQ, to thicken up their sound. Even a very, very small amount of reverb can add nice coloring to the master output. Just remember the adage that a little goes a long way.

As you can see in Figure 10.28, Scene Launch buttons replace clip slots. Playing a scene launches every clip within the selected row and is quite useful for dramatic musical changes or building compositions from intro to verse to chorus and so on. Akin to track titles, selecting any scene and pressing Ctrl+R (OS X: Command+R) lets you rename scenes row by row.

The Crossfader

Crossfaders have been part and parcel of DJ culture for more than 20 years; for many performers, they act as the bridge between two sound sources and have matured alongside

Figure 10.28 Live's master track.

progressions in both turntablism and mixing. Thus, the inclusion of an innovative cross-fader shows Ableton's awareness of the contemporary digital DJ and his kit.

If you are unfamiliar with what exactly a crossfader does, think of it this way. In the early days of disco and hip-hop, DJs had to carefully use two Volume faders, or two motions, to keep a constant equal loudness over the house system so as not to interrupt the energy and the flow of the dance floor. So, what could possibly be easier than two motions? That's right! One motion. The introduction of crossfaders allowed DJs to use a specially constructed horizontal Volume fader to blend two signal sources (turntables) in one smooth gesture. One pervasive example arose once turntablism took this functional need and shaped it into an art form.

Figure 10.29 shows an example of Live's Crossfader and its corresponding Crossfader Assign functions. It's very simple: If neither is selected, the Crossfader does nothing; selecting A assigns that track to the left side of the Crossfader; and thus, selecting B assigns that track to the right side. Easy enough?

Figure 10.29 Assign tracks to Crossfader channel A or B.

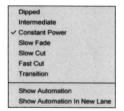

Dipped
Intermediate
✓ Constant Power
Slow Fade
Slow Cut
Fast Cut
Transition

Show Automation
Show Automation In New Lane

Figure 10.30 Use this drop-down list to choose between Live's numerous Crossfader shapes.

Right-click (OS X: Control-click) on the Crossfader, and things get more interesting. The drop-down list (see Figure 10.30) of Crossfader curves determines the Crossfader's "shape," or characteristic. Rather than individually defining them, I suggest that you mess around with different types to hear each curve's independent qualities. Note that these functions are, of course, assignable to MIDI or key commands.

Signal Routing

Arguably, one of the most important concepts for artists to get their heads around involves audio's signal flow. On paper, this idea is fairly simple: The flow of sound within any system moves from a source to a destination. What's more, how a sound moves in between these two points outlines everything you will ever do with audio.

If you are new to virtual studio technology (or any studio technology, for that matter), this simple idea can quickly become overwhelming once multiple signal routings intertwine throughout various signal paths and signal processors (FX, EQs, compressors, and so on). The most straightforward piece of advice on offer here is this: Follow your signal. If you aren't hearing sound out of the speakers, begin at the source and head downstream, section by section, until you hit the output. Think of it this way: As soon as an audio source (mic, turntable, drum machine, and so on) enters a system, it hits a series of checkpoints on its way to a destination—which in our case is the speakers.

Figure 10.31 My patchbays. Yay!

When analog equipment dominated studios, patchbays were (and still are) used as a means of rerouting audio throughout a system. Figure 10.31 shows two of the patchbays that I use at Format Project, my studio in East London. The upper is for audio routing; the lower does the same but for MIDI. Basically, they allow me to reroute (patch) audio and MIDI paths through my hardware. Live's internal signal routing follows a similar concept; however, audio and MIDI sources and destinations are rerouted through drop-down menus using a computer mouse instead of wires—much tidier and significantly more cost effective!

Audio Routing. Figure 10.32 shows an audio track's In/Out section. The labeling is fairly self-explanatory. The two drop-down menus found under the header Audio From are used to configure the where and the how of any incoming audio; simply stated, the top menu tells Live where the audio is coming from, while the bottom menu defines how to receive it.

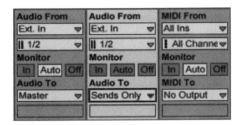

Figure 10.32 The Session Mixer's In/Out section.

There are several input types to choose from: Ext. In implies that audio will be sourced from an external source. Resampling uses Live's master output as the audio track input—a useful feature if you want on-the-fly clip recording of a performance or for creating new loops on the fly. This is especially useful when working with live bands and/or vocalists.

ReWire tells Live to listen for the output of ReWire-enabled applications, such as Propellerhead's popular all-in-one studio software, Reason. And, of course, you can use any audio track as an input for Live's internal signals, such as those from other audio, MIDI, return, and master tracks.

Note: ReWhat? ReWire is the brainchild of Swedish audio software developers, Propellerhead. In their words, ReWire is "an 'invisible' cable that streams audio [as well as MIDI, sync, and other transport functions] from one computer application to another." Not only is ReWire useful to link Reason with applications such as Live, it is also useful to link Live to Apple's Logic, Digidesign's Pro Tools, Steinberg's Cubase, and so on. Check out G. W. Childs' ReWire handbook titled *Using Rewire: Skill Pack*. It helps musicians makes sense of an often overlooked yet incredibly powerful music protocol.

After you configure an audio input, it is important to monitor (listen to) what Live is "hearing." The Monitor section is used to listen to the audio input after it has passed through any and all devices connected to that channel (this also includes aux sends). Different situations require different settings; however, Auto is generally the most appropriate mode. With Auto selected, incoming audio is only heard after the Arm Session Record button is turned on. Audio clips will continue playing until an empty clip slot's Record button is pressed. On the other hand, with In selected, only the incoming audio is heard—in other words, although clips will continue to play, they are not audible until Auto or Off is enabled.

Finally, at the bottom of the In/Out section is the Audio To heading. Using this drop-down menu, you can send an audio track's output to the master, to the return channels (via Sends Only), or through a specified audio interface output—for example, for external processing or effects or for specific advanced external mixing setups.

Tip: If you are using Live as an effects unit, or you are performing with someone who could use a little "Live" effects treatment, engage In from an audio track's Monitor section. Drop a few different types of effects onto that channel strip and directly control the balance of effects on the fly from your hardware controller. A tiny touch of reverb and delay can sit a vocalist nicely alongside the rest of the mix.

Alternatively, choose Sends Only from the Audio To drop-down for "on-demand" effects. This setting ensures that an audio track's input signal is only heard through the return tracks. For example, if you dedicate a handful of return tracks to different effect types, you could use Returns A, B, and so on for reverb, delay, and any other assortment of customized effects devices to apply as needed.

MIDI Routing. Within the "MIDI Track" section, I mentioned that MIDI tracks exist in two states: a standard MIDI track (without a plug-in instrument/effect) and an instrument track (with a plug-in instrument/effect). When it comes time to configure the In/Out section, there are a few important distinctions to remember. Akin to audio tracks, the first two drop-down menus are used to configure the where and the how of any incoming MIDI data; again, the top menu determines where the MIDI is coming from, and the second defines how to receive it.

For example, the defaults of All Ins and All Channels, tell the MIDI track to listen for any incoming control data. If MIDI is sent from a specific source, such as an external MIDI keyboard, another MIDI track, or even the computer keyboard, choose where to receive it from the first drop-down list. The next step (much like with an audio track) is to tell the MIDI track how to receive MIDI data. However, rather than defining an audio input on the external soundcard, you should choose a specific MIDI channel (if All Channels is not relevant).

Similar to that on an audio track, the Monitor section on a MIDI track "listens" for an incoming signal; however, in this case the Monitor section determines how the channel strip will respond to incoming MIDI data. For example, with Auto engaged, MIDI clips play their content, and connected MIDI keyboards are ignored until Arm Session Recording is clicked. Conversely, with In engaged, notes from connected MIDI keyboards are received, and MIDI clip content is ignored until Arm Session Recording is clicked.

Note: Overdubbing? Pay close attention to a MIDI track's Arm Session Recording button. If a MIDI clip's Play button is red, any and all MIDI data (notes, CCs, and so on) received on that MIDI track get recorded into the currently playing MIDI clip. This has benefits in certain situations, such as supplementing notes to a preexisting MIDI clip. However, when they're not wanted, accidentally recorded notes can lead to disastrous results during a performance. You can avoid unwanted overdubbing by disabling the OVR (overdub) button, located at the top of the Live GUI within the transport control bar.

The last major difference between audio and MIDI tracks is located under the MIDI To drop-down list. The default MIDI track only handles MIDI; therefore, the output routing options are limited to other MIDI tracks and/or outputs through a connected MIDI interface to any and all connected MIDI-capable hardware. The most obvious sign of this is before and after a plug-in has been instantiated upon the track. Before a plug-in is loaded, the Output Type header lists MIDI To; after a plug-in is loaded, the header lists Audio To—thus adopting the same Output Type functions as an audio track. Depending on your choice, Figures 10.33 and 10.34 show examples of the two different output types you'll find on a MIDI track. For instance, I have the option to send outbound MIDI through my Fireface and/or Maschine controller physical outputs—for example, to control external hardware. The other, when loaded with a plug-in instrument, gives me the option to route audio data instead—even though it is still a MIDI track that uses MIDI data to control what is ultimately heard at the output.

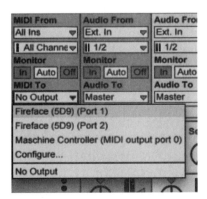

Figure 10.33 A MIDI track's Output Type without a loaded plug-in instrument/effect.

Figure 10.34 A MIDI track's Output Type with a loaded plug-in instrument/effect.

The Live Browser

The Live Browser is essentially a big software toolbox; in use, one of the most common comparisons is with that of OS X's Finder or Windows Explorer. Guaranteed, you will turn to the Browser for many of your Live performance and preparation needs—all the more reason why Ableton designed it for speed and efficiency. Shown in Figure 10.35, the Browser controls are located on the left-hand side of the Live GUI in both Session and Arrangement views. As with all of Live's peripheral windows, the small black triangle (found underneath the Tap and Tempo controls) shows/hides the window from view.

Figure 10.35 Click on one of these buttons to access your plug-ins and other Live content.

The primary purpose of the Browser is twofold: It serves as an organizational tool that provides instantaneous access to both plug-ins, such as instruments and effects, and Live-related files, such as audio, MIDI, and groove clips. The following sections elaborate on this.

Live Device Browser

Basically, Live's Device Browser is a plug-in folder that contains Ableton's Live exclusive audio and MIDI instrument and effect plug-ins. The available devices are broken down into three folders: Instruments, MIDI Effects, and Audio Effects. Most are included with the standard retail version of Live, with a few notable exceptions. For example, if you choose to purchase the Ableton Suite version of Live 8, you gain a series of powerful effects, synths, and samplers and an extensive sample-based sound library. Simply click on the Device Browser button (see Figure 10.36) within the top-left corner of the Live GUI to display the device list you see in Figure 10.37. Remember to check the Ableton website regularly, as the company is constantly adding new Live content.

Figure 10.36 Live's Device Browser button.

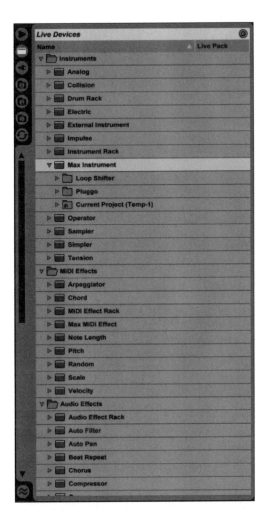

Figure 10.37 Use Live's Device Browser to access Ableton-exclusive instruments and effects.

Plug-In Browser

Live's Plug-In Device Browser uses the same idea as the Live Device Browser discussed a moment ago: It organizes your plug-ins. However, this plug-in folder is dedicated to all third-party VST (Windows/OS X) and AU (OS X) plug-ins—in other words, anything not made by Ableton. Click on the Plug-In Device Browser button (shown in Figure 10.38) to display your installed plug-ins, as I have done in Figure 10.39.

Figure 10.38 Live's Plug-In Device Browser button.

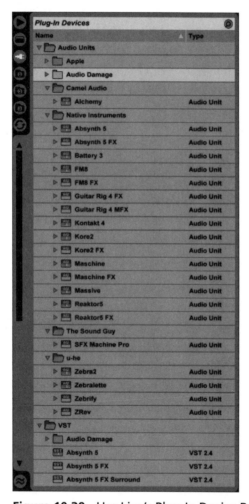

Figure 10.39 Use Live's Plug-In Device Browser to access your third-party instruments and effects.

If you discover that some of your plug-ins have gone missing, double-check a few things:

1. Open Live's Preferences and click on the File/Folder tab.

2. Verify that the appropriate plug-in sources are turned on and that the chosen VST plug-in folder reflects the directory where you have placed all of your

plug-in files (Windows). As an example, many artists using Windows-based PCs create a folder named something to the effect of "VST Plugins" and then drop all of their plug-in files into that folder. Point Live to this folder.

3. Click Rescan and let Live complete a search of your plug-in folders, at which point you should be good to go!

If your plug-ins still don't show up, consider getting in touch with the manufacturer in question.

This process is much easier for Mac OS X users. Most developers place their plug-in files within the same folder: Macintosh HD > Library > Audio > Plug-Ins. The relevant files will all be located under Components (AU) and/or VST (for VST files).

File Browsers

If you're thinking of bringing Live into your DJ performance, picture the File Browser as your digital record crate. Just remember that there is no "correct" way to use Live; some artists prefer the in-the-moment approach, digging through their music library on the fly, whereas others preconfigure their Live sets and never once touch the Browser, and still others use a combination of both methods.

As you can see in Figures 10.40 and 10.41, the Browser displays three numbered folder icons. They are replicates of one another, each intended as a different view into your hard drive. For example, try setting one for loops, one for tracks, and one for MIDI files. However you choose to use the File Browser, note that you can bookmark frequently used locations on your hard drive. To do so:

Figure 10.40   Live's File Browser button.

1. Click on File Browser 1, 2, or 3 from the left-hand side of the Live GUI.

2. Navigate the chosen File Browser to a folder you wish to assign as default.

3. Right-click (OS X: Control-click) on the folder and choose Set as Root, as shown in Figure 10.42.

4. Click on the bookmarks at the top of the File Browser. Choose the option to Bookmark Current Folder, as shown in Figure 10.43. Now, this folder appears within the drop-down menu, allowing you to instantly jump from one location to another without having to dig through file hierarchies.

Look at the bottom of the File Browser. This small window is known as Live's Preview tab (see Figure 10.44)—a useful feature if you want to pre-listen to any source material,

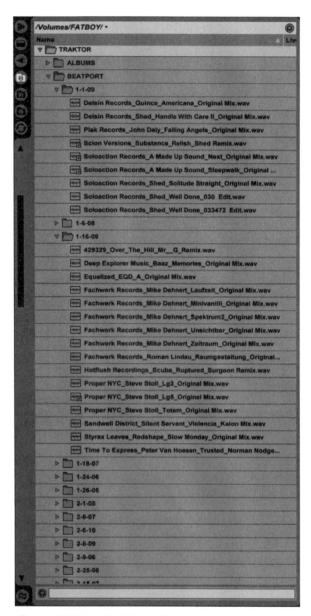

Figure 10.41 Use Live's File Browser to access your Live clips, music files, presets, Live sets, and of course, your tracks.

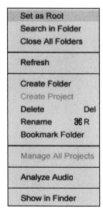

Figure 10.42 Choose Set as Root from the menu.

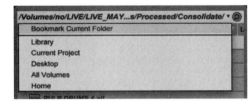

Figure 10.43 Choose Bookmark Current Folder.

Figure 10.44 Use Live's Preview tab to pre-listen or audition your material prior to mixing it to the crowd.

such as tracks, loops, MIDI files, and so on, against the currently playing audio. For example, if your Live set is playing at 120 bpm, click on any audio file within the File Browser, and it will play back in time with the Live set, no matter what the file's original bpm. Click the small headphone icon to enable/disable the Preview tab's autoplay function. Additionally, engage the button labeled Raw from the right-hand side if you would rather hear the file as it was recorded, irrespective of the master tempo.

Using the Browser

Within the previous Traktor chapters I mention my belief that the success or failure of a DJ application is founded upon a handful of core elements. One cornerstone in particular is an application's ability to integrate browser functions that are both immediate and intuitive. Thus, optimizing a transparent "toolbox" is especially crucial for relatively open-ended DJ applications, such as Live.

Loading and Managing Your Plug-In Tools. Thankfully, Ableton made bringing these tools into Live an extremely simple matter. Using behaviors that should be familiar to most computer users, the two primary means of introducing new elements into Live are via drag and drop or via double-click. You can instantly incorporate plug-ins, tracks from your music library, audio and MIDI clips, and even entire Live sets into the current project you are working on. However, one particularly important thing to remember is the situational behavior of each action. For example...

Select an AU (OS X), VST (OS X or Windows), or Live effect/instrument device from the Browser and then drag and drop it into the empty space of the aptly named Clip/Device Drop Area. Depending on the chosen device, Live logically creates an audio or MIDI track and instantiates the device upon it. Alternatively, you can apply the same drag-and-drop maneuver on any track, regardless of type. (Instruments cannot be instantiated on aux tracks or the master.) However, this behavior differs on tracks with preexisting plug-in devices, as you will see in a moment.

Concerning either Live's or third-party plug-in devices, if *no* MIDI track is selected within the Session Mixer, double-clicking an instrument icon within the Browser will create a new MIDI track and instantiate the selected instrument plug-in upon it. On the other hand, if *any* MIDI track was selected within the Session Mixer, double-clicking a new instrument will overwrite any and all existing plug-ins upon that track (for example, instruments and effects) and instantiate the selected instrument upon it.

Effects, on the other hand, can be stacked upon audio, MIDI, and aux tracks, as well as the master. Suppose you want to chain a handful of effects in serial, such as a delay output into reverb into distortion, and so on. Select any track type and start double-clicking away at the effects you want to use. Notice that each new device stacks up within the horizontal Track view window.

Here's a little two-parter for you:

Tip:
- When you are happy with a clip and the assortment of instrument and/or effects devices loaded onto that track, drag and drop a clip (or a selection of clips) back into the Browser. Not only will this action save your clip settings, but it will also take a snapshot of the devices on that channel strip. Now, every time that clip is brought into a Live set, Live will create a new track loaded with all of the relevant devices and their settings.

- Hold down the Shift key on your computer keyboard and use your mouse to select multiple clips within the Live Browser. Drag and drop the clips onto the Clip/Device Drop Area. Notice how the clips align vertically within a newly created track. This behavior is particularly suited when importing a selection of clips to be played in random order—for example, clips with different variations of the same drum loop. Do it again, but this time hold the Shift key and watch as the clips flip to align horizontally across the Clip/Device Drop Area. This behavior is particularly useful if you are playing songs or parts of songs that are to be mixed together from different Session Mixer channels.

These behaviors do not only apply to instrument and effect plug-in devices. Importantly, this is a shared action across Live's entire Browser. Using one of the three available File Browsers, you can introduce audio and MIDI clips to the existing performance, and you can seamlessly merge previous Live sets into the current project. Figure 10.45 shows an example of the four primary icons you will run across while using the File Browser. From the top down: The file with the Ableton symbol is an entire Live set; the file ending in .mid is a standard MIDI file, usable on any MIDI

Figure 10.45 Icons help distinguish between file types.

track; the file ending in .alc is an audio clip file, containing all relevant preset information; and the file ending in .aif (OS X) is a standard audio file—the tiny check mark signifies that the file has been analyzed by Live and is therefore ready to drag and drop into any Live set.

Finally, the Browser also exhibits other standardized computer behaviors, such as Cut, Copy, and Paste (Ctrl/Command+X, Ctrl/Command+C, Ctrl/Command+V, respectively). Right-clicking (Control-clicking) on any file or folder opens a drop-down menu of additional maintenance functions, such as file renaming, searching, and the ability to create new folders. Click the tiny magnifying glass in the top-right corner of the Browser to perform a file search within the directory listed above the text-entry box.

Live's Control Bar

When you are ready to get things moving, turn your attention to the strip of icons arranged horizontally along the top of Live's GUI, known as Live's *control bar*. These parameters range in function from controlling Live's tempo, playback, and recording behaviors, to handling keyboard/MIDI controller assignment functions and status feedback messages. The actions dictated by the control bar are global and thus share the same layout in both Arrangement and Session views. As some features primarily concern the realm of production, I will only cover the handful of controls essential to performance. To get going (or to stop), simply press your spacebar!

In Figure 10.46, you will notice that the control bar is broken into four dedicated sections.

Figure 10.46 Live's control bar.

The first subsection of the control bar regulates Live's tempo behavior. Shown in Figure 10.47, each icon manages a specific aspect of Live's playback timing. For example, artists performing alongside DJs (or live musicians) may find the Tap function particularly useful. From a standstill, hitting Tap four times to the beat of the currently playing track will launch Live's playback in sync to your count-in. If the tempo is not quite

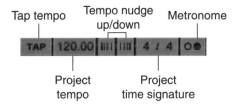

Figure 10.47 Live's tempo controls.

on, keep tapping, and Live will adjust the playback tempo to suit. Note that the Tap button is assignable to computer keyboard or MIDI controller messages—definitely something you should consider in place of tempo tapping with your computer's mouse or trackpad.

Immediately to the right of the Tap function is the Tempo display. No matter whether Live is the master tempo source or synced to external gear, this field reflects Live's current playback bpm. When Live sets the master tempo, click within this field to manually type in an overall bpm value.

Tip: Much like a turntable's or CDJ's pitch fader, the whole number (coarse) and decimal (fine) fields are independently assignable to MIDI controller buttons/faders/knobs for hands-on tempo changes.

If you find yourself performing with other artists, and you are not able to MIDI-sync your setup (for example, you're playing with a vinyl DJ), the next two controls will become your best friends. The two Tempo Nudge buttons are Live's way of allowing you to emulate the vinyl/CD DJ staple of *pitch bumping*, or temporarily speeding or slowing playback to bring drifting tempos back into sync. It should be fairly obvious that these buttons are at their most powerful once they are assigned to some type of controller, be it a computer keyboard or MIDI hardware.

The second subsection of the control bar houses Live's transport functions. Many of the functions shown in Figure 10.48 concern the Arrangement page, so we will skip over those for now. However, pay particular attention to the Quantization menu shown in Figure 10.49. The selection that you make here will determine the global launch behavior of your audio and MIDI clips (with respect to individual Clip Quantization settings). For example, most performers I know use the default option of 1 Bar. In this scenario, all clips using global Clip Quantization settings (described throughout Chapter 11) will launch at the first downbeat of each bar—for example, while Live is playing, if you click the Play button on any clip at the position of 1.1.3, it will flash until it launches at the first downbeat of the next bar, or 2.1.1. (This also applies to stopping clips.) I cannot stress enough the significance of understanding this feature.

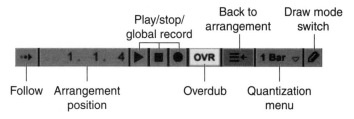

Figure 10.48 Live's transport functions.

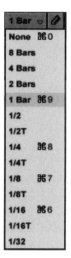

Figure 10.49 Use this drop-down menu to select global quantization behavior.

Whether you're performing solo or with other artists, whatever value you choose here will establish the rhythmic flow of your Live set.

For now, bypass the third subsection and focus on the fourth. In Figure 10.50 you will find the tools for customizing Live's internal control set and observing your system's status feedback. Key and MIDI each engage Map modes (covered in Chapter 12 under the section titled "Mapping Live's Controller Assignments") for either your computer keyboard or your external MIDI control devices. These assignments are useful for everything from simple fader adjustment and mute/solo commands to VST/AU plug-in parameter controls. Once control parameters have been mapped, the two tiny display boxes squished between the Key and MIDI buttons will flash when mapped parameters are received or sent, respectively.

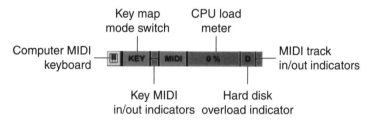

Figure 10.50 Here you will find Live's Key/MIDI Map modes as well as critical system status feedback displays.

To the right, the rectangular box containing a percentage value is Live's CPU Load meter. As you begin adding instruments and effects to your Live set, this percentage will gradually increase as further demands are placed on your CPU. Consider removing plug-ins if you near 80 percent or so, as you will likely begin experiencing unpleasant audio artifacts, dropouts, and so on.

Akin to the CPU meter is the Hard Disk Overload indicator, represented by a box containing the letter D. If Live is demanding audio from your hard drive faster than the drive can provide it, this icon will flash, signifying that your HD is overloaded. If this happens, try loading some of your larger audio clips into RAM instead of streaming them from your HD (discussed in Chapter 11 under the section titled "Sample Box (Audio Clip)").

Finally, the two boxes smashed into the upper-right corner are the MIDI Track In/Out indicators. These indicators will flash when one of Live's tracks is sending or receiving MIDI.

The intent of this chapter was to get you comfortable moving throughout Live's GUI. Knowing what you're reaching for will help speed up the ho-hum mouse-and-software side of things and let you focus on the performance instead. In the next chapter, we'll dive right into the software's single most defining element: the Live clip.

11 Ableton Live: The Clip Concept

If imagery could be used to portray the experience of most contemporary laptop musicians, it would probably be a screenshot of a Live clip (see Figure 11.1). Basically, the clip represents Ableton's elegant redesign of the Post-it note. The primary function of an audio clip is to mark the specific location of an inspired idea—an audio file—on your hard drive. The central purpose of a MIDI clip is to store a specific sequence of MIDI control data: MIDI notes, automation envelopes, and so on.

Dig a bit deeper, and you'll quickly find that, like Post-it notes, clips have multifaceted uses that range from spontaneous musical-note scribbling or doodling, to digital flipbooks of organized ideas.

Tip: Right-click (OS X: Control-click) on any clip and notice that both clips and Post-its share pretty color options, too! This feature is quite useful when filling Live's Session Mixer with the pieces of your Live set.

Audio and MIDI clips are depicted by the small, colored rectangles spread across Live's grid-based Session view or positioned within the horizontally scrolling Arrangement view.

A clip's place in the grand scheme of things is this: Clips make up a Live set's sound source and are organized within horizontal playback structures known as *scenes*. Vertically stacked scenes make up the overall clip slot grid, which is part and parcel of Live's Session Mixer: the focus of these Ableton chapters.

"Playing" Live Clips

Because Live's clips are sort of like its guitar strings, Ableton purposefully engineered multiple ways to play them. Here are some examples:

- With your mouse pointer, click the Launch (triangular "play" icon) button on any audio or MIDI clip.

- Select any audio or MIDI clip with your mouse or MIDI controller and then press the Enter or Return key on your computer keyboard.

▶ MOD BASS

Figure 11.1 Ableton's soul: the Live clip.

- Press Ctrl+M (OS X: Command+M) to enter MIDI Map mode and then assign an audio or MIDI clip slot to any button on your MIDI controller.

- Press Ctrl+K (OS X: Command+K) to enter Key Map mode and then assign an audio or MIDI clip slot to any key on your computer's keyboard.

- Press Ctrl+M (OS X: Command+M) to enter MIDI Map mode and then assign the Track Launch button (immediately above the In/Out section) to any button on your MIDI controller. Note that this feature is only visible when either MIDI or Key Map mode is active.

- Press Ctrl+K (OS X: Command+K) to enter Key Map mode and then assign the Track Launch button (immediately above the In/Out section) to any key on your computer's keyboard. Note that this feature is only visible when either MIDI or Key Map mode is active.

- Simultaneously launch an entire row of clips (known as a *scene*) by clicking any scene's Launch (triangular "play" icon) button from under the master track title bar.

Don't forget that stopping clip playback is equally important. Not only do empty clip slots host individual clip Stop buttons, both audio and MIDI tracks have dedicated MIDI/keyboard-assignable clip Stop buttons directly above the In/Out section. Further, there is also a button within the master track channel strip, clearly labeled Stop Clips. Click this to initiate a global "all-stop" command across the entire Live set. Lastly, just like the play commands, Live's stop commands are all directly linked to the Global Quantization setting located within the Live control bar.

The Clip View

As mentioned previously, a Live clip can be distinguished as one of two types: audio or MIDI. Double-click on any clip, and Live's Clip view will automatically pop open along the bottom of the GUI. No matter whether you selected a MIDI or an audio clip; Live's Clip view looks similar under both circumstances.

For Live to exhibit synchronized performance behaviors, both clip types necessarily share specific playback-related settings. As you can see in Figures 11.2 and 11.3, MIDI and audio clips each share the Clip, Launch, and Envelopes boxes. However, what primarily differentiates audio and MIDI clips is one box unique to each variety: the audio clip's Sample box and the MIDI clip's Notes box. If you are unable to see any of these boxes, enable the Show/Hide buttons located in the bottom-left corner of the Clip view (see Figure 11.4).

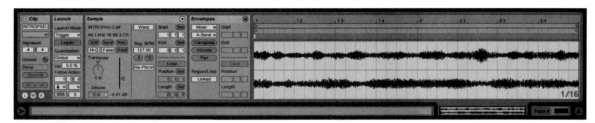

Figure 11.2 Live's Audio Clip view.

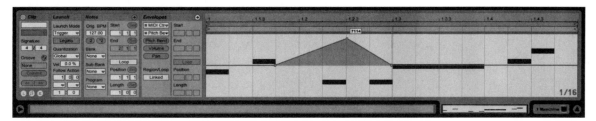

Figure 11.3 Live's MIDI Clip view.

Figure 11.4 Click to show/hide the relevant Clip boxes.

Note: Pressing Shift+Tab switches between Clip and Track view. Pressing Command+Option+L (OS X) or Ctrl+Alt+L (Windows) opens and closes Clip view.

The Clip Box

The leftmost of the Clip view boxes is called the *Clip box* (see Figure 11.5). The Clip Activator, or the tiny on/off button within the top corner of the Clip box, allows you to toggle clip status either on or off. This is useful, for example, within extremely busy Live sets containing clips that you do not want to accidentally trigger, and yet you want access to for the right situation.

Figure 11.5 The Clip box.

Clip Name and Clip Color allow performers to further customize the look and feel of their Live sets via visual cues. Clip Name does precisely what it says and is especially helpful if you need to tag your clip content with text. Clip Color, on the other hand, is particularly useful for visual labeling. For example, within my Live set, I have many of my tracks split into their fundamental stems, such as drums, bass, melodies, atmospheres, vocals, and so on. During my Live set, I constantly jump around to other elements; therefore, assigning the same color to each piece of a "song" provides me with a returning point from my inevitable tangents. Of course, there are dozens of other possibilities, such as assigning specific colors to specific types of instruments or sounds, color-coding clips according to their root keys, and so on.

Signature (Time Signature) lets you dictate how the grid markers fall upon your clips. Although it does not directly change how clips will sound, it does alter the manner in which clips launch in relation to the overall project quantization. For example, if the overall Live set quantization is set to 1 Bar (4/4), and clip quantization (see the upcoming section "The Launch Box") is set to 1 Bar (4/4), clips with a signature of 3/4 will launch every three beats.

Groove

Arguably, the most interesting feature of the Clip box is Live's Groove function. In brief, the term *groove* is most often defined as the "feel" of how a track's parts fit together rhythmically. A lot of electronic music feels mechanically rigid—often the case in house and techno—in that beats fall with systematic precision and with little dynamic variation. Now, of course this has its time and place; however, as an example, drummers often intentionally play a little bit loose. In combination with a human's natural dynamic variations, this injects a certain style, or groove, into their music. Note that groove can be applied in both directions—just as it can breathe new life into static tracks, it can also strip songs of swing and correct imprecise timing.

To add groove to your music:

1. Double-click any clip within your Live set to open the Clip view.

2. Click on the Hot-Swap Groove icon (see Figure 11.6) to directly open Live's Browser to the groove templates. The icon will change to an orange X, signifying that auditioning groove templates is possible.

Figure 11.6 Click this icon to test your clips using new groove templates.

3. To audition the groove templates, navigate to the Live Browser and either double-click your selection or click the orange Hot-Swap Selection button.

4. Once you have found a fitting groove template, click the Groove Pool icon (see Figure 11.7) to open Live's Groove Pool (see Figure 11.8).

Figure 11.7 Groove Pool icon.

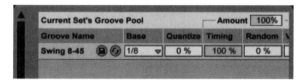

Figure 11.8 Live's Groove Pool.

5. Adjust the various settings as you see fit.

6. Once you are satisfied with the groove settings, click the Commit button within the Clip box. MIDI notes are adjusted appropriately within MIDI clips, whereas Warp Markers are shifted and saved to the relevant audio clips. Note that these settings will *not* permanently alter your audio files.

Finally, the Nudge controls allow you to bump a clip's playback position backward or forward to the degree of your Live set's Quantization setting. Much like Traktor's Beatjumping, this feature can be used when DJing either to line up track phrases so that they smoothly mesh together or to intentionally knock them slightly off beat for creative effect!

Note: Enabling Live's MIDI Learn function opens up a hidden control feature within the Clip box, labeled *Clip Scrub*. Assign this to any endless encoder upon your MIDI controller to emulate vinyl platter control (to some extent). Test out different Global Quantization settings to see which works best for your performance style.

The Launch Box

Directly adjacent to the Clip box you will find the Launch box (see Figure 11.9). Each individual setting within this panel controls specific clip playback behaviors inside Live's Session view; note that they are not found within the Arrangement view. For example, the four options found under the Launch Mode drop-down menu configure how the currently selected clip(s) will play.

- **Trigger.** Routinely the go-to clip playback method, setting Launch mode to Trigger configures the selected clip(s) to play when clicked with a mouse button, computer key, or MIDI control. Clips are stopped via the clip Stop button at the

Figure 11.9 Use Launch box commands to customize clip playback behaviors.

bottom of the relevant audio or MIDI track. Each time a clip is (re)launched, it will start from the beginning at the rate of the chosen Quantization settings.

■ **Gate.** Functions akin to a "hold" command—in other words, the clip is played until the triggering mouse button, computer key, or MIDI control is released. As an example, Gate mode is useful for triggering one-shot samples, such as FX or vocal snippets.

■ **Toggle.** Using Toggle mode turns the clip Launch button into a switch. Press once to launch the clip; press again to stop it. Note that clip playback still follows the chosen Quantization setting.

■ **Repeat.** Holding down a mouse button, computer key, or MIDI control will continuously launch the selected clip at the rate of the Quantization setting—in other words, holding down with a Quantization setting of 1/16 will create the standard machine-gun stutter effect. Upon release, the clip will play as normal. The behavior is similar to the cue functions of a CDJ or Traktor's Cup button.

Legato mode, found directly below the Launch Mode menu, specifically affects the playback position within the currently playing clips. For example, suppose you have a drum track containing four or so clips, with each clip representing different takes, or even fills. If you engage Legato mode, you can seamlessly jump between each of the clips without restarting them—in other words, the playback position across the different clips remains on the same beat/bar/phrase throughout. Skipping across different clips in this fashion can create some interesting and unexpected dynamic changes while retaining the groove and feel of your set.

Tip: When DJing with Live, try cutting tracks into pieces and placing the clips vertically within a track. If you set each clip to Legato mode, you can improvise a remix of your custom track edits on the fly!

I have mentioned the Quantization setting a few times already. With regards to clips specifically, the Launch box provides the option to release individual clips from the Global Quantization settings set within the transport control bar. You can, of course, leave clips to follow the default Global Quantization settings. However, if there are particular clips that you want to play outside the launch behaviors of your overall Live set, use the drop-down list to customize how you want the clip to launch. For example, if your Global Quantization is set to 1 Bar, and you have your clip Quantization set to 1/16, you have 16 "opportunities" to launch that clip in relation to the quantization count of your Live set's Global Quantization.

Directly below the clip Quantization settings, you will find a clip's Velocity Amount, or "sensitivity." As this number moves closer to 100 percent, the amplitude (volume) of a clip will respond to the velocity at which the clip is launched. For example, if you have a velocity-sensitive controller, hitting a key or a pad hard will launch a clip at full volume. In contrast, the softer the message, the softer Live will play the clip's volume.

Follow Actions

Within a performance situation, there are dozens of different angles an artist has to consider in real time. Often a type of "triage" has to be enacted because, in reality, we are only able to handle so many things at once. Specifically, Live's Follow Actions become a valuable asset as Live sets become increasingly more complex. Among other things, they give artists the option to automate one process when they need to focus more intently on another.

Found immediately below the clip Quantization settings inside the Launch box, Follow Actions are essentially automated playback behaviors assigned to a group of clips—a group is defined as a selection of clips arranged in succession upon the same audio or MIDI track. As you can see in Figure 11.10, I have a few groups of clips loaded onto a MIDI track. Let's say that these clips are four different variations of the same drum loop. There are situations when triggering drum loops by hand is a distraction from the overall performance, so assigning Follow Actions to the clips can, for example, automate a sequential progress through the clips or be used to randomly trigger clips within that particular group.

The first option, Follow Action Time, determines how long (bars, beats, and sixteenths) the currently selected clip(s) will play before a Follow Action is triggered. Each clip is given two potential Follow Actions, simply labeled A and B. Whether Follow Action A or B is triggered is determined by the probability entered within the value fields at the bottom. To explain this, if your values are 1:999 (see Figure 11.11), Action A will trigger 1 time in 999: not such great odds. If, on the other hand, you set the odds to 1:1, what will you get? That's right! Action A and B each have a 50-percent chance of launching. Any number can be entered, of course, but the results are more predictable when smaller values are used.

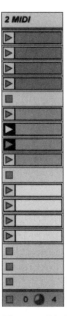

Figure 11.10 Clips assorted into Follow Action groups.

Figure 11.11 Use this dialog to define Follow Action behaviors and probabilities.

Now, the actual Follow Actions themselves are fairly self-explanatory. The only two that might need some clarification are Any and Other. Using Any will trigger any clip within the relevant group—including the currently playing clip. Alternatively, Other will trigger another clip but will never retrigger the same clip. I recommend trying all of the settings to see how they behave within your Live set.

Envelopes at a Glance

As one of Live's most powerful tools, envelopes are an invaluable feature within Live's arsenal that should not be overlooked, if not simply due to the power they hold over clip playback behaviors. I feel that providing an overview of Live's envelopes is particularly important, especially regarding how they can be used to creative effect within a performance environment.

If you click on the Envelope box within Live's Clip view, you should see a red line stretched over the top of your audio or MIDI clip. Also known across DAW applications as a *breakpoint envelope*, imagine that this line is the reflection of a parameter's status changes over time—in other words, playback position scrolls left to right and can represent anything from recorded MIDI controller movements to mouse-drawn volume or pan changes. The envelope can be seen as a container for all of this recorded controller data: a feature known as *automation*.

Double-click anywhere along the line a few times to create a handful of breakpoints. Essentially, breakpoints are markers around which an envelope is bent and shaped. If you look at Figure 11.12, you will see multiple breakpoints around which the audio clip's pitch is transposed. By no means are envelopes exclusive to pitch changes; rather, they can be used as automation for simple features, such as audio/MIDI track volume, pan positions, or solo/mute functions, or for more complex modulations, such as over plug-in parameters or external MIDI-capable hardware (for example, synths, drum machines, and so on).

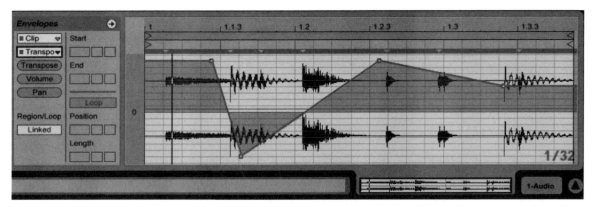

Figure 11.12 A breakpoint envelope transposing the pitch of an audio clip.

While breakpoint envelopes are commonly understood as studio techniques reserved for recording purposes, the manner in which Live has implemented envelopes within audio and MIDI clips translates perfectly to a live performance or a DJ set. One of the main reasons for this is that each clip retains independent automation controller data. You could make a few duplicates of an audio or song clip and assign differing automations within the envelopes of each clip. In effect, the song or loops are the same, but because each clip contains different envelope automations, each clip's sound is completely different.

There are two basic ways to edit envelopes. The first is by simply double-clicking anywhere along the breakpoint envelope (double-click it again to remove it). This will create individual breakpoints that can then be dragged along an envelope's red line. Moving and manipulating these breakpoints will create angular, linear slopes, as shown in Figure 11.13.

The second is known as Draw mode. If you right-click (Control-click) inside the envelope, you should see the menu shown in Figure 11.14. For future reference, bear in mind that all of the options concern envelope-specific editing features. For our purposes, choose Draw mode at the bottom. Depending on how precise you want to "draw" your envelope, use the same menu to choose a resolution from under Fixed Grid. Also shown within Figure 11.12, the chosen grid value will determine how fine

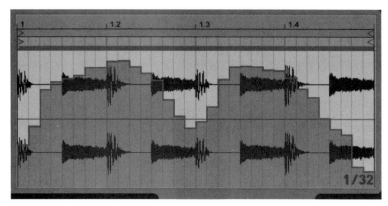

Figure 11.13 Use breakpoint envelopes to automate Live's parameter behaviors.

Cut Envelope	⌘X
Cut Time	⇧⌘X
Copy Envelope	⌘C
Duplicate	⌘D
Duplicate Time	⇧⌘D
Delete	Del
Delete Time	⇧⌘Del

Clear Envelope

Adaptive Grid:

Widest	Wide	Medium
✓ Narrow	Narrowest	

Fixed Grid:

8 Bars	4 Bars	2 Bars	1 Bar	1/2
1/4	1/8	1/16	1/32	
Off				

Triplet Grid	⌘3
Draw Mode	⌘B

Figure 11.14 Right-click (OS X: Control-click) within the Envelope window to access further editing features.

the steps are between your breakpoints—selecting off allows extremely accurate breakpoint editing. Obviously, different situations require different settings, so experiment with these options for a few minutes until you get the hang of using them.

> **Note:** Press Command+B (OS X) or Ctrl+B (Windows) to enter/exit Draw mode.

To assign automations to MIDI or audio clips:

1. Double-click on a clip within an audio or MIDI track to bring up Live's Clip view.

2. Click on the Envelope box. If you don't see it, click on the Show/Hide button in the bottom-left corner.

3. Click on the Device Chooser drop-down menu, shown in Figure 11.15, and choose, for example, Mixer. This will allow you to automate controls available through the Live Session Mixer.

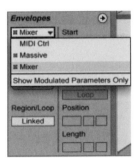

Figure 11.15 The envelope Device Chooser.

4. Click on the Control Chooser and select the specific control you want to automate. As you can see in Figure 11.16, I have selected Track Volume.

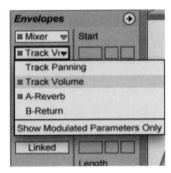

Figure 11.16 The envelope Control Chooser.

5. Double-click anywhere along the red line of the breakpoint envelope to create an individual breakpoint.

6. Repeat Step 5 a few times and randomly drag the breakpoints around, as I have done in Figure 11.17.

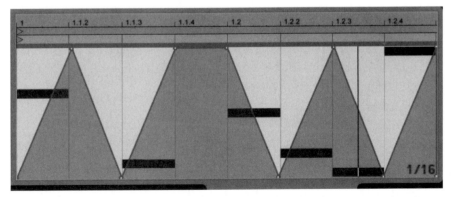

Figure 11.17 Double-click anywhere along the red line to create breakpoint assignments.

7.   Play the clip, and you should see a small red dot appear (and bounce up and down the fader) to the right of the track Volume fader (see Figure 11.18), thus indicating automated volume changes. Play one of your other clips and notice that the behavior goes back to normal.

Figure 11.18 The tiny dot adjacent to the track Volume fader indicates automated envelope data.

Note: Hold Shift and click/drag a breakpoint to overwrite previously existing breakpoints.

Hold Command (OS X) or Ctrl (Windows) and drag a breakpoint to fine-tune envelope shapes. Fine-tuning only operates vertically—in other words, on the amount or depth of the parameter adjustment.

Note that this is a simplified example. You can create multiple complex assignments within each clip—again, totally independent of any other clips within your Live set. For example, if you were automating plug-in parameters, one clip could automate a synth's filter cutoff, filter resonance, ADSR envelope contours, LFO rates, oscillator tunings, internal effects, and so on.

Utilizing the same note sequence across several duplicated clips—each containing independently varied envelope settings—leaves performers with potential that reaches far beyond traditional DJ software applications. Throw some Follow Actions into this equation and see what kind of musical insanity you're left with.

There are a few other features within the Envelope box that require mentioning. By default, envelopes are linked to your clips—in other words, envelopes follow the Loop settings located within the Notes box (MIDI clip) or the Sample box (audio clip). If you click on the button labeled Linked, envelopes become unlinked and gain their own independent Loop controls, found directly to the right of the Link button. From there, you can determine the envelope's start and end points, as well as configure overall looping behavior.

As an example, say that you have automations assigned to a drum loop that is one bar in length. After a while, the loop and its attached automations might get a bit boring. Unlinking the envelope from the loop therefore presents some interesting possibilities for what is effectively still the same one-bar drum loop.

In Figure 11.19 you can see my boring one-bar looped automation envelope. If I click on the Linked button (see Figure 11.20) underneath the Region/Loop header, the envelope will be freed from the loop settings, and I can then adjust how I want the envelope to play back. Notice that once the envelope is unlinked, the audio waveform/MIDI notation disappears. This is because the envelope no longer functions within the clip boundaries.

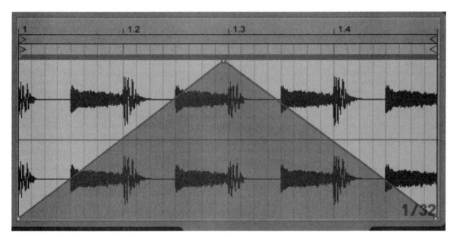

Figure 11.19 A simple one-bar envelope.

Figure 11.20 The Linked button.

Within the bottom Loop field, I change Length from 1 to something like 4 or 8. Notice that the Editor expands across the number of bars entered. From this point, you have several options. For example, you could draw in entirely new automations. On the other hand, if you move the loop bracers to the last bar of the envelope, you could start a clip with several bars of unique automation that end with a loop of the earlier displayed envelope automation (see Figure 11.21).

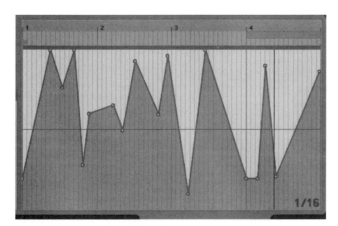

Figure 11.21 Modified four-bar envelope—notice that the last bar is set to loop.

Remember that there are no guidelines for the way you set your envelope parameters. Once you have unlinked envelopes from their respective clips, there is no reason why they have to follow bar-length delineations. In many cases, setting seemingly random values yields results that are more interesting for the dance floor as well as for you.

Sample Box (Audio Clip)

Click on any audio clip within your Live set, and you should find one box titled Sample. If you don't see it, enable the Show/Hide Sample Box button from the bottom-left corner of the Clip view. Thus far, we have seen how the Clip, Launch, and Envelopes boxes share the means of controlling audio and MIDI clip playback behaviors—that is, they manipulate the manner in which clips play in relation to the overall Live set. Unique to audio clips, the Sample box (see Figure 11.22) expands upon these playback behaviors by exerting deeper control over how individual audio files actually sound.

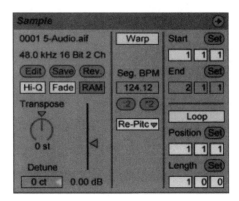

Figure 11.22 The Sample box provides performers with functions ranging from sample editing and loop controls to tuning and Warp Markers.

Note: Live's Notes box is effectively the MIDI equivalent of an audio clip's Sample box (see Figure 11.23). Through the Notes box, a MIDI clip/track's functions are implemented in conjunction with the MIDI Editor—the functional MIDI equivalent to the audio clip's Sample Editor.

Please note that MIDI clip behaviors go beyond the subject matter covered within *Part 1* of this project; however, they are a topic of particular importance to the advanced tips and techniques discussed in *Part 2*.

The feature-laden left-hand side of the Sample box contains the primary sample management functions. Clicking on the file name pops open Live's File Browser to show the file location of the currently selected clip, as well as all other files within the relevant parent folder. If you prefer the audio editing features of an external application, click the Edit button to launch the audio editor chosen within Preferences > File/Folder > Sample Editor. Once you make changes you are happy with, click the Save button to

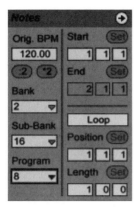

Figure 11.23 Live's Notes box.

preserve the settings of that particular clip—for example, Warp Markers, tuning, tempo, and so on. Within a performance setting, this becomes advantageous as you cycle through tracks and loops that you have used in previous shows. Simply drag and drop the files into any Live set, and your saved data magically reappears.

Note: Remember that unless you edit your audio files within another audio editing application, changes to audio files within Live are nondestructive—that is, they affect the clip analysis files (.asd), not your actual data.

Even though the Reverse button should be relatively self-explanatory, when used sparingly, reversed samples become a very powerful part of sound design—especially when liberally slobbered with effects. Note that the instant you click the Reverse button, Live quickly creates a duplicate, reversed copy of the sample. The name remains, but Live tags the new sample with the letter R. Take a stale piano melody, apply a liberal dose of effects, and then reverse it. BAM—you've extended the sample's sell-by date!

The buttons Hi-Q, Fade, and RAM each apply particular treatments to your clips and how they will ultimately perform within your Live set. Hi-Q engages an evolved audio playback algorithm that improves Live's ability to pitch-shift audio files, though at the expense of CPU. Personally, I find it best to leave this mode engaged. If you find yourself running out of CPU overhead, you are better off axing a few plug-in instruments/effects before lowering your audio fidelity.

The Fade function simply applies a quick fade-in/fade-out on the currently selected clip. If you are not meticulous about editing your loops, leave this setting engaged. Otherwise, files that are not cropped at what is known as the point of *zero-crossing* click or pop at the end/beginning of the loop points. (Naturally, there are countless arguments and examples showing how these clicks and pops can be used musically.)

Finally, engaging the RAM mode places the entire audio file into your computer memory. If you are streaming dozens of clips off of your hard drive, you might experience audio dropouts when, for example, Legato mode is engaged within the Launch box. If the D icon within the top-right corner of Live's interface flashes, your computer is telling you that it's having trouble streaming audio from the hard drive. Because the balance of speed and capacity is of the essence, Ableton recommends loading RAM with short, quick samples and loops or those using Legato mode rather than entire songs.

Located directly below the aforementioned Sample box functions are the Transpose, Detune, and Clip Gain controls. Essentially, when you transpose a track, you are shifting the key of the song in semitone steps. Understanding that there are 12 semitones in an octave, if you adjust the Transpose control to +12 st or −12 st, the track raises or lowers an octave, respectively. For example, if you transpose a track that is in the key of C to +12, the song is still in C, but higher in pitch by an entire octave. This particular setting is particularly useful when matching the relative key of two (or more) tracks.

Jump immediately below to the Detune controls if you need to adjust the pitch with a finer resolution. Essentially, Detune allows tuning micromanagement, with a value range reflected in cents. As 100 cents comprise a semitone, you are given 1,200 steps to work with across an entire octave.

With Live's Warp mode enabled, Transpose and Detune only affect playback pitch, not playback speed. This allows you to match a 110-bpm track with a 130-bpm track without the "Mickey Mouse" effect. On the other hand, when Warp mode is disabled, Transpose and Detune behave more like a turntable/CDJ pitch fader—in other words, it affects both pitch *and* playback speed.

The small fader to the right of the Transpose dial is the clip gain. For the most part, the Clip Gain fader serves the same purpose as a channel gain knob on any typical DJ mixer. As mentioned in earlier chapters, gain allows you to match the relative levels of, for example, volume differences between two separate songs prior to mixing them together with the channel faders.

Sample Display

Upon selecting any audio clip, an overview of the audio file's waveform appears on the right-hand side of the Clip view. Referred to as Live's *Sample display*, this window provides dynamic control over a handful of vital features—most notably, Warp Markers and audio clip Loop functions—but it is also the portal through which you view, zoom, and scrub your clips (both audio and MIDI).

If Warp mode is disabled, zoom in on a sample by clicking and dragging virtually anywhere within the Sample display. With Warp mode engaged, zooming and scrolling are done within the beat-time ruler or within the clip Overview box (see Figure 11.24) at the bottom of the Sample display. Once the small magnifying glass appears, click and drag vertically to zoom in or out or horizontally to scroll through the clip's timeline.

Figure 11.24 Click and drag within the clip Overview to change waveform zoom level and positioning.

If you want the Clip view to follow the playback positioning within an audio clip, engage the Follow switch within the transport control bar shown in Figure 11.25. From Preferences > Look/Feel > Follow Behavior, you can choose whether the clip scrolls across the playhead (think: audio tape) or across the currently zoomed "page."

Figure 11.25 The Follow switch.

Mmmm, Warp Markers...

At the foundation of Live's prominence within the music world lies the Warp Marker. Simply stated, Warp Markers are the reference points Live uses to sync audio clips to one another via the Live set's master tempo. For example, a 4/4, two-bar loop recorded at 120 bpm is 4 seconds; a 4/4, two-bar loop recorded at 90 bpm is about 5.3 seconds. Using the Warp function's time-stretching algorithms, what were once disparate tempo ranges can be creatively merged together. Among other things, this lends itself well to creative reworking of slower hip-hop beats to the tempos of house, techno, dubstep, and beyond.

The way that this works is fairly straightforward; in fact, the Ableton manual uses standard office supplies in its analogy explaining Warp Markers, and it works very well. Using Ableton's example as a guideline, think of time as a ruler, an audio file as a rubber band, and Warp Markers as pins or tacks. If every inch represents a beat, 4 inches make up one bar. So...

Let's say that your Live set's tempo (ruler) is set to 120 bpm. If you used your tacks to stick a 90-bpm track (rubber band) to the ruler, it would stretch over the 4-inch mark... well past your target. Since you want your 90-bpm song to play at 120 bpm, the outer tack must be moved back to 4 inches without cutting or losing any of the audio file's content. As the loop is made shorter, the most visible change is that beat transients are brought closer together. Figure 11.26 shows the 90-bpm track set against our 120-bpm ruler. On the other hand, Figure 11.27 shows our 90-bpm track once it has been brought up to 120 bpm.

Time (the ruler) hasn't changed; however, the track's playback in relation to time (rubber band) has changed. The track plays more of its beats in less time; therefore, the track plays at a faster tempo. If you are one for analogies, moving these tacks bears some similarity to moving Warp Markers.

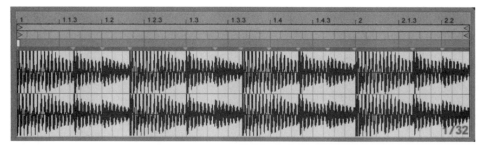

Figure 11.26   Pre time-stretch.

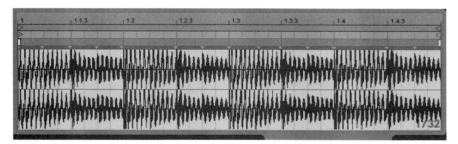

Figure 11.27   Post time-stretch.

Note that these tacks can be used for more than just tempo changes. Take a look at Figure 11.28. Just before the downbeat at 1.3, you can see that the kick hits slightly early. As much as Warp Markers can be used to apply global tempo changes to audio clips, they can also be used to correct imprecise timing. Don't forget: On the flipside, Warp Markers can be just as easily used to disrupt the original flow of those same audio files.

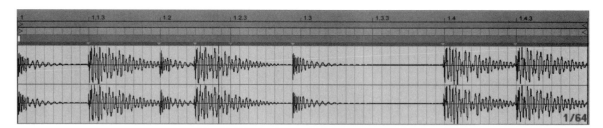

Figure 11.28   Use Warp Markers to fix tempo drifts, such as the early kick at downbeat 1.3.

Tip: Live's Warp Markers are incredibly handy at fixing turntable tempo fluctuations inherent when digitizing or sampling a vinyl collection.

Before working with Warp Markers, you should familiarize yourself with three icons (see Figure 11.29).

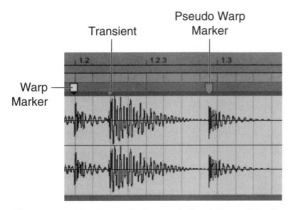

Figure 11.29 From left to right: Warp Marker, transient, and pseudo Warp Marker.

- **Warp Marker.** The previously analogized "tacks," Warp Markers stick a section of an audio file to a specified window of time. Set Warp Markers by double-clicking within the top half of the waveform display or along the gray strip immediately above it.

- **Transient.** Live "intelligently" and automatically places these little gray triangles as logical locations to set Warp Markers.

- **Pseudo Warp Marker.** Gray-colored Warp Marker lookalikes that appear when the mouse pointer hovers over a transient. If the pseudo Warp Marker sits between two yellow Warp Markers, dragging it will create a new, permanent Warp Marker. With no following Warp Markers, dragging a pseudo Warp Marker adjusts clip timing and then reverts to a transient once released.

Using and Setting Warp Markers

To cater to the various needs of performers, Ableton developed several methods to work with and manage Warp Markers. Whether your Live set is composed of music from other artists or from your own music/loops, learning how to work with Warp Markers is a must.

To make track warping easier, Live gives you the option to automate some of the warping process during import. Select one of the Warp options from the drop-down menu from Preferences > Record/Warp/Launch > Loop/Warp Short Samples (see Figure 11.30), and performing with Live quite simply becomes a matter of dropping audio clips into

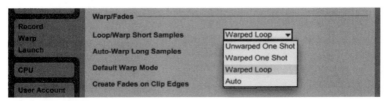

Figure 11.30 Use this dialog box to configure how you want Live to handle the warping of your imported samples.

your set and making a couple of quick adjustments. This is incredibly convenient if you are using your own material, or you regularly edit out custom audio clips from your music collection. In addition, you are given the option to Auto-Warp Long Samples (tracks) and select what Warp mode you want newly created/imported audio clips to use, and you can choose whether or not you want to apply fade-ins/outs.

When it comes down to working on a clip-by-clip basis, Auto-Warping offers several more options. Double-click on any of your audio clips to bring up the waveform within the Sample display. Now, right-click (OS X: Control-click) anywhere inside the visible waveform, and you will see the Sample display's context menu (see Figure 11.31). Within this menu you can find various Auto-Warp options suitable to nearly any imported audio files.

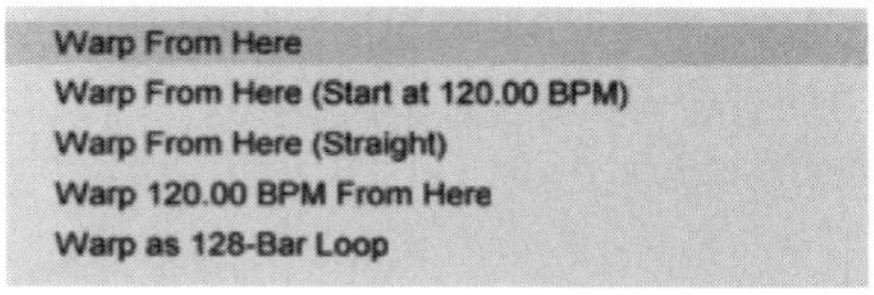

```
Warp From Here
Warp From Here (Start at 120.00 BPM)
Warp From Here (Straight)
Warp 120.00 BPM From Here
Warp as 128-Bar Loop
```

Figure 11.31 Use this context menu to select the appropriate Auto-Warp settings for your audio clips.

- **Warp from Here.** This option applies Live's Auto-Warp to everything to the right of the point selected.

- **Warp from Here (Start at X.X BPM).** Same as above; however, this Auto-Warp method factors in the project tempo to help yield more accurate results.

- **Warp from Here (Straight).** One Warp Marker is used to estimate overall tempo. This method is generally only effective on beat-accurate, machine-driven tempos.

- **Warp X.X BPM from Here.** This option creates a Warp Marker at the project tempo and erases any preexisting Warp Markers to the right of it.

- **Warp as X-Bar Loop.** This option instructs Live to apply warping to create an evenly cut loop. The length of the loop is "intelligently" determined by what Live deems as optimal.

As I have mentioned before, the natural timing drift of human musicians is made plainly obvious when applying Warp Markers to band-based songs or loops. Likewise, if you sample loops and tracks from vinyl records, the inherent pitch fluctuations of a turntable will translate directly to your recorded audio file.

This is one particular area where Live proves more powerful than traditional DJ applications, such as Traktor or Serato. For example, Traktor's Beatgrids can only be globally adjusted against a song—in other words, individual grid markers cannot be manually manipulated to fix imperfect timing.

While Auto-Warping undoubtedly speeds up the preparation of a Live set, be aware that no software is perfect, and Live will make mistakes from time to time. Ableton is well aware of this; through manual Warp Markers, the company has devised an intuitive toolset that allows Live users to individually customize Warp settings across any and all audio files.

Tip: These days, many artists intentionally bounce back and forth between different software tools to exploit the exclusive advantages provided by differing applications. For example, if you prefer the immediacy of DJing with Traktor, you may have noticed at one stage or another that Traktor's internal Sync function does not respond particularly well to tracks with a bit of timing "drift." In this situation, Live's Warp Markers can be used to straighten things out. Simply, bounce out your fixed tracks, re-import the song into Traktor, and you're finished!

The following steps are intended as an introductory "how to" that should help you get comfortable with altering Warp Markers. Once again, bear in mind that these changes are not permanent—you can always start over if you accidentally make a mistake.

Take a look at the one-bar drum loop in Figure 11.32. The kick that should hit on the second downbeat falls a bit past the mark. Bringing this loop back into line is a simple matter of creating a new Warp Marker and dragging it to sit back on the second downbeat, or 1.2.

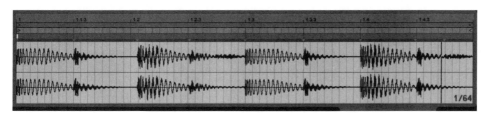

Figure 11.32 As you can see, we're dealing with some dodgy tempo drift here.

Notice the small upside-down gray triangles marking the loop's percussive attacks—these are transients, as mentioned earlier. Think of these Transient icons as Live pointing to where a few Warp Markers might make the most sense. If you downloaded this chapter's Live content from www.formatproject.com/djhandbook1.zip, open the Live set titled live_tutorial.als and follow along with these instructions.

1. Click on the audio clip titled Warp A within the audio track titled WARPS. Notice that this is the same loop as pictured in Figure 11.29.

2. Using the previous example, move your mouse pointer over the kick that hits just past 1.2. You should immediately see a gray pseudo Warp Marker

appear. (Consider using the Zoom function to precisely adjust your Warp Markers.) Hold down Ctrl (OS X: Command), and two "support" pseudo Warp Markers will appear to the left and right of your mouse pointer.

3.   While still holding Ctrl (OS X: Command), double-click the middle pseudo Marker to drop three "permanent" Warp Markers (see Figure 11.33). Alternatively, refer to the clip named Warp B.

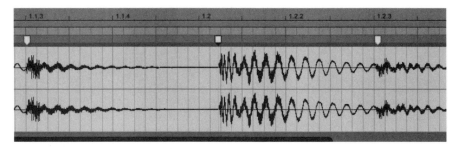

Figure 11.33   A close-up showing our three new Warp Markers.

4.   Click and drag the middle Warp Marker (nearest the second downbeat), 1.2, back in time so that it sits directly on downbeat 1.2 (see Figure 11.34). Alternatively, refer to the clip named Warp C.

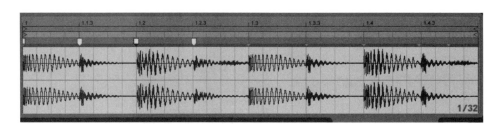

Figure 11.34   Our clip: warped.

5.   While warping your own audio files, if you are unable to move the Warp Markers precisely enough, right-click (OS X: Control-click) within the waveform inside the Sample display and choose one of the settings listed under either Adaptive Grid or Fixed Grid (see Figure 11.35).

Adaptive Grid:
| Widest | Wide | Medium |
| ✓ Narrow | Narrowest | |

Fixed Grid:
8 Bars	4 Bars	2 Bars	1 Bar	1/2
1/4	1/8	1/16	1/32	
Off				

Figure 11.35   Choose the appropriate grid setting to determine the behavior of your Warp Marker movements.

Note that the previous steps are intended simply as a starting point. With just a bit of creative manipulation, Warp Markers can transform any static audio file into something beautiful...or terrifying. Warp within the structure of an audio clip's Grid settings to create rhythmic beds and textures. Or, try altogether unlinking from the clip Grid settings for some seriously unpredictable results. Also, don't forget to test out the various Warp modes, for each will yield its own unique time-stretching effects upon your audio files.

Tip: When you are warping, it often helps to drop a Warp Marker at the very end of your loops—the loop end is thus "pinned" in place. All subsequent warping is therefore bent around and/or contained between the loop's boundaries.

For a general idea of what I'm talking about, check the audio clips titled Warp D, E, F and G. Basically, they are the results of manipulating random Warp Markers as played using a few different Warp modes—however, all stemming from the bog-standard 909 drum loop used from sample clips Warp A, B, and C.

Warp Modes

One great thing about music is that it drops us inside someone else's imagination. Generally speaking, artists intentionally record these ideas at certain tempos and under the frameworks of certain keys. However, yet again referring to the "Mickey Mouse" effect, the tempo changes inherent to DJing alter the pitch of prerecorded audio unless special processing is applied. This special processing is the task of one of Live's numerous Warp modes.

I've already mentioned that Live uses Warp Markers as the means of "tacking" tempo changes to a bpm. More important than the tacks themselves is what happens to the rubber band (time) stretching between them. Given that one song usually sounds quite different from the next, Ableton uses Warp modes to achieve the best results for varying musical content. The drop-down menu shown in Figure 11.36 displays the various Warp modes that Live employs.

Figure 11.36 Use this contextual menu to choose the appropriate Warp mode.

- **Beats mode.** Best suited for tracks and loops that have distinct rhythmic characteristics—for example, percussive house, techno or hip-hop loops, transient bass or rhythm guitar parts, and so on. The way that Beats mode handles audio is fairly straightforward: It loops the end of transients. The Granular Resolution, Transient Loop Mode, and Transient Envelope settings allow you to alter the manner in which this time-stretch function is manifested.

- **Tones mode.** Uses a form of granular resynthesis to time-stretch "tonal" material with extended decay stages—for example, pianos, synths, guitars, or FX-styled noises. The Grain Size parameter should be adjusted to suit the material being processed. As with many things in Live, this is better heard than explained. Play around with this setting, in combination with speeding up or slowing down the overall project tempo. Doing so will give you a better impression of what granular resynthesis does.

Note: In brief, granular resynthesis is the process in which an audio file is "sliced" into extremely tiny fragments (grains) that are played in condensed or sustained loops as the file is compressed or expanded (respectively) with tempo changes. Think of a long line of independently colored marbles where each marble represents one looped grain. As a file is pitched down, the "marbles" are spread apart, leaving gaps between the grains. Granular resynthesis duplicates the frequency (pitch) of each colored marble and fills in the gaps with duplicates, or loops, as the file is slowed down and removes the marbles as the file is compressed, or sped up.

- **Texture mode.** Texture should be used for material that fits the criteria of Tones mode, yet is of richer substance—in other words, piano chords rather than keys, dense synth pads, and so on. Like Tones mode, Texture mode also uses granular resynthesis to process audio clips; however, the added Flux parameter adds a variable degree of randomization to the actual grain sizes to reduce the audible side effects of granular signal processing.

- **Re-Pitch mode.** Used to time-stretch audio by adjusting the pitch, or playback speed, much like that of a turntable. Speeding up the project tempo will in turn speed up the playback and key of all audio files using Re-Pitch—and vice versa.

- **Complex/Complex Pro.** The appropriate selection when time-stretching audio clips that are effectively entire songs—in other words, when using Live "DJ style." Complex (Pro) mode uses a higher-quality time-stretching algorithm designed to adapt to the varying frequency ranges consistent with complete tracks—the "go-to" mode for DJs. The Pro factor simply notches up the quality that much further and should be used if you can hear audio artifacts while using the basic Complex mode.

Where do we go from here? At this stage, you should be gaining a working knowledge of Live and how its internal functions offer up potential for modernizing your DJ set. The only thing missing is how to make that final hands-on move when approaching stage-specific features. Therefore, in the next and final instructional chapter, we will narrow down our focus and examine the specific tools that are naturally adaptable to forward-thinking DJ performances.

12 DJing with Ableton Live

I am generally hesitant to call Live a DJ application, mainly because it is so much more than that, but also because in a traditional sense it isn't a DJ application at all. But does this mean that an artist cannot DJ with Live?

Unlike Traktor or Serato, which (digital/analog aside) are both evolutions of traditional DJ culture, Live seems to have fallen into this category through guilt by association. Nonetheless, DJ culture has unquestionably influenced Live's development as much as Live's development has trickled into applications such as Traktor or Serato. This is plainly evidenced by the recent Live/Serato Bridge functionality.

Advantages and Disadvantages

So, has Ableton become the ultimate DJ application? At the end of the day, bloggers, reviewers, online forums, and so on don't have the answer; it's up to the individual artist.

Although Ableton was more of DJ culture appropriation than say, Traktor or Serato, it still stands among the industry's most powerful DJ tools because of its adaptability. For example, DJs who feel trapped by Traktor or Serato's two- or four-deck structures are free to expand their track-count options inside Live's relatively open-ended design. Along those lines, whereas Traktor and Serato have somewhat fixed signal flows, Live's track-based routing options allow performers to send, receive, and reroute audio virtually anywhere. Factor Max/MSP into the equation, and Live's boundaries expand even further.

If you produce as well as perform music, Live could very well be your one-stop solution. There really isn't any other software on the market that so efficiently allows artists to flip between the studio and the stage. Moreover, it is hard to imagine a better way of adding individuality to a DJ set than through layers of self-made ideas by way of VST or AU plug-in instruments and/or effects. And speaking of effects, no other DJ software boasts Live's potential to create complex effects configurations within a live performance context.

No DJ software application is complete without the addition of a hardware controller. Simply put, the steps to map out controller assignments in Live are likely the easiest of any audio software. Period. Although Live's MIDI mapping does not provide the depth of Traktor's Controller Manager, Ableton's process is significantly more streamlined.

Arguably, Live's most hotly debated "advantage" is that Warp Markers effectively make beatmatching obsolete. When you understand that beatmatching has long been the benchmark separating the proverbial wheat from the chaff, it's no surprise that DJing without it brings such negative scrutiny. Traktor and Serato make manually syncing beats via vinyl or CDs optional. Whereas from Live's perspective, the Bridge creates a balance of both worlds.

Is this an advantage? It entirely depends what you want from DJing.

As we all know, every up has a down. Whenever I do product trainings, my DJ clients tend to avoid certain tedious or time-consuming processes. With that said, DJing with Live requires a lot of preparation and maintenance…and I mean a lot. If maintaining, navigating, and loading a large music collection quickly and efficiently is an absolute must, you will probably be happier with Traktor or Serato, as their Track Browsers are carefully designed for just that purpose. Scrubbing through a song in Live takes a few more steps and simply doesn't work as well in a live setting as the equivalent action within Traktor or Serato. More importantly, the options for multiple cue and loop points are nonexistent as of Live 8—a solution somewhat rectified via the Bridge.

Tip: Even though Live doesn't facilitate multiple cue and/or loop points, it does allow you to cut a song into as many pieces as you like. Unlike in Traktor or Serato, in Live, once clips are cut out of a song, you can edit them to an extent only limited by your imagination. With a bit of patience and experimentation, Live actually lets you do exponentially more with Loops than the other two apps discussed in this book.

Ableton does not display album art, and it also does not recognize standard music file metadata tags (artist, title, and so on). There are little tricks to speed up track browsing in Live; however, one of the most immediate disadvantages of Live as a DJ tool is maintaining a music library. Once you get the hang of setting up Warp Markers, the process does become faster, but Live saves this data in specific .asd files that must be stored alongside your music files. If the reference file is lost, so is all the prep work. Traktor, for example, embeds the data gained from analyzing directly into a file so that the information such as Beatgrids and cue points is never lost. (Again, at some level, these are all concerns that, at some level, are addressed in the Ableton/Serato Bridge.)

Note: Don't let the disadvantages of Live's Browser scare you off—they are neither functional problems nor design flaws. Put simply, Traktor (or Serato) and Live were each originally constructed with a stylistically different artist in mind.

So, when DJing with Live, think of a creative way to store your music and stick with it. For example, create a folder structure by date—in other words, create a new folder every week and dump all of your new music inside of it. That way, you maintain some semblance of organization between new tracks and old tracks. Or, create a "music" folder containing a genre-specific file structure (hip-hop, house, dubstep, and so on). The most important thing here is to ensure that all .asd files are contained within a folder structure that is both easy to maintain and easy to modify.

What Are the Best File Types?

Compressed audio is without a doubt an amazing technological achievement; however, the reason it was conceived in the first place was to solve a problem that no longer widely exists. Several years ago, hard drive space and Internet bandwidth were expensive and in short supply. Today, 4 GB+ HD movies download in well under a half-hour. What is my point?

Simply put, compressed audio formats, such as MP3, MP4, AAC, and so on, are consumer-level file types that are optimized and squished so that we can fit more than 10,000 songs onto our iStuff (iPhone, iPods, iPads, and any other MP3 players). In some respects, this makes sense. However, artists performing as professionals should be using audio in a professionally encoded format. Professional studios never use compressed audio during the recording process, in order to capture audio at its most pristine. So, why should this practice diminish in the performance realm?

Stick with WAV/AIFF files whenever possible. To be sure, Live's versatility is further exemplified by the number of file types that it supports; however, note that all compressed audio formats are "decompressed" into Live's Decoding Cache on import. For example, if I tried to save space with MP3 files, any MP3 loaded into a Live set would then exist on the hard drive as a compressed and a decompressed file—in other words, even more space is ultimately used.

Unfortunately, it isn't always possible to obtain WAV or AIFF (Mac-specific) files through online record shops. Beatport, for example, gives customers that option—granted, at an extra expense. If you have a large CD collection, you already have music files in at least 16-bit, 44.1 kHz, or what is known within the audio industry as Red Book audio. With regard to importing, Apple's iTunes is probably the most direct process available—and it's free.

Note: Mac users have it slightly easier. Double-click on the CD icon from the desktop (or select it within the OS X Finder). Simply "lasso" and then drag and drop the AIFF files wherever you store your audio files—done!

If you choose to use iTunes, remember that the import settings do not automatically default to WAV or AIFF. Go to iTunes Preferences > General > Import Using. Click the drop-down menu and choose WAV Encoder (see Figure 12.1). Insert your CD, right-click (OS X: Control-click) on the CD's icon within the iTunes Browser, and choose Import CD.

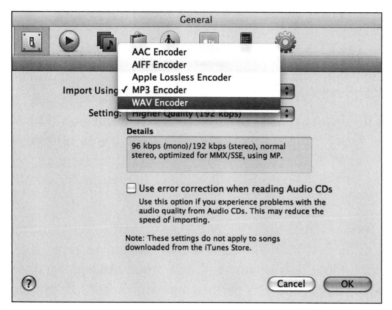

Figure 12.1 Configure iTunes to import files in WAV format.

What you do with the imported files is then up to you, but as I have said before, think of a formula and stick with it! Regrettably, the analog versus digital / WAV versus MP3 debate is far too complex a discussion for *Part 1* of this project, but rest assured that I will broach this subject in *Part 2*.

Ripping Vinyl

What about our precious vinyl collections? As a Live user, you're already a step ahead. It's a safe bet that if you own vinyl, you probably still own a DJ mixer. Note that unless you are using an audio interface with a built-in phono preamp (NI's Audio 4 or 8), you will have to route through your DJ mixer and then connect the mixer's output to an input on your audio interface.

The process from here is simple.

1. Ensure that your hardware is connected properly—in other words, route the DJ mixer's record out or master output (even a monitor output) to the appropriate stereo input on your audio interface.

2. Select the audio track into which you want to record.

3. Choose Ext. In from the Input Type drop-down menu.

4. Select the appropriate stereo input pair from the Input Channel drop-down menu (see Figure 12.2).

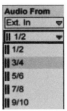

Figure 12.2 Choose the soundcard input channel that your DJ mixer is plugged into.

5. Enable the Arm Session Recording button upon the audio track (see Figure 12.3).

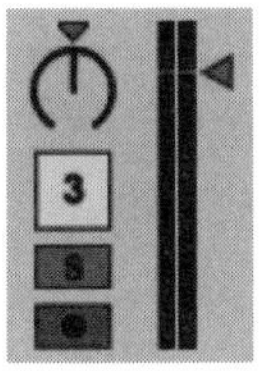

Figure 12.3 Click Arm Session Recording to tell Live that it's time to record some vinyl.

6. Leave Monitoring set to Auto; this way you can verify what got recorded once you are finished. Cue up a few locations on the record to verify that the inputs are not clipping. Analog distortion = nice. Digital distortion = not so nice.

7. Click the Record button on an empty audio track clip slot (see Figure 12.4).

Figure 12.4 Click any clip Record buttons to start recording incoming audio.

8. Use the clip Stop button to stop recording and then move on and cue up the next track from your vinyl!

Ripping Other Sources

Now, if you do not own CDs or vinyl, streaming audio resources permeate the Internet. The legality of what you choose to record is ultimately your responsibility, but that aside, this type of sampling presents virtually limitless possibilities. Quite a few methods of capturing these audio streams exist; however, Mac users in particular have two powerful options worth noting.

Cycling '74 Soundflower

From the makers of Max/MSP (and, of course, Max for Live), Soundflower is a Mac OS X system extension that allows users to spread virtual audio cables across their applications, thus removing all the messy wiring. Soundflower presents itself as an available audio input/output option within practically any application that allows customized audio routing.

For example, if you wanted to send audio from Traktor to Ableton Live, Soundflower (2ch) shows up within both Traktor and Ableton's respective input/output preferences right alongside any other connected hardware audio interfaces. If you require more advanced routing, Soundflower also offers a multichannel option that provides up to 8 stereo (16 mono) input/output channels. Thus, you could conceivably assign several third-party software applications, such as Internet radio apps, their own dedicated output and route each one directly into its own independent Live audio track input.

Figure 12.5 displays Soundflower's configuration window upon the OS X taskbar. Much like working with soundcard audio drivers, modifying Soundflower's buffer size is possible according to the demands placed upon it. You can find more info at Cycling '74's website: www.cycling74.com/products/soundflower.

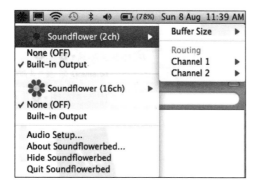

Figure 12.5 Configure Soundflower's preferences from the OS X taskbar.

Audio Hijack

Rogue Amoeba's Audio Hijack Pro (see Figure 12.6) is simply a no-fuss audio recording application. It can just as easily be used with a microphone input as it can with the audio output of virtually any application on your computer. Moreover, if you have a life away from your laptop, you can set a timer to record the output of nearly any application at a specified date and time—for example, for Internet radio stations.

You can copy ripped streams to your hard drive in several different formats, drop in AU (OS X) and VST (OS X and Windows) effects over the top of your recordings, combine Audio Hijack with AM/FM software streams to record "proper" radio content, use it to break DRM encoding if you have any encrypted music files—and, of course, you can also record samples from all of your favorite DVDs. Finally, tell

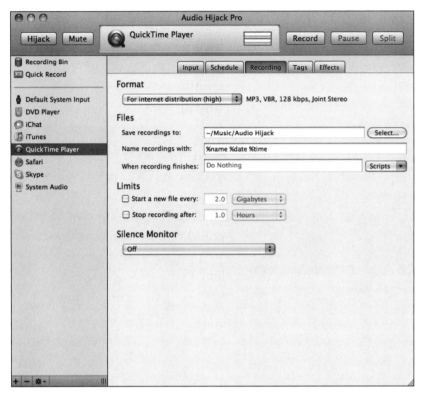

Figure 12.6 Audio Hijack's GUI is straightforward and gets right to the point.

Audio Hijack to record your Skype phone/video calls; later, you can blackmail all of your friends when they annoy you, or just blend some of the absolutely priceless garbage that they say into your tracks/DJ sets!

Configuring Live for a DJ Set

The difficulty with defining how to use Live as a DJ tool is made slightly complex by the fact that there is no single way to do it. With that said, the intent of this section is to provide a bit of context so that you can decipher your own workflow. Therefore, I have constructed a simple DJ-focused Live set to help guide you through the rest of this chapter.

Before proceeding, please download and open the Live set file titled dj_tutorial.als from www.formatproject.com/djhandbook1.zip.

Tip: When you configure a layout that works, save it as a default template. Go to Preferences > File/Folder > Save Current Set as Default. Click Save, and the current configuration will load every time you launch a new Live set. This feature is especially helpful if you constantly reuse the same workflow—in other words, things such as key/MIDI/macro mappings and plug-in inserts are always reloaded within a custom default template.

Shown in Figure 12.7, the Live set I have put together is relatively straightforward. Although there are six tracks in total, remember that this setup is intended purely as a guideline. You are encouraged to add, subtract, and modify as you see fit. I have labeled the tracks as such:

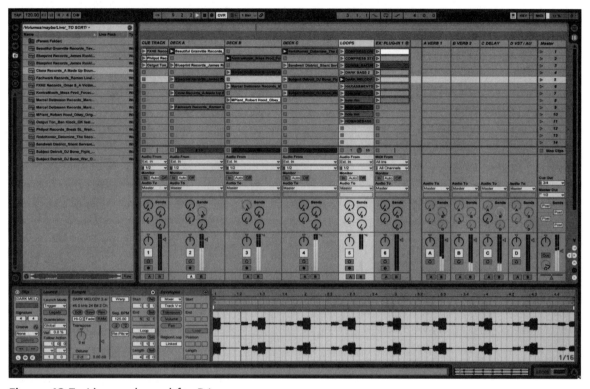

Figure 12.7 Live: reshaped for DJs.

- **Cue track.** Used to earmark tracks dragged directly from the Browser. If desired, the cue track's Solo/Cue button can be left on at all times for instant pre-listening. Additionally, it helps keep each of the playback decks clearly organized.

- **Deck A–C:** The playback decks act as digital turntables, giving performers three sound sources for their music library. Notice that Decks A and B are assigned to A and B of the Crossfader (see Figure 12.8). Drag Live's Crossfader left/right to blend between any audio, MIDI, or aux tracks. Of course, if you don't want to use the Crossfader, simply disable the A or B from the relevant track. In addition, all mixable tracks are preloaded with Live's EQ Eight. One way to use this device is to assign the low-cut and high-cut filters to knobs on your control surface. Doing so simplifies the DJ standards of filter sweeps, bass cuts, high cuts, and so on. As an alternative, the EQ Three device has Low/Mid/Hi On/Off kill switches. If you would rather punch the EQ in and out, try assigning these functions to a button on your control surface.

Figure 12.8 Use the Crossfader to smoothly blend between your tunes.

- **Loops.** Simply an audio track intended to play back your own audio loops, edits, atmospheres, sound effects, a capellas, and so on. Although the tunes that get loaded into Decks A–C will probably change quite often, your loops may not. If you save the Live set with the loops in place, you have a semipermanent arsenal of sound beds right at your fingertips.

- **Ex Plug-In 1.** Used as an example for pushing your Live set into the gray area between a DJ performance and a Live performance. Nothing is loaded for compatibility purposes, but create a MIDI track or two, and you can expand your performance with Live's instrument devices or any third-party plug-in. For example, NI's Maschine is the perfect complement to an Ableton-based DJ set because, among other things, drum machines let you compose your own percussive layers on the fly.

- **Return Tracks 1–4.** These "FX return" tracks merely scratch the surface of Live's powerful effects routing. As an example, A Verb 1 is but a simple reverb. On the other hand, B Verb 2 is followed by a side-chained compressor—in other words, the reverb tail is squashed based on the dynamics of the audio content fed into the compressor's side-chain input. In our example, I have the output of the B Verb 2 feeding into the side-chain input—in short, this means that any audio sent into the reverb on Return Track B will influence the compressor's behavior as a result. (You could, of course, switch this input to the output of any other track.) Load and play any clip and use Send B to route signal to Return Track B to hear what I mean. From there, C Delay houses a few different Live delay types, ready to be switched on or off as needed. Finally, D VST/AU is simply to encourage the use of third-party effect plug-ins as well.

Tip: Like feedback? Take a quick look at the return tracks in our sample Live set. Notice how only a few of the sends are enabled, while the rest remain disabled. One often-overlooked feature of Live's effects routing is the fact that you can send the output of one return track to the input of another. Moreover, you can also use a send to pipe audio directly back into the same return track's input, generating feedback. Try applying this concept across a range of return tracks, and you can create unbelievable feedback networks—just watch your ears!

Preparing Your Music Collection

Whether you make Traktor, Live, or Serato your DJ application of choice, analyzing the music collection is part of set preparation. Each company takes a different approach, and the result of the process is unique to each application; however, no matter which way you go, the process is relatively straightforward.

For instance, I keep a sort folder named "To Sort" for music that I haven't bothered to go through yet. To analyze these new files, I simply right-click (OS X: Control-click) on the folder from within the Live Browser and choose Analyze Audio (see Figure 12.9).

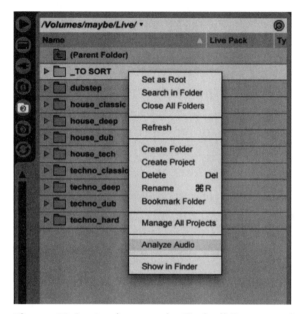

Figure 12.9 Analyze tracks "in bulk" to speed up Live's file optimization process.

Now, there are a few options to note. First, let's say that I want Live to automatically apply Warp Markers to my music files while they're analyzing. Because song files are fairly long, I need to instruct Live what to do. Navigate to Preferences > Record/Warp/Launch and turn on the Auto-Warp Long Samples option.

Second, I have mentioned this already, but Live provides numerous situation-specific warp algorithms (see Figure 12.10). Many performers opt for Re-Pitch, because it provides a good balance of sound quality and CPU resourcefulness. On the other hand, the two Complex modes theoretically use the most appropriate algorithms for entire tracks. Try a few options and judge with your ears. When you settle on the best-case Warp mode, go to Preferences > Record/Warp/Launch and choose it within the Default

Figure 12.10 Test out Live's warp algorithms with some of your tracks to determine what sounds best for you.

Warp Mode drop-down menu. In the future, each time a folder of music is analyzed, Live will default each track to the selected Warp mode.

Finally, each track will need to be judged on a case-by-base basis. If the default Warp mode doesn't cut it for a particular track, apply a different setting within the clip-specific Sample box. Additionally, Live does its best to optimize Warp Marker placement, but auto-detection is not perfect. As I said when working with Traktor's Beatgrids, find a couple of perfectly warped tracks and use them as your reference. Play the reference tracks alongside those that need warping in order to help you fine-tune the process. If necessary, refer back to the Beatgrid tutorials found earlier within the Live chapters.

Previewing Tracks

Despite the lack of a few DJ-focused features, the Live Browser is still an incredibly intuitive search tool. If you have dedicated an output on your audio interface to the cue out, auditioning your music collection is simply a matter of selecting a track inside the Browser window. The selected track will pop up within the Preview tab (see Figure 12.11) at the bottom of the Browser and play from the output selected from the Cue Out drop-down menu (see Figure 12.12). Alternatively, try dedicating and pre-listening to tracks from a dedicated cue channel, as in our sample Live set. As you can see here, I have my cue out routing to outputs 3/4 of my RME Fireface. With the Preview (headphone) button enabled, tracks will automatically play when selected. By default, clips audition in sync with the project tempo; click the Raw button to hear them as they were recorded.

Figure 12.11 The selected track appears in the Preview tab.

Figure 12.12 Use these two menus to separate your cue mix from the master out.

Note: You can audition more than just audio files with the Preview tab. You can test Live clips incorporating plug-in instruments and/or effects devices against the currently playing music without having to actually load the clip, instruments, or effects.

Editing Tracks

Without question, the dub, re-edit, or remix remains a foundational element at the heart of DJ culture. It's fairly safe to assume that every DJ has heard at least one track that he feels could have or should have been constructed differently: a little more percussion here; rearrange, loop, or entirely remove the vocals there; extend the intro/outro; and so on. Even if you prefer the more traditional experience of Traktor or Serato, don't forget that Live is an exceptionally powerful audio editor.

Note: Remember that Live's editing tools are all nondestructive. As mentioned earlier, a clip is simply a reference to an audio file stored on your hard drive. Live executes all edits in real time, so there is never any permanent damage to your music.

From the get-go, using Live to edit your music files should feel somewhat familiar. Established word processor functions, such as Cut, Copy, Paste, Delete, Undo/Redo, and so on, are all readily applicable to clips via standard OS X/Windows key combinations. Conveniently, Ableton created a list of these (and other) hotkey combinations and stuck it right at the end of the user documentation. I won't go over every function here, but let's quickly take a look at what editing a track might look like.

1. If you are not there already, press the Tab key to flip to Live's Arrangement view.
2. Open the Browser and find a track that needs some editing. Drag the song from the Browser and drop it onto any empty lane within the track display.
3. The track display's default view size is too small for proper editing. Using Figure 12.13 as a reference, navigate to the right-hand side of the GUI and drag downward on the bar bordering the Edits box and directly above the Deck A track name. This expanded view makes precision editing significantly easier.

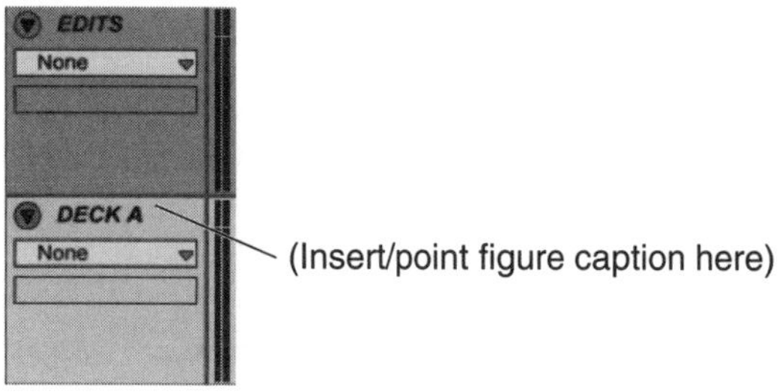

Figure 12.13 Drag downward on this bar to resize the view.

4. Suppose you only want to keep two bars of your sample track. If you move your mouse up to the beat-time ruler (above the loop brace) shown in Figure 12.14, the mouse pointer will change into a magnifying glass. Click, hold, and drag up or down with your mouse to zoom in or out of the song's waveform, respectively. Additionally, you can drag left or right to optimally position the waveform for editing purposes.

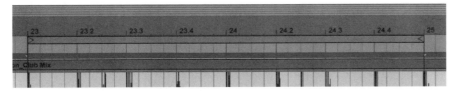

Figure 12.14 Drag up or down on Live's beat-time ruler to zoom in or out of your tracks, respectively.

5. Following my example displayed in Figure 12.15, click and drag directly on the waveform within the track display to highlight the section you want to edit. Press Ctrl+L (OS X: Command+L) to engage the Loop switch. Press Play to ensure that the loop points are where you want them. If everything is good to go, press Ctrl+E (OS X: Command+E) to split, or slice, your loop into a new clip. Alternatively, if you won't be using the rest of the track you are editing, press Ctrl+J (OS X: Command+J) to consolidate the loop into an entirely new audio file, independent of the song from which it was taken. One advantage here is that when you're using the Collect and Save feature, you'll use less disk space.

Figure 12.15 Our pre-slice loop.

6. Select your new loop by clicking on the clip's colored title bar. You can use Ctrl+C/Ctrl+V (OS X: Command+C/Command+V) to copy/paste the tracks into the Session Mixer; drag it from the track display and drop it into an appropriate folder within the Live Browser (for example, Loops); or click and hold on the clip's title bar, press the Tab key to flip to the Session Mixer, and then drag and drop it onto an empty clip slot.

The previous exercise merely serves to introduce Live's audio editing potential. Experimentation is the key; try cutting a section (for example, drum hits, vocal parts, or even micro-sampled clicks and cuts) into small slices, consolidate the parts into new files and rearrange them into your own customized version. Further, drag and drop the edits into one of Live's sampling instruments, such as Impulse or Sampler, and use the instrument's control parameters to manipulate and mangle the audio data. I guarantee that you will be surprised by the results.

Slice to New MIDI Track

An altogether different type of slicing is Live's powerful Slice to New MIDI Track option. In short, this feature takes an audio loop, slices it into segments, instantiates a new drum-rack device onto a new MIDI track, and then maps each individual segment to its own MIDI note inside a new MIDI clip. Each MIDI note can then be rearranged and reshuffled to form an entirely new drum loop in a fraction of the time it takes to edit an audio file. Moreover, if you are performing with a MIDI keyboard or MPC-styled drum pad, each slice can then be triggered (played) live.

If that sounds confusing, think of it this way: Imagine that you have a two-bar drum loop that you want to slice up and rearrange. The file sequences something to the effect of kick, open-hat, closed-hat, snare, and so on. Using the default Slice to New MIDI Track option places, for example, the kick on C1, the open-hat on C#1, and so on. This behavior is common with a few other powerful sample-based applications on the market. Of particular note: Propellerhead's ReCycle loop editor and Native Instruments' Maschine groovebox, as well as its Kontakt 4 sampler. Each of these applications spits out audio loops and/or MIDI files that are designed specifically for reconstruction.

This feature is especially useful for DJs who like performing with personalized re-edits. Cut the good stuff out of an otherwise mediocre song and use the Consolidate command to turn it into a new audio clip. Let's try it for ourselves. First, right-click (OS X: Control-click) on a short loop and choose the Slice to New MIDI Track (see Figure 12.16).

Once the loop is chosen, a box containing various slicing options will pop up (see Figure 12.17). The upper drop-down menu tells Live how and where to make slices within your audio clip, whereas the lower menu contains different Slicing Preset configurations, such as chain effects and macros. I recommend testing these out on your own, but pay particular attention to the macro controls—tweaking them can yield some interesting results.

Tip: After you have sliced your audio clip, take note that each drum-rack pad is able to hold individual effect chains. Dropping different types of effects onto random pads often leaves you with some pretty crazy results.

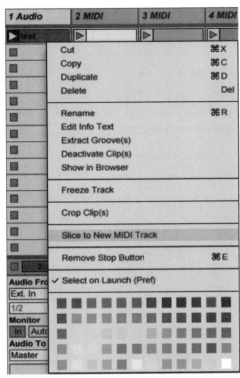

Figure 12.16 Try using the Slice to New MIDI Track command on sections of old songs that you've grown tired of. Afterwards, you'll look at your music library in a whole new light.

Figure 12.17 Use the context menus to define how your loops get sliced to a new MIDI track.

As soon as you start digging through tracks to chop up, bear in mind that this feature maintains a ceiling of 128 slices. Therefore, rather than trying to slice a whole song, carve out shorter audio clips and slice those up instead. Figure 12.18 shows one of my audio clips after using the Slice to New MIDI Track command. The Track view of your new MIDI track displays the new drum rack and all of your slices as played from Live's Sampler instrument device. As you can see, I have clicked on Slice 16 from the Pad section. This correlates to the highlighted slice within the Sampler's Sample display. So what is the best way to learn how this all sounds? Experiment for yourself!

Finally, refer to the Live manual for more information about the Slice to New MIDI Track command as well as the devices it uses. A few features were added since the

Figure 12.18 Tweak the macros and/or the Sampler's parameters to drastically alter the sound of your sliced audio clip.

release version of Live 8, a theme that may continue with future updates. With that said, the user documentation should reflect the specifics.

Looping

Given that Live so efficiently handles audio looping within a production context, its onstage efficiency is hardly surprising. It's simple: Loop controls are global, meaning that once assigned to a MIDI control surface, the same controls are used to manipulate any clip you select within the Session Mixer. Figure 12.19 displays the Loop controls, which are found within both the Notes box (MIDI clip) and the Sample box (audio clip).

Figure 12.19 Test out these Loop parameters to determine how they can enhance your performance.

Logically, the Loop button turns looping on and off. The Set Loop Position button drops the left side of the Loop Bracer (loop-in) at the current playback position—the point where looped playback will begin. This is followed by the Set Loop Length button, which drops the right side of the Loop Bracer (loop-out) at the subsequent playback position—the point where playback will jump back to the beginning of the loop.

Note: If the Loop section is grayed out, either the audio clip isn't warped or Warp mode is disengaged. If necessary, warp the relevant audio clip, and you should be good to go.

So now you're looping. This function becomes even more interesting once you fiddle around with the numbered boxes below both the Set Position and Length buttons. Arranged in bar/beat/sixteenth fashion, each box is MIDI assignable and allows for real-time loop adjustment. Specifically, the Loop Position controls shift the entire Loop Brace by the assigned amount—in other words, if your MIDI controller is assigned to the Bar command, the loop will jump forward/backward by one bar length. On the other hand, the Loop Length controls move only the loop-out point, thereby manipulating how long the loop plays—in other words, if your MIDI controller is assigned to the Beats command box, the loop end will step inward/outward by a single beat. Importantly, all of these commands act as events that follow the Global Quantization settings—in other words, your looping will never fall out of sync.

Tip: Even if you don't use Live's looping functions while you're playing, you should still consider setting loop points at the end of your tracks and loops. Doing so will let you hold onto your mixes longer as well as prevent accidentally "running out of record."

Looping in Live versus looping within, for example, Traktor is an entirely different animal. For example, Live's looping functions are much more hands-on. When you're preparing a DJ set, fine-tuning loops is faster and more precise with a mouse. Live provides this option; Traktor does not. However, Traktor gives you infinitely more loops per track than Live, and as mentioned before, Traktor takes this information and embeds it as metadata within your audio file. The Ableton workaround (or advantage, depending on how you look at it) is that rather than embedding loop or cue point markers inside a track, you can simply slice out an infinite number of audio loops, one-shots, and so on from a single audio file. Digital song files thereby become sampled audio treasure troves—all for the taking!

Effects

Effects have got to be my favorite topic. Manipulating audio files definitely creates amazing results, but effects let you place preexisting sounds into entirely new environments (and here's the key) quickly and easily. The two main reasons why Live's effects are so (ahem!) effective is that Ableton accepts the VST/AU plug-in standards and then lets you route, process, and control them in a logical, modular fashion. In addition to hosting third-party effects, an extensive list of Ableton's own effects devices is located inside the Audio Effects folder within the Live Device Browser. For more information on the specifics of these devices and what they do, please refer to the Live user documentation.

There are two primary ways to go about using effects within Live.

Insert FX

Insert effects are exactly as they sound: effects that are directly "inserted" into the signal flow. For example, if you drag and drop an effect device onto an audio track, the signal passes through the effect unit before heading to the master track output. The amount, or degree, of the original signal that is affected is referred to as the *wet/dry* mix.

Traditionally, the intent of an insert effect is to replace the existing sound (dry) with a treated sound (wet). Dynamics processors (compressors, limiters, and so on), EQs, and filters are generally used to reshape, modify, or optimize a specific sound source. In most practical cases, EQing or filtering a sound would be illogical if 50 percent of the signal escaped untreated. Take a look at Live's EQ Eight and Simple Delay devices in Figure 12.20. In particular, notice that the EQ Eight has no Wet/Dry control, whereas the Simple Delay does. The reasons for this are simple, as you will see.

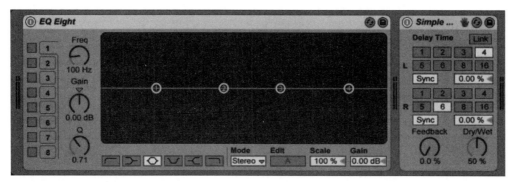

Figure 12.20 EQs are designed to treat and replace an entire signal, whereas delays are generally used to creatively blend the dry/wet signals.

Now, there are circumstances when control over an effect's wet/dry balance makes sense. Depending on the result you are going for, wet/dry balance on a reverb can create a subtle sense of space with a low wet/dry ratio. However, a full-on wet reverb could be equally powerful when used to creative effect. Any number or type of effect is usable as a channel insert effect, but remember two things: In a live context, the same effect copied across several tracks simply creates more (somewhat needlessly) to think about and sucks up significantly more of your precious CPU power—hence, the creation of Live's return tracks.

Send FX

Send effects, on the other hand, are designed for an altogether different purpose. Think of them in two ways: First, return tracks are the meeting point for related sends—for example, all Send A's come together at Return A. One standard practice saves CPU power by utilizing return tracks. Using the same plug-in on multiple tracks can unnecessarily suck up loads of precious CPU headroom. Instead, drop the relevant effect on a return track and "send" groups of signals to the single effect unit.

Note: Pre versus post: You may have noticed that the master track doesn't offer send pots. Yet, for each return track created within the Session Mixer, a switch displaying Pre or Post appears instead.

By default, send pots operate post-fader—for example, sends do not "send" any signal when the track Volume fader is down.

On the other hand, prefader sends continually transmit signals regardless of the track volume position. Thus, you will still hear your effects even if the track Volume fader is brought down. When used with the right audio source, such as vocals, this trick causes quite an ethereal effect.

Second, send levels can also be viewed as the wet/dry mix for multiple, yet entirely independent signals. For example, slap a reverb on return track A. If audio track 1 is a drum loop, 2 is a synth line, and 3 is an a capella, tracks 1 and 2 may not need as much reverb as track 3. Therefore, sends allow each source signal to be treated with a different amount of the same reverb—in other words, independent wet/dry balances for the same effect. Try applying this line of thinking to various effect types.

Additionally, notice that return tracks also have their own send pots. Many effects types sound great when mashed together; using return track sends, you can choose what effects get sent where. With a little toying around, you can even create some great feedback networks. (Just be careful of your ears.)

Finally, sends can be combined with return tracks to incorporate hardware effects into your Live set, such as delay pedals or Korg's popular Kaoss Pads. If you look at Figure 12.21, you'll notice that I am about to assign return track B's output to output 5 of my RME. From the hardware side of things, my particular signal goes: RME output 5 (mono) > Empress Effects Superdelay > either a mixer FX return or back into the RME (and a Live audio track). Now, every time I use send B, audio is routed out to my hardware delay. In some situations, I route the delay pedal back into a dedicated audio track. This way, I can send the delayed signal into other return tracks—for example, reverb, vinyl distortion…or send those effect outputs back through my Superdelay.

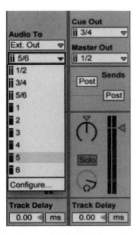

Figure 12.21 You can also use return tracks to bus audio to an external source, such as a delay pedal.

Tip: There are dozens of effects pedals on the secondhand market, eBay, Craigslist, and so on. Finding the perfect unit requires a bit of patience and research, but they're usually comparatively cheap and always a hell of a lot of fun!

When working with effects, remember that even though there are generalized guidelines, these usually exist to achieve a specific result. If "established" isn't your thing, remember that the best results are often achieved through experimentation.

Live's Virtual Gear Racks

Racks are one of the most compelling, potent, versatile, misunderstood, and, unfortunately, often overlooked features within Live's device arsenal. By themselves, Racks don't do much, but dump a few plug-ins into a Rack, and an entirely new realm of sound will be unveiled.

Three particularly important details concerning Live Racks are:

- Racks house both Live and third-party devices as either instruments or effects.

- Signal flow is significantly more flexible and therefore somewhat more complex than when dropping instruments/effects directly on an audio/MIDI/return track.

- Racks enable the use of macro control parameters.

Creating a Rack is straightforward. To keep this example as simple as possible, open the Live Device Browser and drag and drop one of the four Rack types onto the Clip/Device Drop area. This way, Live will automatically create the relevant track type for you. Depending on what type of Rack you selected, you have the option to create a series of devices that are able to handle any and all incoming signals in serial or in parallel.

To put this in perspective, remember that when you drop instruments onto any Live track, signal flow begins at the leftmost device and then proceeds rightward through what is known as a *device chain* connected in serial. You can turn devices on and off, of course, but the signal flow inside the Track view remains the same.

Suppose we wanted to thicken up a vocal loop. Figure 12.22 shows some effects devices paired in serial. Each effect adds its own color to the source audio. Repositioning the four effect units might alter the sound at the output; however, the signal always moves from the left to the right.

Figure 12.22 A simple device chain connected in serial.

Racks, on the other hand, join several serially connected devices into parallel groups. When dropped into a Rack, the aforementioned example would represent one of several parallel device chains. Within Figure 12.23, you can see how the Audio Effect Rack contains three chains. The first chain contains exactly the same configuration as the example back in Figure 12.22; however, it shares Rack space with two others. Each chain receives the same vocal loop as its input. The vocal is then independently processed in serial through each individual device chain. Finally, the signals meet and blend at the Rack's output stage.

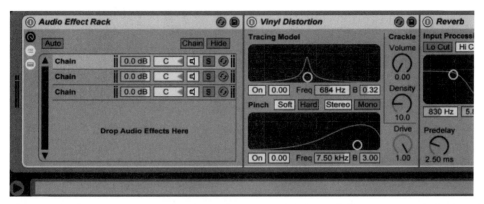

Figure 12.23 You can use Racks to house multiple serially connected device chains in parallel.

Now consider this: Racks behave like all other devices loaded into a Track's device chain. An effect Rack can follow an instrument Rack. Moreover, an instrument Rack can hold chains of other instrument or effects Racks. You can mold cascading "tiers" of Racks into a complex hive of sound sources and/or sound processors.

How is this kind of complexity a benefit during a performance?

Right-click (OS X: Control-click) on any device parameter inside your Rack. As you can see in Figure 12.24, you can map any assignable parameter directly to a macro command—and thus, your MIDI controller.

| Show Automation |
| Show Automation In New Lane |
| Copy Value to Siblings (2) |
| Edit MIDI Map   ⌘M |
| Edit Key Map   ⌘K |
| Edit Macro Map |
| Map to Macro 1 |
| Map to Macro 2 |
| Map to Macro 3 |
| Map to Macro 4 |
| Map to Macro 5 |
| Map to Macro 6 |
| Map to Macro 7 |
| Map to Macro 8 |

Figure 12.24 Use this context menu to assign and manage your macro commands.

But there are so many controls and only eight macros....

Luckily, one macro can hold several assignments. For example, try assigning delay time and delay feedback, chorus feedback, and reverb wet/dry to the same macro. Map this macro to any knob on your MIDI controller, and you have an incredibly powerful effect for building dance-floor tension using only one movement. Stretch this kind of behavior across a controller like Novation's APC40, and you have a seriously devastating combination of sounds.

Note: If your macro list becomes unmanageable, click Edit Macro Map within the context menu shown in Figure 12.23. Use this Macro Mappings window to view and manage all of your macro assignments accordingly.

Regrettably, the depth of what is possible with an instrument/effect Rack goes beyond *Part 1* of this project; however, *Part 2* of *The Laptop DJ Handbook* will dive into the various ways artists can exploit Racks onstage. Fortunately, Live's user documentation provides a healthy description covering what precisely the Rack is. Definitely flip through it when you have a chance.

Tip: If you find yourself reusing certain effect chains, simply highlight all of the effects devices, right-click (OS X: Control-click) on any device header, and choose Group (see Figure 12.25) from the drop-down context menu. Afterwards, click the Save Preset button (see Figure 12.26) upon the newly created Audio Effects Rack device. Do this a few times, and you can quickly drop complex effect chains into any of your Live sets.

Figure 12.25 Group together effects that you use regularly—it's a big timesaver.

Figure 12.26 The Save Preset button.

Mapping Live's Controller Assignments

Concerning Live, almost everything I have discussed so far relates to the functions and features available to nonconventional DJing. When does this information become practical? With controller assignments…

Live is truly born (man, I love a cheesy pun) after these features are given some type of tactile interaction. Whether you are on an airplane with a computer keyboard and mouse or onstage with a tabletop of gear, Live's controller assignments seamlessly bend around situational need. Onstage or off, Ableton's impressive design choices are apparent through the simple fact that mapping never hinders preparation, practice, or, most importantly, performance.

For example, while I was performing a few years ago in Hamburg, almost immediately one of my controllers decided that it would be funny to commit suicide in front of a few hundred people. I won't name the manufacturer (even though the incident spelled the death of my second unit), but two things saved me: First, Live didn't skip a beat and continued to loop the clips that were playing; second, I was luckily performing with a couple of other controllers. The dead device was mapped to Live's track volumes and sends; about a minute later, everything was reassigned to the living, breathing devices, and I finished up my set a little bit sweatier than usual. Afterward, my dead controller joined his buddies Becks, Heineken, and Budvar in the club's trashcan!

Getting back on track…the simplicity of Ableton's Mapping function clearly saved me from an embarrassing outcome.

Key Mapping

Basically, Ableton broke controller assignments into two types: key mapping and MIDI mapping. Key mapping opens up the assignment of Live's internal functions to a computer keyboard. Track Mutes, Solo/Cue, and Arm Session Recording are as readily assignable as clip start/stop, Select Track, or transport functions. As an example, try mapping any track's send pots to the computer keyboard, and you can toggle a 100-percent send level on/off at the tap of a button. To use Key Mapping mode:

1. Enter Key Mapping mode by clicking the Key button (see Figure 12.27) within the top-right corner or pressing Command+K (OS X)/Ctrl+K (Windows). Notice that the Key Mapping Browser pops out in place of the Live Browser.

Figure 12.27 Click the Key button.

2. Use your mouse to click on whichever Live parameter you want to assign to the computer keyboard—for example, a clip slot, Solo/Cue button, send pots, and

so on. A bracket surrounds the chosen parameter, while the status bar at the bottom of Live's GUI indicates that the parameter is ready for assignment.

3. Click any key on your keyboard, and you will see it appear on the relevant parameter. In Figure 12.28, you can see that I have assigned Send A to the d key on my laptop's keyboard. Notice also that the assigned parameter is now situated within the Key Mapping Browser.

Figure 12.28 I assigned Send A to my d key.

4. If you are assigning keys to parameters that utilize scalable values, such as track faders or send pots, you can use the Key Mapping Browser to fine-tune the Min/Max values that Live receives. Let's say that I want the send to route only about half of its output range. Using the previous example, Figure 12.29 displays the send pot, or A-Return, assigned to keyboard key d. Pay particular attention to the slider located under the Max heading. Because I adjusted the Max value to −20 dB, every time I hit the d key, the send pot now only jumps to about 50 percent. Try this with other parameters, such as Live's instrument or effects devices, as well!

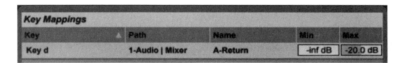

Figure 12.29 Use the Key Mapping Browser to assign parameter Min/Max ranges.

5. Click the Key button, press Command+K (OS X)/Ctrl+K (Windows), or press Esc on your computer keyboard to exit Key Mapping mode.

Note: Don't forget that you can also use the computer keyboard as a MIDI keyboard to send note values to your MIDI tracks. If you would rather use the computer keyboard to control Live's functions instead, make sure that you disable the Computer MIDI Keyboard button (see Figure 12.30) located in the top-right corner of the Live GUI.

Figure 12.30 The Computer MIDI Keyboard button.

MIDI Mapping

Although both MIDI and key mapping employ a virtually identical process, MIDI controllers are decidedly more diverse than computer keyboards; therefore, configuration involves a few additional steps. Live breaks controller types into two camps: those that have native support and those that don't.

Natively supported control surfaces boast one overarching advantage: plug and play. Through what Live calls *instant mapping*, you can connect up to six supported devices simultaneously. In most cases the mapping for each device is automatically configured through a drop-down list of preselected devices—in other words, there is no need to load any custom template files.

Instant Mapping. One distinct advantage of Live's native support is that it offers a type of focused control over the currently selected instrument/effect device. For example, say that you have two audio tracks: AudioA and AudioB. Upon each track you drop Live's Auto Filter effect device. Using a natively supported controller, the hardware knob that sweeps the filter cutoff on AudioA is exactly the same knob that sweeps the filter cutoff on AudioB. As you switch between the two tracks, the knob "intelligently" switches to the focused device. Simple as that!

Note: If you don't see your controller within the drop-down list, proceed to the following "Manual Mapping" section. Your controller will still work great; the process is just handled a bit differently.

Now, if you would prefer that AudioA's filter cutoff remains "locked" to the previously mentioned knob, simply right-click (OS X: Control-click) on the device title bar and choose Lock to Control Surface (see Figure 12.31). Locking the assignment lets you grab the intended filter cutoff irrespective of where the Live GUI is currently focused. Be aware that some natively supported MIDI controllers do not offer this behavior. If you don't see the Lock To option, it is probably not supported by your hardware.

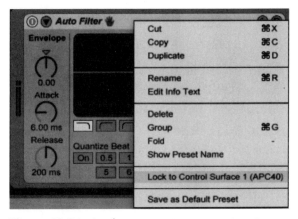

Figure 12.31   Lock your go-to parameters to a control surface for instant access to crucial functions.

Open Live's Preferences and click on the MIDI/Sync tab. As you can see in Figure 12.32, I have used the Control Surface drop-down menu to choose two natively supported controllers: the AKAI APC40 and the Novation Launchpad. The Input and Output options are just as simple; Input tells Live where to listen for incoming control data, and Output sends outbound status feedback to a controller. In other words, changes made in Live (send levels, clip status, and so on) are instantly reflected on controllers that support such behaviors.

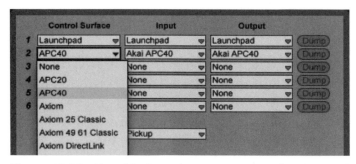

Figure 12.32   Use this drop-down menu to assign any and all natively supported control surfaces.

For some controllers to operate with Live, they may require what is referred to as a *preset dump*. If you look immediately to the right of the control surface output chooser, you will find the dump icons. To receive this preset transfer, your controller will have to be waiting for Live to transfer the information. How the device is readied for preset dumps varies with the make and model, so refer to your user documentation for further information. Logically, if the icons appear deactivated, your controller does not use preset dumps.

If you find that you need to perform some further customizing, simply open the MIDI/Sync Preferences and enable the relevant controller's Remote On button. Once it is engaged, you can use Live's standard manual MIDI mapping to overwrite existing instant mapping commands.

Manual Mapping. Manual mapping serves two purposes. First, it allows you to construct custom controller mappings that link a fixed hardware component (fader, knob, pad, and so on) to a software parameter; second, it allows you to take specific instant mapping assignments and override them with customized manual mapping parameters. For example, APC40 applies instant mapping to the Pan and Send knobs located within the Track Control section. Personally, I don't often pan any audio within my Live sets because it was already done during the production phase. Instead, I drop a Low-Cut Filter plug-in on Tracks 1 to 8 and then assign each respective Cutoff Frequency parameter to the hardware Pan knobs 1 to 8.

Figure 12.33 shows the bottom half of the MIDI/Sync page within Live's Preferences. MIDI Ports displays any and all connected MIDI-capable devices. In particular, note

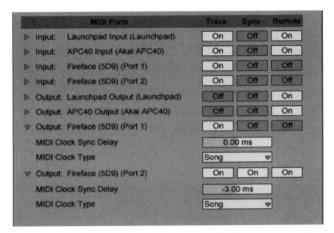

Figure 12.33 Use the bottom half of Live's MIDI/Sync Preferences to customize how your hardware interfaces with Live.

that devices are repeated; all hardware will offer both Input and Output controls. However, unlike with the instant mapping Input/Output previously discussed, the manual Input and Output controls are broken down into three types.

Switches	MIDI Input	MIDI Output
Track	Engage for any device used to send MIDI data to Live's tracks—for example, MIDI keyboards.	Engage for any device used to receive MIDI data from Live's tracks—for example, MIDI clip data to an external synth.
Sync	Engage at ports where Live is receiving external sync—for example, syncing Live to an external drum machine's internal clock.	Engage at ports where Live is sending external sync signals—for example, syncing a drum machine to Live's internal clock.
Remote	Engage for any ports linked to external control devices—for example, controllers that do not support Live's instant mapping or devices requiring manual mapping.	Engage for any ports linked to external control devices that provide real-time status feedback—for example, backlit endless encoder knobs that reflect, for example, Live's send levels.

Note: Clicking the triangle on the left-hand side of any device exposes further control options. These comprise the advanced control configurations discussed within *Part 2* of this book project.

Note: Due to the unpredictable latencies across various audio and MIDI hardware devices, it may be necessary to adjust Live's incoming/outgoing MIDI clock sync delay. Slowly adjust the offset value until the devices are all playing back in time with one another.

To begin manual mapping for yourself, try the following:

1. Enter MIDI Mapping mode by clicking the MIDI button (see Figure 12.34) in the top-right corner or press Command+M (OS X)/Ctrl+M (Windows). Notice that the MIDI Mapping Browser pops out in place of the Live Browser.

Figure 12.34 Click the MIDI button.

2. Use your mouse to click on whichever Live parameter you want to assign to the control surface—for example, track volume, clip slot, Solo/Cue button, send pots, and so on. A bracket surrounds the chosen parameter while the status bar at the bottom of Live's GUI indicates that the parameter is ready for assignment.

3. Manipulate the control surface feature that you want to bind to the Live parameter—in other words, if you are assigning a hardware fader to Live's track volume, click the Track Volume slider within Live and then move the hardware fader. You should see a MIDI parameter tag pop up on the Track Volume fader. In Figure 12.35, you can see that track volume is now tied to a fader value sent from my control surface. The first number lists the fader's MIDI channel, while the second lists the CC number (or MIDI note value). Notice also that the assigned parameter is now situated within the MIDI Mapping Browser.

Figure 12.35 The track volume is tied to a fader value from my control surface.

4. If you are assigning a control surface to parameters that utilize scalable values, such as Track faders or send pots, you can use the MIDI Mapping Browser to

fine-tune the Min/Max values that Live receives. Let's say that I want the Track fader to pipe only about half of its output range. Pay particular attention to the slider located under the Max heading. As you can see in Figure 12.36, because I adjusted the Max value to −15 dB, every time I move the hardware fader, the Track fader now only jumps to about 50 percent. Try this with other parameters, such as Live's instrument or effects devices, as well!

| 1 | CC 14 | 1-Audio | Mixer | Track Volume | -inf dB | -15.0 dB |

Figure 12.36 Use the MIDI Mapping Browser to assign parameter Min/Max ranges.

5. Click the MIDI button, press Command+M (OS X)/Ctrl+M (Windows) or press Esc on your computer keyboard to exit MIDI Mapping mode.

With the vast number of control surface options come a vast number of controller behaviors. One important factor to be aware of is specifically how a hardware device sends data to Live. In most cases these values are best defined as either absolute or relative. A Volume fader, for example, controlling absolute MIDI values 0–127 transmits 0 as off and 127 for full output. On the other hand, some hardware controls send relative MIDI values—in other words, incremental steps upward or downward. For example, if a Live send was completely off, and a hardware knob was completely on, slightly touching the knob would jump the send value full on, which might sound terrible if done by accident. A relative value in this circumstance would incrementally step the value up or down relative to the software positioning, rather than taking a huge leap to the absolute hardware position.

Have a look down on Live's status bar when manually mapping out your control surface. Use the drop-down list shown in Figure 12.37 to tell Live what type of data your control surface is sending. Refer to your hardware's documentation if you are unsure about what data is sent by specific knobs, faders, and so on. For further information about Live's supported data types, refer to the operation manual.

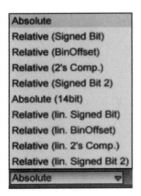

Figure 12.37 Use this drop-down menu to assign absolute versus relative controller values.

Live's Hidden Controls. Some of Live's most powerful control features remain otherwise hidden outside of the MIDI mapping context—precisely the reason why they are so easy to miss. Although it is fairly easy to see that tracks and their clip slots are assignable to key or MIDI commands, additional controls exist that provide another slant on performance control. Engage MIDI Mapping mode and have a look for these hidden control options.

- **Track Launch.** Once you engage MIDI (or Key) Mapping mode, Track Launch (see Figure 12.38) appears directly above the Track Pan/Volume controls. When assigned, this command launches whichever clip slot is currently in line with the current scene—that is, rather than launching an entire scene of clips (as done by the Scene Launch button), only the clip slot within the relevant Track Launch's channel strip is played. If no clip is loaded, the clip Stop button is engaged, stopping any clips currently playing in that track.

Figure 12.38 Assign Track Launch to globally control an entire channel strip's clip playback.

- **Scene controls.** The four controls located below the Stop Clips button (see Figure 12.39) supply direct control over Live's scene navigation. If you assign Scene Launch to a MIDI (or key) command, pressing any button launches the currently selected scene of clips. Scene Up and Scene Down step the currently selected scene up or down, respectively. Finally, Scene Select is a control

Figure 12.39 Assign these parameters to your control surface to quickly navigate through scenes in Live's Session Mixer.

intended for a MIDI endless encoder pot—once configured, twisting one direction steps scenes up, while twisting the other steps them down.

- **Crossfader Left/Right position.** Find these two hidden controls bookending Live's Crossfader. As you can see in Figure 12.39, the Crossfader Left/Right controls only appear once MIDI Mapping mode is engaged. Assign each of these controls to a button to flip between Crossfader assignment levels. For simplicity, only one command needs assigning to one of the Left/Center/Right options. This allows toggling between Crossfader A and Crossfader B positions, respectively.

- **Clip Scrub control.** Although this feature was already mentioned, it needs restating. The basic function of clip scrub is to jump through a track's playback position. Engage MIDI Mapping mode and find the Clip Scrub control within the Clip box of the Clip view (see Figure 12.40).

Figure 12.40 Scroll through clip playback positions with the Scrub control.

Multiple Assignments and Multiple Controllers. If you find yourself running short of hardware knobs, faders, buttons, or pads, keep in mind that a single hardware control is able to manipulate multiple Live parameters. Just to demonstrate a couple of wide-reaching examples, you could assign all of your track sends to one single hardware knob. Alternatively, you could even make a couple of "awesome buttons," which launch preconfigured clip slots unlinked to the rules of horizontally regulated scenes.

To make sense of this, take a quick look at Figure 12.41. Notice the seemingly random assortment of MIDI mapping assignments—if you look closely, you will see that each is assigned to 8/A2, or MIDI Channel 8, MIDI Note Value A2. Instead of using a Scene Launch that strictly follows horizontally related clips, you use a single button to fire off precisely assorted clip slots—kind of like a preprogrammed "reset" if a Live performance drifts too far off message. The only limitation to assigning multiple parameters to a single hardware control is that vertically organized clip slots cannot use the same

MIDI assignment—individual audio or MIDI tracks are only able to play one clip at a time.

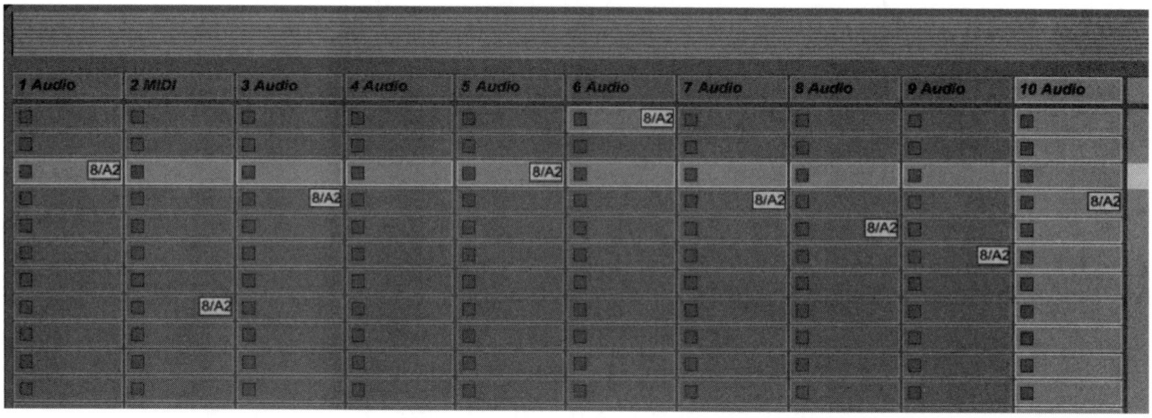

Figure 12.41 Link multiple assignments to a single "awesome button."

Finally, you can also combine various hardware devices irrespective of make and model. For example, the tiny Korg nanoKONTROL paired with a wireless USB computer keyboard is an ultra-compact, ultra-portable fader/pot and Clip Launch/Session Mixer combination.

Syncing Live

I touched on this within the Traktor chapter, and now it comes up again. The potential of applications such as Live (as well as the Bridge) and Traktor creates a powerful assortment of tools for adventurous performers. MIDI clock allows an artist to harness the strengths of various hardware and software developers and merge them together to creative effect.

Part 2 of *The Laptop DJ Handbook* will expand upon the advanced concepts mentioned here. For now, we will take a look at how to prepare Live for a MIDI-synced setup.

Live as Master

Using this configuration, Live acts as the Master Clock source—in other words, the MIDI clock sync signal is sent from Live to a separate slave destination. You could use this signal to sync another application on the same computer, another computer running Live, Traktor, or Maschine, as well as any number of other MIDI-capable hardware drum machines, effect units, and so on.

1. Ensure that your hardware is connected and configured properly—in other words, the output of your sending MIDI interface (master) connects to the MIDI input of the receiving device (slaved computer, drum machine, and so on). Ensure that the slave device is set to receive MIDI clock. If the slave happens to

be another computer running Live, also refer to the following "Live as Slave" section.

2. Navigate to Preferences > MIDI/Sync Tab.

3. Find the appropriate MIDI output device from within the list and check the On button located under the Sync header (see Figure 12.42).

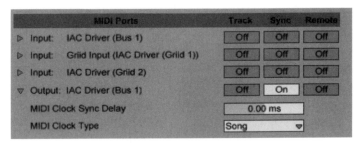

Figure 12.42 Send MIDI clock from a Live-as-master scenario by enabling the Sync output button.

4. Press Play from Live's transport control bar. You should see the slave device begin playback.

5. You will probably need to adjust the sync signal's offset. The best way to equalize the difference is by setting all devices to play obvious, rhythmic material—drum loops, for example. While monitoring the playback of all devices, adjust the Sync Delay slider (refer to Figure 12.42) until everything properly falls into place. If you do not see the Sync Delay slider, click the small triangle to the left of the MIDI output device.

Live as Slave

Using this configuration, Live serves as a slaved device—in other words, Live receives the MIDI clock sync signal from an external Master Clock source. This signal could also be used to sync other applications on the same computer, another computer running Live, Traktor, or Maschine, as well as any number of other MIDI-capable hardware drum machines, effect units, and so on.

1. Ensure that your hardware is connected and configured properly—that is, the input of your receiving MIDI interface (slave) connects to the MIDI output of the sending device (master computer, drum machine, and so on).

2. Navigate to Preferences > MIDI/Sync Tab.

3. Find the appropriate MIDI input device from within the list and check the On button located under the Sync header (see Figure 12.43).

Figure 12.43   Receive MIDI clock from a master source by enabling the Sync input button.

4.   After you enable the sync input, the Ext button (see Figure 12.44) will appear in the top-left corner of the Live control bar. Click on Ext to activate Live as slave.

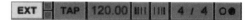

Figure 12.44   Click the Ext button, and Live will listen for any incoming MIDI clock signals.

5.   Press Play from the master device—for example, a computer or drum machine. You should see Live begin playback. Notice that the small indicator light to the right of the Ext button flashes in time with the incoming MIDI clock signal.

6.   You will probably need to adjust the sync signal's offset. The best way to equalize the difference is by setting all devices to play obvious, rhythmic material—drum loops, for example. While monitoring the playback of all devices, adjust the Sync Delay slider (refer to Figure 12.43) until everything properly falls into place. If you do not see the Sync Delay slider, click the small triangle to the left of the MIDI input device.

And Next...

In my eyes, one of the most important things about Live is that it manages to thrive within this functional gray area between DJs, musicians, studios, and stages. Sure, it's not a DJ application in the traditional sense, but it can certainly be used for DJing. Pointing out this simple fact through example was the intent of these Live-focused chapters.

Yes, Live and its parts can seem deeply complex to those new to digital DJing; however, Ableton has constructed Live in such a way that the intuitive thought process behind every action permeates the application as a whole. It's a perfect example of software that was purposely designed to capture *the* artistic experience. Even where that experience has nothing to do with recording, Ableton has done its job when Live adapts around our creative moments.

So, you have reached the end of *Part 1*'s content. Within the next (and final) chapter, I will briefly summarize what we've covered thus far with the slant of introducing where *Part 2* will take us.

13 Parting Thoughts for Next Time

When I started this project, I assumed that 350 pages (or so) would be sufficient to complete a music technology manual of this sort. However, by the time I was about halfway through it, my editors and I reached the conclusion that the project would make more sense in two parts: an initial volume for beginner/intermediate users followed by a second volume aimed at a somewhat more experienced audience. As a result of this decision, I am able to make the project altogether more comprehensive.

This initial volume is intended to offer a bit of introductory direction to a wide-ranging DJ audience—although more specifically, it is directed at the gear freaks who share a common interest in the tools that make modern DJ culture tick. By no means does this book exhaust every option on the market, but it does present the three products central to shaping the future of digital DJing.

For these two parts, taken as a whole, I felt that it was important to approach digital DJing from a particular context. These days, it's common to meet artists who use laptops to perform, to dig for music, as record crates, as home studios, and even as mobile offices to run their record labels. These artists might use Ableton to produce their tracks, bounce out those ideas, and then directly import them into Traktor or Serato. Because Traktor doesn't offer support for third-party plug-ins, they might run Ableton in the background as an advanced effects rack. If that's not enough, the option is there to just stick with Ableton alone and sync up a drum machine in order to inject live elements into a DJ set.

Despite all of the choices, the unifying theme here is the ubiquitous laptop, which in and of itself is digital DJing's double-edged sword. The upside: Computers provide artists with possibilities that would be virtually unaffordable (if not entirely impossible) to spread across individual hardware equivalents. The downside: Jumping into bed with any digital music software assumes a certain degree of computer proficiency. Loosely, it's sort of like playing the guitar—if a string breaks, then what?

For these reasons, the first few chapters are constructed to help explain this potentially confusing subject matter. Each subsequent chapter is thereby designed to define and demonstrate the potential offered by three innovative software packages: Traktor Scratch Pro, Serato Scratch Live, and Ableton Live.

And what about *Part 2*?

My goal within the forthcoming second volume is to shift gears from this discussion and create a guide aimed at a more experienced, intermediate/advanced user base. The intended reader ideally has some familiarity with any combination of the previously discussed hardware and software—maybe even with a bit of supplementary production experience. Just remember, it doesn't matter if you're new to laptop DJing and/or production; there is no reason to steer clear of advanced material. To be honest, I generally find that diving in at the deep end is usually the best way to learn.

Some highlights:

- Descriptions and diagrams of advanced performance workflows, techniques, and stage setups catered to contemporary digital DJ sets.

- Advanced performance techniques with the new Traktor Pro S4 and Traktor Kontrol S4 bundles.

- Powerful Ableton Live performance and production techniques with a focus on MIDI clips, the Arrangement view, Max for Live, and third-party plug-ins.

- In-depth performance tips for the new Serato/Ableton collaboration, the Bridge.

- Embracing the new digital DJ tools of NI's Maschine and Kore 2, but also introductions to Max/MSP and how to make the most out of nonspecific hardware controllers, such as the Monome and Apple's iPad.

- Artist interviews, tips, tricks, and techniques.

- And of course, much more...

In conclusion, if I had to attach any single experience to my motivations behind this book, it would undoubtedly be the window of time that I spent working from the Hollywood-based Native Instruments office. It was an environment of creative professionals who didn't take themselves too seriously, yet who provided a professional level of service across some very serious music software products.

The relaxed ambiance of the office was operated with a managerial resourcefulness that recognized the viability of a mobile workplace. This flexibility allowed me to create a position where I was able to spend a few months out of the year gigging in Europe, handle customers midweek via email from random WiFi-enabled hotels and coffee shops, spend some time working with my colleagues in Berlin, and then eventually land safely back at my desk in L.A. several weeks later—only to discover that my colleagues had casually piled their unwanted junk all over it. (Jerks!)

All the same, the day-in-day-out (sometimes heated) interactions with DJs, producers, composers, sound designers, and all other manner of audio freaks led me to appreciate certain ideas that every music lover appreciates—the same ideas that I do my best to pass on to my clients while freelancing for NI, performing solo, or developing my own independent messes inside my East London studio....

Index